Sport as Symbol

Sport as Symbol

*Images of the Athlete in
Art, Literature and Song*

MARI WOMACK

McFarland & Company, Inc., Publishers
Jefferson, North Carolina, and London

Lyrics from "Mrs. Robinson," ©1968 Paul Simon,
used by permission of the Publisher.

LIBRARY OF CONGRESS CATALOGUING-IN-PUBLICATION DATA

Womack, Mari.
Sport as symbol : images of the athlete in art, literature and song /
Mari Womack.
p.   cm.
Includes bibliographical references and index.

ISBN 0-7864-1579-7 (illustrated case binding : 50# alkaline paper) ∞

1. Sports in art. I. Title.
NX650.S83W66   2003   704.9'49796 — dc21   2003012455

British Library cataloguing data are available

Cover art: George Bellows, "Both Members of This Club,"
1909, oil on canvas 45" × 63",
Chester Dale Collection, National Gallery of Art, Washington, D.C.

Manufactured in the United States of America

*McFarland & Company, Inc., Publishers
Box 611, Jefferson, North Carolina 28640
www.mcfarlandpub.com*

To Victor Turner,
a pioneer in the anthropological study of symbols,
who was the first to recognize the importance of my study
of professional and high-level athletes

Table of Contents

Preface

In his account of a golf game on the legendary St. Andrews golf course, Michael Murphy writes, "I can think of no better way to say it — those final holes played me." That perfectly expresses my experience in researching and writing about athletes. I did not seek out this game; the game sought me.

It seems to be the only explanation for why I, neither an athlete nor a sports fan, came to have such a privileged perspective from which to study and write about professional and high-level athletes. My involvement with athletes began when I was a graduate student in the anthropology department at UCLA, looking for a suitable laboratory to test the relationship between risk and ritual. I was looking for a population with varying degrees of physical danger, great potential for winning and losing, and conditions of social stress. I found my population when Dennis Abgrall, a professional hockey player with the Los Angeles Kings, invited me to watch his team play.

After years of interviewing and observing tennis players, auto racers, and athletes in various types of team sports, I concluded in my Ph.D. dissertation that rituals aid performance by helping the athlete to screen out distractions and prepare mentally for the game. At the time of my study, sports psychologists and other scholars were dismissing athletic rituals as "superstition." But the athletes and their coaches knew better, and I learned from the experts, the athletes whose lives, limbs and livelihoods were on the line. Now the importance of rituals for dealing with stress has become conventional wisdom among sports psychologists, and a whole new field of medicine and psychology has developed around the idea that stress can be dealt with through changes in behavior.

As I was completing my research on risk and ritual, I became interested in another aspect of sports, its role in articulating and reinforcing social values. I introduced the topic in my dissertation and developed the model of the athletic hero that is given in the present work. But my professional life led me in another direction, back into my previous career as a journalist.

I was hired by Voice of America, the second most influential radio broadcasting organization in the world at that time, after the BBC, to cover the Los Angeles Olympics for an international audience. I covered the preparations and behind-the-scenes negotiations prior to the Olympics as well as the Games themselves. I

1

also covered the international competitions leading up to the Games. I was privileged to witness many great sporting events at the Los Angeles Olympics, including the running of the first women's marathon in the modern Games and Mary Lou Retton hitting perfect tens in the floor exercises and vault. I later covered a number of international sports competitions and the 1988 Calgary Winter Games. However, as a general assignment reporter based in Los Angeles, I was also responsible for coverage of politics, the film industry, scientific developments, and other events. Eventually, these assignments led me away from covering sports.

One day, as I was working on another assignment, I got a phone call from Friends of Mexico, which was funded by Televisa, the Mexican television network. The caller offered to fund me to conduct a cross-cultural study of the portrayal of athletes in art and literature both historically and in the present. I almost turned him down. Ultimately, in spite of my already heavy workload, I accepted the offer because I couldn't resist the subject matter. Over the next few weeks, I worked essentially another full-time job sifting through piles of books at UCLA's Art Library.

My object was to locate portrayals of the athlete in works that were not considered sporting art. I wanted to get beyond stereotypes of the athlete embedded in American culture, which tends to view athletes as mindless hulks. My own experience of professional and high-level athletes had convinced me that this view is false. Successful athletes must be as focused and dedicated as successful writers. Athletes study the strategy of their sport with the same dedication that neurosurgeons study the human brain. Even in sports that require massive strength, such as football and weightlifting, this is not brute force. There is a strategy for weightlifting, just as there is a strategy for tennis, auto racing, or removing an appendix. A consistent comment by athletes in all the sports I studied is, "It's a mental game."

And indeed, it is so. I have watched athletes defy pain and attempts to distract them. I have seen a physically more talented figure skater lose in competition to a less talented rival who was able to break her concentration.

In surveying images of athletes in art and literature, I wanted to examine the way in which portrayals of athletes reflect the way in which particular groups of people see themselves. The Puritan heritage lives on in the United States in anxieties about the human body expressed in stereotypes about athletes. British ideals about manly courage are acted out in their sports. Athletic pursuits in China and the ancient Middle East reflect attitudes about the responsibilities of rulers to their subjects.

Athletes are integral to the society in which they appear. They provide a mirror in which we see ourselves reflected. As we come to know and understand our unspoken assumptions about athletes we come to know ourselves. Within two years of completing my initial survey of athletes in art and literature, I quit my job at Voice of America to write *Sport as Symbol*.

A book of this scope could never have been produced without the aid and encouragement of many helpers along the way. Thanks go to S. Minanel, who scoured the earth for a suitable publisher and never lost faith in me throughout this long effort. The orientation of this book was first presented at a panel organized by the UCLA Center for the Study of Religion, and UCLA continues to support my work through my affiliation as a research scholar with the UCLA Center for the Study of Women.

Though members of an author's family are usually the last to be given credit for their contribution, my family really deserves first mention for their multiple contributions. I grew up in a family that encouraged intellectual exploration and took it for granted that reading, writing and debate were suitable jobs for a woman. My children — Laura, Jeff and Greg Womack — both endured the demands that authorship makes on a mother and actively supported my efforts. They, in turn, are actively supported by their spouses, Richard Williams, Michelle Gravatt Womack and Kathy Freeman Womack.

I have drawn considerable support from a number of professional areas. Chief among these are my media friends from my days at Voice of America. Especially notable are Ray Kabaker, for giving me the job of covering the 1984 Los Angeles Olympics, and Sean Kelly, who fostered my journalism career. Many thanks also to Ivo Alonso, with whom I covered many sporting events. Members of my dissertation committee encouraged and supported me when the idea of studying professional athletes was viewed with suspicion. They are anthropologists Jacques Maquet, Allen W. Johnson, Douglass Price-Williams, and sociologist Ralph Turner. Those who are familiar with these area of study will recognize that I had a sterling dissertation committee.

I am also grateful to members of The Association for the Anthropological Study of Play, especially Kendall Blanchard, Alice Cheska, Andrew Miracle, John Roberts and Brian Sutton-Smith. I was privileged to be among this pioneering band of scholars. Through my TAASP membership I was able to present papers and discuss ideas that later provided a foundation for this book. Through this group I also met Mihaly Csikzentmihalyi, who has long recognized the importance of play and creativity for psychological well-being, and Allen Guttman, with whom I happily disagree. My friends and neighbors, Jeff Law and Mary Lewis, provided the kick that thrust me across the finish line.

First, last and always, I owe a tremendous debt to all the athletes who have contributed to my understanding of the value of sports in human social life. They have much to teach us, and I still have much to learn.

PART 1. SPORT AS SYMBOL

One

Heroic Dramas and
Athletic Actors

Life is the game that must be played.
Edward Arlington Robinson, Ballade by the Fire

The apostle Paul often compared the Christian life to sports. In the first Epistle to the Corinthians, he writes: "Do you not know that in a race all the runners compete, but only one receives the prize? So run that you may obtain it" (I Corinthians 10:24).

Paul then proceeds to mix his sporting metaphors. In the most enthusiastic of sports writing traditions, he races from the track to the boxing ring. "I do not run aimlessly," he writes, "I do not box as one beating the air; but I pummel my body and subdue it, lest after preaching to others I myself should be disqualified" (I Corinthians 10:24). At one point Paul wearily sums up his successes and failures, finally consoling himself with the thought: "I have fought the good fight, I have finished the race, I have kept the faith" (I Timothy 4:7).

Paul was using sport as a metaphor to illustrate complex ideas about the appropriate approach to life. He is not alone in making this connection. The twelfth-century Persian poet Nizami advised his readers: "The Horizon is the boundary of your polo ground, the earth is the ball in the curve of your polo stick. Until the dust of non-existence rises from annihilation, gallop and urge on your steed because the ground is yours."

Sport is often used as a symbol, expressing meanings that go beyond its significance as diversion or physical training. Sport has been called ritualized warfare, but this is only one aspect of its metaphoric role. In the art and literature of Asia, the Middle East, Europe, and the United States, there is a pervasive use of sport as a symbol for sexuality, courage, spiritual striving, and a range of other epic themes. Nor is sport symbolism confined to these traditions. Native Americans, Africans, and indigenous people of many other parts of the world use sport as a metaphor for various types of conflict. In fact, it would be difficult to find a culture that does not link physical contests to some form of conflict resolution.

Symbols are powerful because they express complex ideas dramatically and succinctly. They engage private emotions in the service of public expressions of values. They are an effective way to communicate social values because they reason from the simple to the complex and from the known to the unknown. People react to symbols viscerally since symbols unite intellectual, emotional, and biological energies. In the symbolism of sport, there is a continual conceptual flow from the playing field to everyday reality to transcendence of the mundane world and back again. In the multivocal language of symbols, the "game" takes place on several levels at once.

Sport and Ritual

Symbols gain power by being acted out in ritual, and sport plays a part in this process. Many sports originated in religious ritual. Prior to the conquest of Mexico and Central America by the Spanish in the sixteenth century, a ball game formed part of the cosmology of the region. The Mayans of southern Mexico and Guatemala and the Aztecs of central Mexico developed complex civilizations marked by elaborate religious beliefs. Some of the most important of these involved the ball game.

The Central American ball game, *pok-tapok* among the Maya and *tlachtli* among the Aztecs, is ancestral to both soccer and basketball. Spanish conquistadors were astonished to see the people of Central America playing with rubber balls that rebounded "incredibly into the ayer." Europeans at that time were playing with inflated pig bladders or stuffed leather balls. The Central American ball game was played with a hard rubber ball in a high walled court with two stone rings. Without using their hands players tried to put the ball through the stone rings, a nearly impossible and hazardous enterprise.

The ball game was performed as part of religious rituals, and either the winning or losing team was sacrificed to the gods, perhaps depending on the region. The court was viewed as a microcosm of the universe, and the Aztecs believed the sky was a *tlachtli* court for the gods, who used the stars for balls. The Maya believed the sun and moon were originally ball players who defeated the underworld gods of sickness and death.

To understand sport as a religious rite, it is important to remove oneself from the often austere religious observances with which Westerners are most familiar. These reflect the influence of long centuries of constraints aimed at taming religious fervor. In the Western Christian tradition, especially, the body and its passions are seen as dangerous and immoral. In most traditions — both historically and in the present day — religious celebrations provide the setting for frenzied expressions of joy and despair.

One must imagine a great religious festival — similar to a fair — drawing people from all parts of the region. Colorful banners hang from buildings and images of gods and goddesses writhing in agony or contorted in transports of joy punctuate the square. Streets are crowded with people calling out greetings to friends and relatives, while buying food and other wares from street vendors. Feasting, dancing, and ritual performances of all kinds entertain the crowds. There may be theatrical enactments of traditional myths. From time to time, the crowd parts to make way for priests bearing flower-bedecked images of the gods, followed by penitents and petitioners making their way across the square. In the midst of all this activity, arenas are set aside where local heroes meet to wrestle, to vie against each other in races, or to compete as teams in ball games.

Participants in these sacred sporting events do not simply conduct a ritual performance, though the games contain aspects of both ritual and theater. All three types of performances enact dramas of life and death, but the way in which these themes are presented differs. In religious ritual and theater, the outcome is predetermined, removing an element of danger present in sports. Believers can be assured that religious ritual will maintain their relationship with the gods and natural forces on an even keel. Audiences at theatrical performances know that Good will triumph in the end, or at least, that the play's author has plotted a culturally appropriate conclusion.

But spectators at sporting event experience an additional source of anxiety: No one can predict how the game will end. Good may, in fact, lose to Evil. Or a superior team may be defeated by a lesser team. As one National Hockey League athlete put it, "Professional teams are so nearly equal in skill, any team can lose to any other on any given day."

There may be an added burden on athletes and spectators in a religious sporting contest. The athletes must use all their strength and skill on behalf of the gods to keep Evil and Chaos from overpowering heaven and earth. The Raramuri or Tarahumara Indians, who live in a mountainous region of northern Mexico, act out a cosmic conflict between God and Satan in a stylized battle that is probably similar to the origins of many sports. The Raramuri were introduced to Roman Catholicism by Jesuit missionaries early in the seventeenth century, but after that, remained somewhat isolated. In the ensuing centuries, the Raramuri developed their own interpretation of Christian theology, reflecting their experience of social life.

Unencumbered by European views of celibacy and monasticism as a religious ideal, the Raramuri place greater value on marriage and family solidarity. God and Satan, like the Raramuri, have family loyalties and responsibilities. The rivalry between God and Satan is not based on abstract moral principles, but on relationships within and between families.

The Raramuri believe that God is often in danger from his treacherous rival, Satan. They consider God especially vulnerable during Holy Week, just before Easter, when they must protect Him from onslaughts of the Devil. Throughout the week, the Raramuri purify themselves and their church by fasting and ritual cleansing of themselves and the church grounds. The people are divided into two groups: The Pharisees represent the forces of the Devil; the Captains are charged with the responsibility of protecting God from Satan's evil power.

On Holy Saturday, the people spend much of the day encircling the church in a ritual procession aimed at protecting the church, and by extension, God and God's wife, the Virgin Mary. William L. Merrill, an anthropologist who studied

Kim Hong-do was famous for his scenes from daily life, taking ordinary people as his subjects. This scene is from an album of 25 leaves, each organized in a circular composition focusing on a single figure or group. A leaf from the album shows wrestlers encircled by spectators, as a peddler offers a tray of *yot*, sticky rice treats (National Museum of Korea, Seoul, Treasure No. 527).

the Raramuri, describes the tremendous responsibility felt by participants in the ritual: "The fate of the universe rests on the Raramuri's shoulders during this period, for they must prevent the Devil from vanquishing God and destroying the world" (1987:381).

The activities of the Pharisees reflect a complex form of role-playing. They both protect God from the Devil and act on the Evil One's behalf. As representatives of the Devil, the Pharisees provide a visible, and therefore manageable, enemy. At the same time, the dual role of the Pharisees ensures that everyone in the community is involved in protecting God, regardless of the ritual parts being played. Thus, this vital work becomes a unified effort, reinforcing the solidarity of the group, while providing an opportunity to act out group conflicts.

On Holy Saturday, Captains and Pharisees engage in wrestling matches, battling for control of statues of Judas and his family, believed to be relatives of Satan. Regardless of who wins, the Captains take possession of the Judas images, shooting arrows into them and setting them on fire. Thus the evil forces that threaten the universe and the social life of the Raramuri are vanquished for another year (Merrill 1987).

It is not hard to see how sporting events arise from just such symbolic combat. Though the somewhat subdued religious observances with which we are most familiar may seem far removed from the apparent chaos of these vigorously enacted religious festivals, both express variations on common symbolic themes: responsibility to one's peers, duty to one's god, and the quest for some form of immortality.

Sport and Society

Sport reflects society. That is generally agreed upon by observers as removed in time and space as Greek poets, Chinese scholars, and contemporary social scientists. Sport is considered a subset of play, which is set apart from ordinary reality so that "real-life" values and relationships can be practiced without threatening the social fabric. Thus, play is seen as a creative wellspring that enriches society.

Though sport is a subset of play, it occupies a unique niche in social organization. Whereas some other forms of play may be exuberant and spontaneous activities with virtually inexhaustible creative potential, sport is more rigid both in form and social organization. Sport is defined by rules that must be adhered to regardless of the shifting social context. Sandlot leaguers in baseball must follow, in general, the same rules of the game as seasoned professionals, with some adaptations to compensate for differences in size, strength, speed, and experience. There is a hierarchy in sports just as there is a hierarchy in contemporary society. Nations have monarchs, presidents, or prime ministers; sports teams have managers, owners, and coaches.

Sport also inherently involves conflict. The Swiss philosopher Johan Huizinga notes that ball games pit village against village, school against school, and he might have added, nation against nation. Sport is defined as a contest involving physical strength, agility, speed, or endurance. The contest need not be against other people. In such sports as hunting, fishing, and hang gliding, the athlete may contend against nonhuman or even inanimate opponents.

Symbolic battles acted out in sports are often substitutes for the real thing. When the colonial administrators outlawed warfare in the Trobriand Islands, off the coast of New Guinea near Australia, cricket was introduced as a way of acting out traditional rivalries. Trobrianders adapted their warfare insignia and magic to the cricket field.

The modern Olympics have provided an arena for acting out political conflicts. For many years the Soviet Union and the United States fought the Cold War through the Olympic contests. For most of that time, the United States took a pummeling in a number of sports, including ice hockey. However, the U.S. ice hockey team reversed that relationship by defeating the Soviets during the 1980 Winter Games, at a time when the American public was feeling particularly vulnerable. Hostages had been taken at the U.S. Embassy in Iran, and the Soviet Union had invaded Afghanistan. Paul Conrad, cartoonist for the *Los Angeles Times*, depicted the U.S. ice hockey team raising the American flag in an image modeled after the famous painting of U.S. Marines raising the American flag on Iwo Jima during World War II. Thus, the triumph on the ice was equated with a victory on the battlefield.

Another newspaper also drew an explicit link between the outcome of the game and war: "Revenge is oh so sweet — especially when it involves the Russians.... It was also the biggest shot in the arm of America since the Canadians helped 6 Americans escape from Iran.... After Finland, bring on Afghanistan."[1]

Iwo Jima was the scene of the longest, most intensive shelling of any Pacific island during World War II, involving the U.S. Air Force, Navy, and Marines. U.S. military strategists considered the capture of Iwo Jima to be essential for launching air raids against Japan and determined to seize the island at all costs. Air bombardments began in June 1944. Three days before the planned invasion date, Navy vessels bombarded the island. Then shortly after 9 A.M. on February 19, 1945, U.S. Marine divisions began hitting the beach. On February 23, Marines fought their way to the top of Mount Suribachi, an extinct volcano that forms the southern tip of the island, and raised a small American flag atop the mountain. Taking control of the summit was significant both strategically and symbolically. Capturing the mountain gave American troops a command post, and the sight of the flag inspired troops at the base to greater efforts. That afternoon, when the U.S. military had secured the mountain, a larger flag was raised by five Marines and a Navy hospital corpsman.

Raising of the flag inspired a Pulitzer Prize–winning photo by Associated Press photographer Joe Rosenthal. The photo, in turn, inspired a sculpture by Felix W. de Weldon, then on duty with the U.S. Navy. Three of the six who raised the flag survived the continued fighting on Iwo Jima and posed for the sculpture which now stands as the U.S. Marine Corps War Memorial.

The historic scene on Iwo Jima became an important symbol of courage and

This image by Paul Conrad depicts the win of the U.S. hockey team over the Soviet team in the 1980 Winter Olympics. It is modeled after the raising of the U.S. flag on Iwo Jima during World War II (*Los Angeles Times*, February 25, 1980).

hope in the aftermath of the destruction by terrorists of the Twin Towers of the World Trade Center in New York on September 11, 2001. Two commercial airliners, hijacked while en route from Logan Airport in Boston to Los Angeles International Airport, were flown into the Twin Towers, reducing them to fiery rubble. Two other airliners were hijacked on the same day. One crashed into the Pentagon, a symbol of U.S. military might; another crashed into the countryside outside Pittsburgh when passengers resisted the hijacking. Their courage thwarted plans of the hijackers to inflict even more damage on the American psyche.

Since the Pentagon was the only military target, the hijackings were widely interpreted as an attempt to demoralize the American people through destruction of the Twin Towers, symbols of U.S. economic might. In defiance, three firefighters raised the U.S. flag atop the rubble of the World Trade Center as others worked to rescue potential survivors among the thousands of people buried in the rubble.

The gesture was especially poignant since several hundred firefighters and police officers died in the rescue effort. The image of the firefighters' dedication and defiance was a rallying call for Americans, evoking crises of the past that had been overcome and signaling hope for the future. Veteran journalist Tom Brokaw choked up as the image flashed on the television screen, then hastily apologized, explaining, "I was caught off guard by a rush of emotion when I saw that flag." Both the image and the reaction of a seasoned journalist dramatically underscored the range of emotions, including national pride, evoked by terrorist attacks on treasured cultural icons.

Admiral Chester W. Nimitz's assessment of the U.S. military effort on Iwo Jima could also apply to recovery efforts following the destruction of the Twin Towers of the World Trade Center: "...uncommon valor was a common virtue." A recurring theme of the three images — on the mountain, on the ice, and atop the rubble of the Twin Towers — is triumph in the face of adversity. This is a theme that evokes national pride among Americans. Conrad's image of the flag being raised on the ice illustrates the close symbolic relationship between sports and other aspects of social life.

Sports can also be used as an arena for political negotiation. A shift in international political alignments was signaled at the 1976 Montreal Olympics when the Taiwanese team was stripped of the right to march under its own flag in the opening and closing ceremonies. Mainland China had been isolated from participation in the Olympics after Mao Zedong seized control of the government in 1949. The United Nations ousted Taiwan from its General Assembly in 1971, and the United States and mainland China exchanged liaison offices in each other's capitals in 1973. China threatened to boycott the 1976 Olympics if Taiwan were permitted to march under its own flag, since mainland China claimed to be the sole government representing China. The International Olympic Committee reached a compromise by requiring Taiwan to march under the official Olympics flag.

After Soviet troops occupied Hungary in 1956, Hungarian nationals expressed their frustration in a hard-fought water polo match between the two countries. As one Hungarian water polo player proudly described the scene to me: "The pool was red with blood." Hungarian water polo players later denied that the match had been that violent, but the legend lives on in popular imagination, because it reinforces the pride of the Hungarian people. Though the Soviets dominated the Hungarian countryside, Hungarians dominated the pool, winning Olympic gold medals in water polo in 1956, 1964, and 1976, surrendering to the Soviet Union only in 1972. There are decided advantages to fighting symbolic battles with a heroic army. The athletic victory is just as sweet as that on the battlefield, and there are no cities to be rebuilt or (usually) bodies to be buried.

The contesting aspect of sport makes it especially powerful as a symbol. The physical context becomes a metaphor for the challenges that all human beings meet in going about their daily lives. Sports symbolism usually expresses themes of epic proportions: responsibility to oneself and others, the moral choice of Right and Wrong, the dilemmas of power, and the agony of loss and betrayal. Often, it is clear the "game" is life itself, played out in a hazardous universe.

The Hero Myth

Sporting achievements figure prominently in the careers of heroes, ranging from the Celtic warrior Cú Chulainn to the ancient Sumerian king Gilgamesh. Even Siddhartha Gautama, the historical Buddha and founder of Buddhism, proved his prowess in athletics.

Before his enlightenment, when he was a young man still living in the world of sensual pleasures, Siddhartha sought for his wife Yasodhara, daughter of a noble family of his own Sakya tribe. Prior to this time, Siddhartha's father, King Shuddhodana, had never denied his son anything. Since the young man's birth, the king had surrounded Siddhartha with pleasure to prevent him from leaving home to pursue the religious quest that had been foretold for him. The king had never even allowed his son outside the palace gates for fear the boy would see something that would distress him and cause him to question the meaning of life. When Siddartha expressed his desire to marry Yasodhara, King Shuddhodana set off to see Yasodhara's father to arrange yet another of his son's desires. But in this case, the aims of the king were balked. Though Siddhartha was a wealthy prince, the woman's father hesitated to approve the match, saying:

> My lord, your son has been brought up in luxury; he has never been out-
> side the palace-gates; his physical and intellectual abilities have never
> been proven. You know that the Sakyas only marry their daughters to men
> who are skillful and strong, brave and wise. How can I give my daugh-
> ter to your son who, so far, has shown a taste only for indolence?

King Shuddhodana despaired at hearing these words. For the first time, he could not give his son what he wanted. However, the king had not counted on his divine-born[2] son's innate wisdom and physical prowess. When King Shuddodana reported his conversation with Yasodhara's father to Siddhartha, the prince merely laughed, saying, "My Lord, you are needlessly disturbed. Do you believe there is anyone in Kapilavastu [his kingdom] who is my superior in strength or in intellect?"

The king quickly set about arranging a contest pitting Siddhartha against the wisest and strongest men of the region. In the first two events, writing and mathematics, the prince easily bested all the others. In the athletic contests, the prince effortlessly won at running and jumping. In wrestling, he merely touched his opponent, who would then fall to the ground. Siddhartha's most dramatic demonstration of skill came in the archery event:

Then they brought out the bows, and skillful archers placed their arrows in targets that were barely visible. But when it came the prince's turn to shoot, so great was his natural strength that he broke each bow as he drew it. Finally, the king sent guards to fetch a very ancient, very precious bow that was kept in the temple. No one within the memory of man had ever been able to draw or lift it. Siddhartha took the bow in his left hand, and with one finger of his right hand he drew it to him. Then he took as target a tree so distant that he alone could see it. The arrow pierced the tree, and, burying itself in the ground, disappeared. And there, where the arrow had entered the ground, a well formed, which was called the Well of the Arrow [Herold 1954:33–37].

Thus the prince won his bride. But destiny was not to be balked. After Yasodhara had given birth to a son, thus continuing the royal line, Siddhartha was given permission to venture outside the gates of the palace, where on successive visits, he chanced to see an old man, a sick man, and a dead man. The sight of human suffering so distressed the gentle prince that he set out on his successful quest to understand why humans were born to suffer and die. The success of Siddhartha's quest earned him the title of Buddha, or Enlightened One. As Buddha Sakayamuni (enlightened sage of the Sakya tribe), he attracted a band of followers, the first Buddhists.

Alteration of the natural landscape, such as that described in the account of the archery contest, is a recurring feature in heroic legends. In altering the landscape, the hero is symbolically demonstrating his control over nature, thereby taking on some of its power. Control over nature — though less dramatically expressed — is central to a number of sports, including mountain climbing.

One reason for the prominence of sports in the careers of heroes is that it allows them to demonstrate their worth. Not only is physical prowess conceptually correlated with other heroic abilities, but sports provide a context in which heroes can display character traits that make them gracious winners. At the same time, the conflicts and ethical dilemmas that form the basis for heroic stories are precisely those themes that are acted out in sports: moral and physical courage and responsibility to one's peers. The hero is a public symbol who, through his own personality and moral choices, acts out the conflicts that are recurring features of human psychological and social life. The hero myth can present an ideal model for dealing with real-life crises, but is often a cautionary tale, providing an example of how *not* to behave.

According to psychologist Carl Jung, the hero is a symbol of transformation acting out the human life cycle from birth to death. Jung suggests that the hero myth illustrates the process of growth from a state of dependency to adulthood. The myth accomplishes this, Jung writes, by drawing on libido, or energy from biological drives: "The finest of all symbols of the libido is the human figure, conceived as a demon or hero" (Jung 1956:171).

A story of transformation is dramatized through the sport of hunting in Ernest Hemingway's short story, "The Short Happy Life of Francis Macomber." Macomber is a man dominated by his wife. On a big game hunt in Africa, Macomber's "weakness" is embarrassingly apparent to the "manly" safari leader, Robert Wilson, an example of the guide who often assists the hero in myths of this genre.

Macomber's flaws are first dramatically displayed by his cowardliness in hunting a lion. In the primal confrontation between man and beast, the beast demonstrates its superiority. The story implies that this is a reversal of the natural order. The man must overcome his own fear by facing down and killing the lion. Macomber's failure at hunting extends to sexuality when his wife leaves him to go to the bed of the more "masculine" safari leader. Impotence in the hunt is mirrored by Macomber's powerlessness in sexually controlling his wife. Later, while tracking three buffalo, Macomber becomes transformed by the excitement of the chase and transcends his own troubles and anxieties in pursuit of a higher game. Macomber's personal transformation also transforms the relationship among Macomber, his wife and the safari leader:

> Macomber felt a wild unreasonable happiness that he had never known before.
> "By God, that was a chase," he said. "I've never felt any such feeling. Wasn't it marvelous, Margo?"
> "I hated it."
> "Why?"
> "I hated it," she said bitterly. "I loathed it."
> "You know I don't think I'd ever be afraid of anything again," Macomber said to Wilson. "Something happened in me after we first saw the buff and went after him. Like a dam bursting. It was pure excitement."

By transcending his human failings, Macomber also frees himself from his wife's domination. He has conquered his fear, the animal, and his wife in one splendid moment of total engagement. As if in retaliation, he is killed by his wife in a hunting "accident." It is clear that, for Hemingway, Macomber's "short happy life" refers to those brief moments before his death when he is wholly dedicated to the primal contest between man and beast. Hemingway's terse prose describes the life of the hero from beginning to end.

According to Jung, the career of the hero is an arc, which is also the trajectory of the sun when viewed from earth. Jung's model was based on the career of the Greek hero Icarus, who flew too close to the sun on wax and feather wings constructed by his father Daedalus. To Jung, the prototypical hero was the sun-god, known as Surya in Hindu mythology and as Apollo in Greek mythology. The trajectory of the sun symbolizes the human life cycle:

> Just as the sun, by its own motion and in accordance with its own inner law, climbs from morn till noon, crosses the meridian and goes its downward way towards evening, leaving its radiance behind it, and finally plunges into all-enveloping night, so man sets his course by immutable laws and, his journey over, sinks into darkness, to rise again in his children and begin the cycle anew [Jung 1956:171].

According to Jung, those who hear the hero myth identify with the hero and learn from the triumphs and sorrows of the hero how to deal with the triumphs and sorrows in their own lives.

The hero myth also deals with the role of the individual in society, spelling out one's responsibility to one's peers. Many heroes are culture givers, and this is a recurring theme in the art and literature of sports. In some cases, the hero battles forces of nature that threaten to overwhelm society; in others, he fights on behalf of those weaker than himself. The hero myth is in one sense a warning that superior gifts must be used on behalf of society, and the hero fails when he turns inward, away from society.

To Jung and other writers on the hero, this symbol of transformation is typically portrayed as male, and therefore I have used male pronouns in discussing their work. However, the idea of the hero as male is due to a traditional cultural bias in psychology and the social sciences that defines males as social actors and females as marginal to social processes. In fact, there have been many female sports heroes, and female participation in sporting activities is documented for as long as we have historical records.

The adventures of the hero act out the process of conflict resolution. The myth typically centers on a battle with a powerful enemy or enemies, which provides the context for an exploration of the hero's character. The enemy can be a personified as an external force or a demon within. The overall trajectory of the hero myth is consistent cross-culturally, but the hero drama may vary, depending on variations in cultural values and on the psychological and social dilemmas the hero represents.

Based on my research among professional and high-level athletes, I identified four hero types, each of which embodies lessons that point the way to growth and transformation. They also provide models that conform to or challenge prevailing cultural mores. The four hero types are the *Paragon*, the *Rogue*, the *Outlaw*, and the *Rebel* (Womack 1981, 1983). As has been noted by Jung and other scholars, we learn not only from the triumphs of the hero but also from his or her mistakes.

The Paragon exemplifies social virtues. He is cited as an example to youth and is considered the ultimate in human achievement. The role of the Paragon is to abide by the rules and embody social values. On the other hand, the Rogue emphasizes pleasure over principle. He is self-indulgent and represents a lifestyle seemingly free of the cares that beset the rest of us. The Rogue conforms in many respects to the Trickster, a prominent figure in American Indian mythology. The Trickster is often portrayed as an animal who prevails through cunning and subverting the rules (Radin 1948). The Rogue may be regarded as the untamed aspect of ourselves that resists conformity to social demands without challenging the legitimacy of the social order itself.

Whereas the Paragon and the Rebel ultimately uphold the social order, the Outlaw and the Rebel illustrate important social lessons by rejecting conformity to social rules altogether. The Outlaw provides an object lesson by breaking the rules and failing. His downfall illustrates the hazards of failing to conform. The Rebel challenges the social order in hopes of changing it. Whereas the Outlaw proclaims

"I am guilty," the Rebel proclaims "The social order is guilty." Through their different styles of conformity or nonconformity to social norms, sports heroes help to define appropriate social roles by acting out and negotiating the implicit rules that underlie social life.

Defining the Rules—The Paragon and the Rogue

It is important that the Paragon do battle against an external enemy who represents the character flaws alien to the hero's own superior nature, but which give rise to the conflicts that are essential to the unfolding of the myth. The life of Siddhartha Gautama is characteristic of the career of the Paragon. Since the Buddha was a great spiritual leader, he could not be subject to weakness of any kind. His troubles, when they arose at the height of his career, were due to the machinations of his would-be rival Devadatta. Devadatta's attempts to supplant the Enlightened One are a recurring theme in the Jatakas, stories about the previous lives of the Buddha. The Buddha represents the ideal; Devadatta represents an illicit challenge to that ideal

The Paragon model is also represented in the life of the fifteenth-century French heroine Joan of Arc, the Maid of Orleans. During her brief but splendid life, she rallied her compatriots in their battle against the English. Though she was burned at the stake by the English while still in her teens, she continues to live as a symbol of French national pride.

In sports, the Paragon is exemplified by the African-American U.S. track star Jesse Owens. On the eve of World War II, Adolf Hitler planned the 1936 Berlin Olympics as a showcase for what he considered Aryan superiority. Jesse Owens invalidated that claim by winning four gold medals during those Games and by helping the U.S. relay team set a world record that lasted for twenty years. Jesse Owens faced the ultimate adversary in Hitler, an evil dictator whose designs included control of the world and eliminating those he deemed inferior. The athlete's triumph was heightened by defeating his adversary on Hitler's own turf. This is a real-life sporting event that captures the essence of the heroic conflict in portraying the dramatic triumph of Good over Evil. The message is especially satisfying because the hero represented a disadvantaged underclass facing a seemingly invincible opponent.

The life of U.S. baseball player Joe DiMaggio is a variation on the Paragon myth. In this case, the heroic conflict included the dramatic element of tragedy. DiMaggio's symbolic stature developed from his excellence in baseball, itself a symbol of the "American way of life." The athlete's demeanor, combining strength with restraint, expresses U.S. cultural values relating to self-reliance and male avoidance of emotional display. DiMaggio's story took on a note of tragedy as a result of his brief but romantic marriage to another American symbol, Marilyn Monroe. Her early death enhanced the tragic myth, as according to popular legend, he continued to send a single rose to her grave every day.

During the social and political upheaval of the 1960s, Joe DiMaggio's association with the "American way of life" brought him a different type of symbolic prominence. In the Simon and Garfunkel song "Mrs. Robinson," composed for the film *The Graduate*, the baseball player is called upon as a metaphor for a simpler past:

> Where have you gone, Joe DiMaggio?
> A nation turns its lonely eyes to you.
> (Wo, wo, wo.)
> What's that you say, Mrs. Robinson
> "Joltin Joe" has left and gone away?
> Hey, hey, hey — hey, hey, hey.

The film was itself a rallying call for disillusioned youth of the 1960s who had rejected the values of their parents, a generation that represented the materialism, unbounded optimism, and suburban lifestyle of the post World War II era. The story line of *The Graduate* expresses the conflict between parents who gained affluence through adherence to the work ethic and their offspring, who rejected the materialism and hypocrisy they saw in their parents. The song reflects the ironic view that, though the nation may long for its heroes, real-life problems often call for more complex solutions. Thus, the symbolism associated with Joe DiMaggio acquired a double-edged significance. While acknowledging the heroic status of the baseball player, the song rejects what it implies are simplistic values.

Rogues are among the best loved heroes because they are more accessible than the Paragon. The Rogue lifts us beyond our routine existence and allows us to experience his lifestyle vicariously. Since the career of the hero is an arc, we can be reassured that the Rogue must ultimately pay for his excesses. We can soar with him to his heights and watch him fall from a safe distance.

One of the most renowned athletes of classical times was the wrestler Milo of Croton, who is said to have lived during the sixth century B.C.E. Milo had an unusual training regimen. As a boy he carried a newborn calf on his shoulders each day. As the calf grew, the weight borne by the athlete naturally increased. When the calf was fully grown, Milo was able to walk around the Olympic stadium bearing it on his back. The hero triumphed in all four major Greek athletic festivals. He began his Olympic career with a victory in the boys' wrestling event in 540 B.C.E. He later won the men's event in five successive Olympiads from 536 to 520 B.C.E. He also won seven times at the Pythian Games at Delphi, ten times in the Isthmian Games, and nine times in the Nemean Games. Milo was five times holder of the Periodonikes, a greatly esteemed title earned by the winner of all four major athletic festivals in the same cycle. The wrestler held a high command in the Croton army. He spurred his men to victory by going into battle wearing his Olympic crowns, along with a lion skin and club that symbolically linked him to Herakles (Hercules).

Milo's arrogance brought about his own death. While walking in a forest, the wrestler saw a tree trunk that had wedges inserted in it to split it. In an ostentatious attempt to demonstrate his strength to his companions, he opened the split with his fingers. However, the trunk closed on his hands and, unable to free himself, Milo was killed and eaten by a pack of wolves (Harris 1966:110–113).

Heroes are bigger than life. Their virtues are great; so are their faults and so is their misfortune when it occurs. One who hears the myth participates vicariously in the hero's triumphs and learns from the example of his misfortunes. Our heroes do not serve us by remaining remote from human dilemmas, but by "coming to grips" with them, by "wrestling" with them, so that we may experience the full drama of the conflict.

Lords of Misrule — The Outlaw and the Rebel

Anthropologists have long noted that some categories of individuals and some festivals reinforce cultural values and social relationships by challenging them. One example is the Lord of Misrule characteristic of Medieval European Christmas celebrations. The Lord of Misrule was chosen by lot a month before Christmas, and during the period leading up to that sacred event, he presided over festivities that flaunted all normal rules of behavior. The Lord of Misrule was given full license to indulge in whatever pleasures he desired, enticing his "subjects" to join him in his indulgences.

Crowning a Lord of Misrule dates back to the Roman Saturnalia, a ritual observance that culminated in sacrifice of the king of revelry to the somber god Saturn. During the Middle ages, an effigy was burned instead. Such rituals of rebellion actually reinforce the social order by allowing members of the group to express emotions and act out conflicts held in check by ordinary rules of behavior (Gluckman 1952). Sacrificing the Lord of Misrule, either literally or in effigy, puts a dramatic end to the period of disorder and reaffirms social norms.

In sports, the Outlaw and the Rebel similarly reinforce the social order by challenging it, though they accomplish this in different ways. The Outlaw seems unable to follow the rules that govern the rest of us. Outlaws may repeatedly be arrested for drunk driving or some other infraction of the rules. The annals of sports are replete with Outlaw figures. In the 1990s, the football player O. J. Simpson plummeted from Paragon to Outlaw in the eyes of the public when he was accused of the murder of his estranged wife Nicole Brown Simpson. Though he was acquitted in the case, the conduct of the trial and Simpson's later behavior reinforced the popular view that he was guilty of the crime. Further, Simpson's private life was revealed to fall far short of behavior expected of the Paragon.

On the other hand, boxer Mike Tyson broke both the rules of society and the rules of the ring by biting off a piece of the ear of his opponent Evander Holyfield. This single act of assault brought him more notoriety than the jail time he served for the sexual assault of some female companions. As an Outlaw, violating criminal law was consistent with his symbolic image. In assaulting his boxing opponent, he violated the rules of the ring. Ultimately, neither challenged his heroic role. In fact, he drew greater boxing revenues through his illegal behavior than through his athletic performance. Spectators still cheered Tyson on, not because of his athletic skill but because of his challenge to the social order.

Outlaws are heroes in the Jungian sense because their lives embody social lessons and because they engage the attention of the public. Outlaws uphold values by providing a warning of what happens to those who don't follow the rules. In a sense, the Outlaw is a tragic figure. In spite of his great athletic gifts, his life is a lesson in disorder. By breaking the rules and suffering the consequences, the Outlaw reaffirms the social order.

It is sometimes important to question society, to challenge rigidity and outmoded concepts. This is the job of the Rebel. Tennis player Billy Jean King battled the sporting establishment almost as effectively as she faced her on-court opponents, winning significant financial rewards for female athletes. The role of the Rebel is usually a thankless one. Athletes are expected to uphold the social order, not challenge it. African-American athletes who gave the Black Power salute on the victory stand at the 1968 Mexico Olympics were virtually consigned to oblivion after the Games. Though Billie Jean King won greater prominence for women athletes, she failed to win the hearts of the American public.

Boxer Muhammad Ali took on the role of the Rebel in refusing to serve in the war in Vietnam. In spite of his stint as a Rebel, Muhammad Ali is one of the best-loved of American athletes, but not because of his challenge to the social order. During much of his boxing career, Ali played the role of the Rogue, a much more endearing heroic figure than the Rebel. After his retirement, Ali's role as a hero shifted to that of the Paragon, as Americans recognized his contribution to popular culture.

Sport is often used to metaphorically challenge society. Oscar Wilde once described English nobility engaged in foxhunting as "the unspeakable in full pursuit of the uneatable." The writer is deriding an entire social class through his image of the fox hunter. It is often our most deeply held values that invite parody, because it is such a small step from the sublime to the ridiculous. Sentiment quickly fades into sentimentality. It is when we try hardest to be dignified that we are most likely to appear absurd. Social life has a dual face: the emperor must be balanced by the clown, who makes fun of all that the emperor represents.

The Hungarian scholar Zoltan Kovesces suggests that sports represent "possible worlds," where ideals are perfectly conceptualized but imperfectly acted out. Sporting symbols typically express the ideal order, but the very intensity of that expression is a reminder that disorder lurks nearby.

Heroic Lessons

The idealistic view of the athlete as contender in a game that is larger than life reached a pinnacle in Greek art. In this tradition, famous athletes assumed the stature of minor gods. Important athletic events, including the Olympics, were held in honor of the gods, and victorious athletes were immortalized in statues, on vases, and in poems and songs. The statues of some legendary athletes were believed to have the power to heal the sick. The poet Pindar was often commissioned to commemorate an athletic victory, as in the following poem celebrating the winner of a boys' boxing event in 176 B.C.E.:

> For Olympian victors, such acclaim
> is laid in store
> without limit, and I
> am eager to tend it with my song.
> for a man flourishes
> in wise understanding,
> as in all things,
> through a god's favor.
> Know now, son of Archestratos,
> Hagesidamos, because of your boxing victory
> I will sing, and my song will be
> an added adornment
> to your gold olive crown....

In his epic poem *The Odyssey*, Homer describes a stop on Odysseus' journey home where he is entertained by Alcinous, king of Phaiacia. The king's son Laodamas invites Odysseus to compete, saying: "Come along, father, have a try at the games yourself, if you ever learnt them. A man ought to know about games. Game is the best way to fame while you're still alive — what you can do with your arms and legs."[3] No hero could resist such a challenge. Odysseus springs to his feet, picks up a huge weight, and throws it farther than any of the younger men. After this prodigious display of strength, he declares that he can beat them all at wrestling, boxing, running, or the javelin, but his listeners decline to test his claim.

Athletes are often used to illustrate cautionary tales that warn against the dangers of early fame or excessive pride. A. E. Housman's 1896 poem "To an Athlete Dying Young" acknowledges the idea that the athlete competes on behalf of the town, but tells the dead youth he is fortunate to go before his glory fades and he is forgotten by the crowds who formerly idolized him:

> The time you won your town the race
> We chaired you through the market-place;
> Man and boy stood cheering by,
> And home we brought you shoulder-high.
>
> To-day the road all runners come,
> Shoulder-high we bring you home,
> And set you at your threshold down,
> Townsman of a stiller town.

> Smart lad, to slip betimes away
> From fields where glory does not stay,
> And early though the laurel grows
> It withers quicker than the rose.

Housman's poem underscores a pervasive theme in the symbolism of the sports hero, that the athlete does not compete on his own behalf, but as a representative of the group to which he belongs. The athlete represents aspirations of the group, not the individual. The individual excellence of the athlete is "owned" by the group. As Jung notes in his model of the hero, the athlete fails when he forgets his responsibilities to the group. Ernest Lawrence Thayer's 1888 poem "Casey at the Bat" warns against such arrogance:

> There was ease in Casey's manner as he stepped into his place,
> There was pride in Casey's bearing, and a smile on Casey's face,
> And when, responding to the cheers, he lightly doffed his hat,
> No stranger in the crowd could doubt t'was Casey at the bat.

Casey knew how to work the crowd. Tension rises among the fans as Casey lets ball after ball go by him, aiming to demonstrate his utter control of the plate. Alas, glory was snatched from his grasp:

> Oh! Somewhere in this favored land the sun is shining bright;
> The band is playing somewhere, and somewhere hearts are light;
> And somewhere men are laughing and somewhere children shout,
> But there is no joy in Mudville — mighty Casey had struck out.

Though his image may be a bit tarnished, Casey remains a folk hero. Ironically, through his failure, the fictional nineteenth-century baseball player achieved an honor long denied the real-life twentieth-century baseball player, Pete Rose. Although he was more successful at the plate than Casey, Rose was denied admission to the Baseball Hall of Fame in 1991 after suffering legal problems arising from his passion for gambling. On the other hand, Casey's statue holds a place of honor at the Baseball Hall of Fame in Cooperstown, New York. Seemingly unchastened by his humiliation at the plate, Casey stands leaning nonchalantly on his bat, as though daring the pitcher to throw the ball — a true rogue.

Sport is often used as a metaphor for lost youth or for an inability to deal with the complexities of life. In *Goodbye, Columbus* (1959), Philip Roth's character Ron Patimkin views all of life, including his coming marriage, in terms of sports:

> And at dinner Ron expanded on the subject of responsibilities and the future.
> "We're going to have a boy," he said, to his mother's delight, "and when he's about six months old I'm going to sit him down with a basketball in

A statue of the fictional baseball player Casey exhibits the casual arrogance typical of the Rogue. The work is on display at the National Baseball Hall of Fame in Cooperstown, New York (National Baseball Library, Cooperstown, New York).

front of him, and a football, and a baseball, and then whichever one he reaches for, that's the one we're going to concentrate on."

"Suppose he doesn't reach for any of them," [Ron's sister] Brenda said.

"Don't be funny, young lady," Mrs. Patimkin said.

For Philip Roth, Ron Patimkin's preoccupation with sports symbolizes artificial middle class values, as well as the inability to move beyond the games appropriate to youth. The author seizes upon sport as an appropriate metaphor for complex relationships, including the special place given to Ron Patimkin over his sister Brenda.

Throughout history, writers, poets, and artists have been similarly inspired to look to sport to elucidate troubling aspects of human existence. Sport mirrors other aspects of everyday reality, but with a clarity and precision that escapes most real-life events. After conducting a small-scale study of softball, a sport in which she participated, one of my students put it this way:

> There are many rules in softball. Just like there are many rules in society. The difference is that the rules in a softball game are more up front and everybody must abide by the same rules. Unlike a society where the rules are sometimes hidden and they do not apply to everybody.[4]

This student has accurately pinpointed the significance of sport as a symbol. Sport is like society without the confusion or contradictions.

Sport and Conflict Resolution

Some scholars assert that all sports developed either from hunting or warfare, and the essential component of these activities is the contest. This assertion is not entirely accurate. Some sporting events arise from other activities. Foot races engaged in by many North American Indian groups celebrated the speed and social value of messengers. Though these runners were of great importance in carrying messages during battles, they were essential at all times for carrying messages between spatially isolated groups.

One of the most satisfying aspects of sports is that it pits the athlete against a worthy opponent. The combatants are wholly engaged and, at times, even their lives may be at stake. The contest and the total commitment of the participants provide an idealized context for conflict resolution.

Sport is a symbol, a mechanism for acting out and resolving conflict. Metaphorical symbols, based on the principle of reasoning by analogy, make complex concepts accessible by encoding them in compelling images. In battling dragons, evil dictators, and countless other horrors, the hero acts out our own nameless terrors and our own struggles with the seemingly endless demands of social life. Sport dramatizes this ongoing conflict, objectifies it, and provides an arena in which to resolve it.

Conflict can take place on a number of levels: social, moral, and psychological. Social life is rife with competing goals and demands, as well as with inherent contradictions that must be resolved or mediated. Moral or ethical dilemmas arise from the struggle to uphold social norms that run counter to what seems to be individual self-interest. Psychological stress arises, in part, from the attempt to balance fulfillment of personal goals against the need to meet expectations of others. All these forms of conflict are expressed in the symbolism of sport. The athletic hero is judged by how well he or she meets social obligations and fulfills cultural expectations while achieving the maximum in human potential.

The heroic contest in sports is organized in this book according to three recurring themes expressed in the art, literature, and song of sports: the fight for survival as expressed in a contest against an adversary in nature; the fight against a powerful human adversary; and the fight against an even more dangerous and elusive adversary, the enemy within.

The type of opponent generally shapes the sporting event. The contest with nature is typically expressed in images of the hunt, discussed in Chapter Two. Chapter Three, on the domestication of the hunt, traces the development of sport through its various aspects as ritual and pageant. The human adversary is encountered in such sports as boxing and wrestling, and the various types of ball games. Chapter Four examines warfare as represented in combat sports ranging from jousting to boxing. In addition, this chapter explores the way in which combat sports express such themes as social responsibility, spiritual striving, and aesthetics. Sport is also associated with warfare in the various forms of ball games. These are treated in Chapter Five according to their social dynamics, as expressed in the style of play.

Perhaps the most dangerous adversary in sports is the opponent within, the part of oneself that must be conquered to excel in the game of life. Chapter Six deals with the contest against one's inner self, represented in such sports as racing and mountaineering. Although there may be a fiercely competitive aspect to these activities, the adversary is no longer met in hand-to-hand combat. Rather, the opponent serves as a spur to greater effort, so that the contestant wins by transcending baser elements of his or her own nature. Ultimately, it can be argued, this is the essential contest in all sports. Sport also serves as a metaphor for other aspects of human aspiration, including erotic love and religious transcendence. These permutations on the symbolism of sport are explored in Chapter Seven.

Chapter Eight, which focuses on the relationship of the athlete to society, discusses the differing experiences of athletes and spectators. This chapter also summarizes the process of secularization of sport, especially as it relates to ethics, violence, and group identity. It also describes recreational aspects of sports that serve to *recreate* the experiences of individuals and the dynamics of society as a whole.

Sport, in its many variations, has engaged the attention of artists, writers, and musicians all over the world. Sport communicates through the language of symbols and, like art, it dramatizes complex ideas that cannot readily be expressed in words.

PART 2. THE ADVERSARY IN NATURE

Two

The Hunt:
Power of Life and Death

There is a passion for hunting something deeply implanted in the human breast.

Charles Dickens, *Oliver Twist*

The hunt is among the most pervasive of sporting symbols. In fact, hunting art may be traced to neolithic cave paintings. Technically, these early hunts are studied as subsistence activities rather than sport. However, there appears to be a great deal of sport associated with subsistence hunting, both prehistorically and at present.

The first record of hunting art dates from about 32,000 years ago, during the Upper Paleolithic, by which time modern Homo sapiens had displaced earlier hominid species. We have an abundant record of cave art and decorated objects from the Upper Paleolithic. Scholars are at a loss to precisely explain the plethora of creative expression dating from this period. Originally, it was thought that "primitive" artists were using magic in an attempt to enhance their success in the hunt. According to the principle of sympathetic magic, killing the animal in the image helps the hunter to kill the animal in the flesh.

Some representations of animals display puncture marks indicating that they were stabbed, perhaps ceremonially, after being painted. More recently, archaeologists have noted that most paintings do not display such marks and that many of the animals depicted were not hunted for food. Thus it seems unlikely that magical kills were the only or even the primary motivation for producing the art. Further, humans from the Upper Paleolithic, when the art was produced, were highly skilled and effective hunters. Far from being primitive, these foragers were skilled both in their technology and in their knowledge of animal habits and anatomy. They were also skilled and imaginative artists. Some works of art use the topography of the cave to give a three-dimensional image of the animal being depicted. Representations of animals that have survived to the present day on the walls of European caves demonstrate artistic skills comparable to those of artists trained in modern academies.

A striking feature of European cave art is that animals are depicted realistically, whereas humans are often represented as stick figures and with non-human features. Some human figures were depicted as having bird heads or features of some other animal. Since these early artists clearly had the skills to paint human figures realistically, why did they choose not to do so? David Whitley, a rock art expert and U.S. representative to the International Council of Monuments and Sites, suggests that some of these images represent states of trance experienced by shamans.

Shamanism is a cross-cultural phenomenon in which individuals trained in the practice enter an altered state of consciousness by taking hallucinogens, fasting, drumming and dancing, or some other method. The resulting altered state of consciousness is described by shamans as a "journey into the spirit world." In some societies, shamans experience themselves as transformed into animals or as interacting with animal helpers. Whitley suggests that, in the Coso mountain range of eastern California, the ability to bring rain was symbolically equated with killing a mountain sheep. Whitley writes: "The majority of the Coso motifs, as the ethnography demonstrates, were graphic expressions of the visions of rain shamans that, themselves, were metaphors for the rain shaman's supernatural control over weather (1994:363)."

Whitley's analysis of cave art as representing an early form of shamanism is controversial, as are other explanations for these depictions of humans and animals. It is unlikely that we will ever know for sure what these early artists were thinking when they painted these animals in meticulous detail and presented humans only sketchily. However, the animal features attributed to humans evokes a characteristic forager pattern of myths and legends in which humans transformed themselves into animals and vice versa.

Man the Hunter or Woman the Gatherer?

Contrary to popular belief, our earliest hominid ancestors were probably not ferocious hunters, and their quest for food most likely centered on gathering plant materials, rather than hunting for meat. The !Kung of Africa's Kalahari Desert, a group of foragers who have survived into recorded history, have long been looked to for clues to the lifestyle of early hominids, though the equivalency is not exact. The !Kung diet consists primarily of plant materials gathered by females, including tubers, melons, and protein-rich mongongo nuts. Meat provided by males through hunting is less available, and therefore, more highly valued. Among contemporary foragers, meat makes up the major portion of the diet in areas where plant materials are scarce, such as among the Inuit (mistakenly called Eskimos), who live above the Arctic Circle.

Anthropologists have long questioned why the division of labor in contemporary foraging societies assigns the task of gathering plant materials to females and hunting game animals to males. The traditional explanation for this division of labor was that males have greater physical strength, especially the upper body strength needed to pull a bow or throw a spear. In addition, women in many forager societies

This prehistoric rock art from eastern California depicts a hunter about to kill a sheep with a bow and arrow. Among shamans of indigenous people of the Coso mountain range, killing a sheep symbolized the ability to make rain. The hunter wears a headdress that duplicates the horns of the sheep. (© David Whitley, International Council on Monuments and Sites, Comité d'Art Rupestre.)

nurse their children for as long as three to six years, which would require them to remain accessible to their children. In all societies, women assume the primary care for infants.

In recent decades, anthropologists have called into question these simplistic explanations of male and female roles. Among the Agta of the Philippines, many women hunt large game animals, such as deer and wild pigs, and nearly all women assist men in hunting by driving the game. Agnes Estioko-Griffin notes that Agta men typically hunt alone whereas "women are team hunters":

> [Women] work with other women or with their men. They almost always prefer to drive with dogs and favor killing with long knives instead of bows and arrows (arrows are apt to endanger the dogs). They are seldom the fanatics that men are, but for some women, love of the hunt dominates all their work [1993:226].

Girls are taught to hunt by their mothers, fathers, or husbands. Some women hunt with bows and arrows, though the bows used by women are typically smaller than those carried by men. Estioko-Griffin describes one grandmother, Taytayan, as being an especially enthusiastic hunter:

I recall the time she ran a deer for two days, until its feet were raw and bloody and exhaustion had slowed it to the point it could be shot. She had given up the hunt the first day, but the next day, she took her dogs, found the deer, and chased it until it collapsed. Other times she and [her husband] Littawan hunted, Taytayan leaping ahead to shoot and kill, then asking Littawan to carry the carcass home. The kill, she felt, was fun, but lugging a pig home was no joy at all [1993:226].

Estioko-Griffin's description of Tatytayan and her husband almost evokes contemporary images of women shoppers with their husbands in tow to carry their parcels. But who takes care of the children while Agta women hunt? Estioko-Griffin notes that some women carry smaller children on their backs while chasing deer and wild pigs. Older children are left with babysitters, or if they are able, assist in the hunt.

Because they hunt in groups and use dogs, Agta women bring home more meat per hunting venture than all-male groups or men who hunt alone. Mixed teams of men and women have the highest success rate per hunting venture. Overall, males bring home more meat because they hunt more often than females. Even so, Agta females provide more food than males since women are responsible for gathering plant materials and tending family garden plots, more reliable sources of food.

Women can hunt successfully. They are not constrained by biology, either in terms of strength or the need to care for children. Limitations in strength can be overcome by the use of dogs or a shift in hunting tactics. The need to care for children can be offset by cooperative care taking. The Agta further indicate that women are not constrained by an innate repugnance for the kill. Agta women delight in both the chase and the kill, and are adept at killing game at close quarters with a long knife.

Hunting by males is often explained as meeting the need for animal protein, but in many societies, females also supply animal protein in the regular course of their work. Forager women, such as the !Kung, collect small animals, including snakes and lizards, as they gather nuts, melons, and tubers. Women may also be primarily responsible for fishing in environments where fish are an important component of the diet. Jacques Lizot describes a fishing expedition undertaken by Yanomami women who live in the tropical rainforests of Venezuela:

Next day, the women leave for the forest. They cross a part of the garden before reaching the cool shade under the forest canopy. They walk in single file, without hurrying; the carrying baskets on their backs rock in rhythm with their steps, and fat, whimpering infants ride on their hips. Little girls run swiftly back and forth between them [1985:64].

It is clear from Lizot's description that Yanomami women are skilled at fishing and that one woman, at least, "catches enough fish to provide handsomely for the noon meal" (1985:66)

In all societies, male and female roles are defined as being separate and complementary to each other. Women are responsible for providing for the biological needs of the group, ensuring the availability of food and shelter, and producing and caring for offspring. Wherever we look, we find that women are engaged in providing a reliable source of food. Gathering, gardening, and fishing are more reliable as sources of food than hunting, which depends on availability of game and the skill of the hunter. Women gather, garden, and under many circumstances, fish.

Some patterns of gender roles appear to be pervasive in human groups. Women provide and sustain life within the domestic unit, whereas men establish and sustain relationships within and between groups. Women cook for the family; men cook at ceremonial events. Women are innately powerful by virtue of their ability to give life through childbirth and to entice men sexually. Male power is validated through socially recognized achievements: conducting ceremonies, presiding over exchange between groups, demonstrating their courage in warfare, and prevailing over game in the hunt.

Hunting and Male Potency

The hunting ritual of Yanomami males of Kohari village begins after dark, three nights before the actual hunt. Young men and older boys walk arm-in-arm around the perimeter of the central clearing of the village, singing *heri* [hunting songs] owned by the village:

> Those of Kōbari carry their blowguns
> tightly under their arm.
>
> The *waika* imitate the *kirakirami* bird,
> like the *kirakirami* bird do the *waika* whistle.
>
> The macaw swishes its tail,
> its long blue tail.
>
> The moon tree has been called.
> The jaguar's tail unrolls, unrolls, unrolls.

The *kōbari* is a bird whose call is considered a bad omen. *Waika* is a derogatory term for neighbors of Karohi villagers. The *kirakirami* bird is a kind of parrot. According to Napoleon Chagnon, the jaguar is a recurring symbol of ferocity in Yanomamö[5] myths:

> In mortal form, the jaguar is an awesome and much-feared beast, for he can and does kill and eat men. He is as good a hunter as the Yanomamö are and is one of the animals in the forest that hunts and kills men — as the Yanomamö themselves do. He is in that sense like Man, but unlike Man, he is part of Nature, not of Culture [1992:105].

The hunting potency of Kohari youths is symbolically linked to sexuality. The *heri* ritual includes obscene jokes and, at its conclusion before dawn, the hunters conduct a ritual sexual conquest of women of the village, pelting the faces, genitals, and buttocks of sleeping women with mashed banana pulp that is "sticky like sperm": "This mock fight represents not only the antagonism of men and women, but also that of day and night, of silence and noise. Its sexual connotation is obvious" (Lizot 1985:144). As dawn approaches, girls of the village retaliate by attacking the young men as they try to sleep in their hammocks.

After three days and nights, in which young men and women alternate in attacking each other, the young men set off for the hunt, carrying manioc cakes prepared by the wife of the village headman. The young men do not hunt for themselves, but to present the headman with game for a feast he will host for another village. The young men are not permitted to eat their game during the hunt, but subsist on roast caterpillars and birds, supplemented by the entrails of some animals that are allowed to them. When they return and all have feasted on their game, the bony remains of the animals will be displayed in the shelter of the headman, as a symbol of prosperity and the hunting ability of the men, as well as to ensure success in future hunts. Thus ultimately, the Yanomami hunt does not symbolically reinforce the biological potency of young males, but the social potency of older males.

Hunting and Female Fecundity

Among the Ainu of northern Japan, women were not allowed to hunt. They were not even allowed to go into the mountains, where bears dwelled. Bears were the highest ranking deities of the Ainu pantheon, and Ainu believed that deities were repelled by menstrual blood and the blood of parturition associated with females. Since bears come in both male and female versions, it may seem odd that an animal in which female fecundity is essential to the continuation of the species should be offended by markers of fertility among human females. The answer is not to be found in the preferences of bears but in the social organization of humans, especially the organization of gender roles. Regardless of its biological sex, the bear was symbolically equated with males, and was therefore presumed to be repelled by the fecundity of human females.

Among the Ainu, concepts of sacredness and pollution shaped their spatial orientation, the organization of their household and daily activities, and the activities of men and women. Central to the Ainu view of the universe and social organization was the importance of hunting. Hunting was strictly a male domain, and much of a man's social status depended on his success in hunting.

Ainu distinguished between "soul-owners" and inanimate objects or features. Every Ainu, animal, and plant was believed to have a soul, as did some objects made by humans, such as tools, kitchen utensils, and grass mats. Every soul-owner required a ritual observance upon its death and a sacred space dedicated to disposal of its bones. Humans, bears, cooking pots, and other soul-owners each had their own bone-pile.

Some soul-owners were viewed as deities, and these were classified according to the place in which they dwelled. In general, these were Deities of the Shore, Sea and Water Dieties, Sky Deities, and most important of all, Mountain Deities, called "mountain people" by the Ainu. Ainu symbolism associated with these deities reflects the relationship between males and females.

The most important sky deity was a female who manifested in two forms, as the sun (daytime moon) and the moon (dark moon). The Goddess of Sun and Moon mediated between the Ainu and other deities. All ritual activities were conducted in the morning, when the Goddess of Sun and Moon was in a good mood, and no rituals could be held during the last half of the month, when the deity was believed to be crying. She was not able to deliver Ainu messages to the other deities when she was in a bad mood.

Among other sky deities were dragons. Though dragon deities lived in the sky, they sometimes came to earth to drink from rivers and lakes or just to visit. Thunder was believed to result from the sounds of dragon deities fighting each other; the flashing of their swords produced lightening. In general, though dragon deities were believed to be beneficial, relations between humans and dragon deities were sometimes problematic. In two stories, women served as mediators between dragon deities and humans.

In one story, a dragon deity fell from the sky during a storm and blocked the entire mouth of the bay that provided the village passageway to the sea. A wise old woman told the people to stay inside and went to the top of a high cliff near the bay. While waving her underwear, she prayed to the dragon deity, who climbed the cliff and returned to the sky.

Just as deities in general were offended by the blood of menstruation and parturition, many deities disliked needles, used by women to sew garments and footwear from plant materials, animal skins, and fish skin. Dragon deities were especially afraid of needles, as indicated by the following story.

A handsome and well-dressed man began to visit an Ainu woman at night, and eventually they were married. One day, the woman happened to see him as he was leaving the house and realized he was a dragon deity. "Being afraid of him, she secretly inserted a needle in his garment when he returned. He went out again the next day but never came back. She went to the lake, where she found a dead dragon deity with a needle stuck in his body" (Ohnuki-Tierney 1974:104).

As these two stories illustrate, there is a link between dragon deities and female sexuality. Dragon deities are both sexually attracted to and afraid of human females, who have the power to command them and to destroy them through that typically female weapon, the needle. A psychoanalytic analysis would suggest that the dragon deity stories are a projection of Ainu male anxiety concerning female sexuality, which is both alluring and dangerous. Significantly, no rituals were addressed to dragon deities.

The bear, the highest ranking of mountain beings, was both hunted and viewed as a deity. It symbolically provided a synthesis among deities, animals, and humans. Above all, the bear provided a means of acting out male potency in a number of realms, especially in the bear ceremony, which took place over a period of two years. The object of the ceremony, which culminated in a bear sacrifice, was to celebrate the close relationship of humans to bears, then release the bear from its body so it could return to its relatives on the mountain bearing gifts and messages from its "relatives" in the settlement.

The ceremony began with a bear hunt that involved a confrontation between human male potency and animal female fecundity. In the spring men went to the mountains to capture live a newborn bear in the den or a cub strolling with its mother after coming out of hibernation. The family of the man who captured the bear became hosts of the ceremony. The cub, which could be of either sex, took on the dual identify of deity and grandchild. Any woman in the settlement who was nursing would also nurse the cub, if it was a newborn, but the oldest woman of the host family was officially in charge of caring for the bear. The bear lived with the host family until its claws developed to the point of becoming dangerous. At that time, it was transferred to a bear house outside the family house, in the sacred space near the "bone pile" of Grandmother Hearth.

All members of the settlement participated in care of the bear, providing it with the best food available even when food was scarce. Bathing the bear allowed young men of the settlement to prove their valor. When the bear was removed from the cage to be taken to a river or the seashore for bathing, young men were encouraged to charge directly at the bear, which was restrained from the rear by a rope held by other men. The young man was supposed to grab the ears of the bear and retreat immediately. In this, timing was crucial. Ohnuki-Tierney notes:

> If a man fails to grab the ears, the bear will grab him instead and perhaps harm him seriously. Or if the bear retreats just as he charges, the youth may fall in front of the bear and become its prey. If a man [charges the bear] successfully, it is said that he will become a great leader in the future [1974:49].

The bear ceremony was held at the beginning of the cold season following the capture of the cub, then 1½ years old. The ceremony was held when the new moon first appeared, when the Goddess of Sun and Moon was in her best mood.

On the evening before the ceremony, a shaman would ask Grandmother Hearth to deliver the messages of the Ainu to the bear deities. After a night of feasting and dancing, the next day's festivities began at sunrise with dancing around the bear's cage, a single line of men followed by a single line of women. The bear was then taken out of its cage and tied to a tree, bifurcated at the top and regarded as a ritual object. Both men and women, dressed in their best clothes, presented gifts to the bear to carry back to his or her home in the mountain. After this, only men could participate in dispatching the bear. Just as women were believed to have the power to harm dragon deities, they also had the power to prolong the bear's suffering.

A male elder reminded the bear of the hospitality he had received from the host family and the settlement in general and expressed gratitude for the bear's stay, inviting the animal to return to live among them once again. The elder then purified the bear by waving a ritual stick over it. A specially chosen marksman, not a member of the host family, shot the bear, and two male dogs were sacrificed as offerings to the bear deities and as servant-companions to the bear being sacrificed.

Both men and women participated in preliminary feasting in front of an altar. The bear, now a pelt, participated in the feast and was given some of its own flesh to eat. On ordinary occasions, Ainu expressed an aversion to raw food, but on this ritual occasion, men consumed the brain raw and drank the bear's blood. Women were tabooed from consuming any part of the bear's head, and members of the host family could not eat any part of the bear, since it was a member of the family. During the ceremony, sexual intercourse of any kind was forbidden. Those who breached this taboo were believed to become sick or lose their minds.

Ainu social life was bifurcated with respect to gender, just as the sacred universe was represented in the bifurcated poles used in the bear ceremony. The fecundity of parturant and menstruating females was distinguished from the nurturant qualities of post-menopausal women. For the most part, both were distinguished from the hunting potency of men. In addition to the opposition between male potency and female fecunity, there is an opposition between young and old. As is true of the Yanomami, the hunting potency of young males contributed to the social status of powerful male elders. Both males and females, if successful, gained social potency with increasing age: male potency resided in commanding the hunting potency of younger males; female potency resided in their ability to participate in ceremonies tabooed to younger, fecund females.

Ainu foragers provide important lessons about male-female relations, for understanding various kinds of power relations, and in illustrating the shifting balance of power that emerges in the human life cycle. In youth, both male and female power is conferred biologically: in males, through masculine prowess; in females, through fecundity and the desirability of feminine sexuality. Elders gain power through their social roles. Both males and females gain power by controlling the potency and fecundity of younger men and women.

The Noble Hunter

The essential theme of the hunt is the contest between human beings and nature, a contest which may also reflect status among humans. Depictions of the hunt in foraging societies stress the interdependence of humans and nature, and the contest between man and beast appears almost equal. With the emergence of settled, agricultural populations and the rise of stratified societies in many parts of the world, hunting became a sport of the elite. Images of noble hunters emphasize mastery over nature.

In Asia and the Middle East, kings and nobles are depicted as they dispatch lions, sheep, and other game with bows and arrows. The men are often on horseback, their bearing erect and regal, their gaze intent on the fleeing game. In these works, hunting serves as a metaphor for nobility and the power to command. Hunting is often symbolically linked to the leader's ability to protect his subjects from the predations of human enemies, from the uncontrolled forces of nature, or from some otherwise nameless evil.

Paintings of the elite also emphasize the thrill of the chase, showing hunter and hunted locked in a life-and-death struggle. In some cases, one can almost hear the panting of the deer or the rattle of the horse's bridle as the pursuit nears its finish.

In either case — whether the hunt focuses on the implausible composure of the nobility or the excitement of the hunt — the images are often technically accurate, so they can almost serve as manuals on the paraphernalia and techniques of the hunt. The artwork may also provide historical records, documenting particular hunts or historic personages.

Symbolism of the hunt as sport reflects values about the relationship of humans to nature and to each other. In Asian tradition, the emperor is held accountable for the harmony of heaven and earth, as expressed in his success in the hunt or other evidence of his command over nature. In the art of the ancient Middle East, the monarch is looked to as a bulwark against encroaching nature and the forces of chaos. European royalty held a privileged position with respect to nature. They "owned" the wild animals, and commoners were barred from "poaching," or stealing the king's game.

Though hunting art, literature, and song never omit the social context, the contest between humans and animals may also be depicted as a quest for communion with nature, and having come full circle, the identity of the hunter may be merged with that of his prey.

Dogs tear at a downed stag in the foreground as another tries to flee its pursuers in a 17th-century Flemish painting, *The Stag-Hunt*, by Frans Snyders. Just as the forest gave way to the plow, the deer falls under the onslaught of the dogs. (Musées Royaux des Beaux-Arts de Belgique, Brussels.)

The Mandate of Heaven

Chinese emperors were viewed as having a special relationship with nature, since they ruled by the "Mandate of Heaven." When the monarch held heaven's mandate, his people lived in prosperity and even the wild animals of the country benefited from the perfect coordination of earthly, human, and divine forces. A poem from the Confucian *Book of Songs*, dating from around the eighth century B.C.E., describes the balance of natural forces during the idyllic rule of a monarch favored by heaven:

> The king stood in his "Park Divine,"
> deer and doe lay there so fine,
> so fine so sleek; birds of the air
> flashed a white wing while fishes splashed
> on wing-like fin in the haunted pool.[6]

The word "haunted" used in an idyllic setting may seem jarring to Western ears since the English term has negative associations. A haunted person or place is seen as not being at peace or rest. The difficulty lies in the translation from Chinese calligraphy to English characters. The English alphabet is literal, whereas Chinese calligraphy is pictorial. The word-pictures characteristic of Chinese and other East Asian writing systems must be interpreted in their context.

Further, Chinese view the spirit world differently than do English speakers, so there is no equivalence in the use of language. In the Western tradition, spirits of the dead go to reside in a distant place called heaven or hell. In Chinese belief, spirits of the dead, or ancestors, retain their place in the family. Ancestors, as progenitors and elders, are entitled to the respect and care provided by their living relatives. In return, the ancestors are responsible for the material well-being and general good fortune of their descendants. Thus, the English word "haunted" does not accurately portray the continuing responsibility of Chinese ancestors to their living descendents.

Though the role of the emperor is grounded in Confucianism, a number of religious/philosophical traditions, including Taoism, contribute to the imagery of the poem. Whereas Confucian philosophy orders relationships basic to the conduct of everyday life, Taoism defines the nature of the universe and the place of human beings in it. The Taoist concept of heaven differs from the Western view of Heaven as the home of an all-powerful God looking down on His creatures. According to a text written in the sixth/fifth century B.C.E., the manifest universe is composed of energy, or *chi*, which can be either male (*yang*) or female (*yin*). This energy emerged from the Original Source or Tao. From *yin* and *yang* emerged heaven, earth, and the watery underworld.

Male energy is creative, hot, active, and light; female energy is receptive, cold, yielding, and dark. Harmony reigns when there is a balance between male and female energy. This balance is represented in the yin-yang (female-male) symbol.

Disaster, illness, bad luck, and lack of productivity result from an imbalance of energy. Male and female energies are balanced through manipulation of the five elements: wood, fire, metal, water, and earth. The religious scholar Michael Saso writes that Taoist ritual is aimed at "striking a sacred feudal contract with the spiritual powers of the cosmos, asking for the blessings of new life in spring, maturity and full crops in summer, rich harvest in autumn, and rest and security in the old age of winter" (1991:350).

The poem depicts harmony because all the elements are in their appropriate place. The king, the deer and doe, birds, fish, and ancestors represent the natural relationships between things. There is a balance among the three manifestations of the cosmos: Heaven, Earth, and Water.

Natural disasters, political upheaval and famines were signs that the emperor had lost the Mandate of Heaven. Thus, the Chinese philosophy differs from the European concept of "divine right of kings," which held that monarchs ruled by the will of God and therefore could not be overthrown. The Chinese concept of the Mandate of Heaven both reinforced the power of the emperor when times were good and justified revolution when they were not. According to the second of the five Confucian classics, *The Book of Documents*, "Heaven's mandate is not given in perpetuity."

The emperor could prove his worthiness to rule by protecting his people during times of war or by demonstrating his prowess at the hunt. While the emperor held the mandate of heaven, game would be plentiful. Another poem from *The Book of Songs* praises the grandeur of the noble hunter:

> Our chariots are strong,
> Our horses well matched.
> Teams of stallions lusty
> We yoke and go to the east.
> Our hunting chariots are splendid,
> Our teams very sturdy.
> ....
> My lord follows the chase
> With picked footmen so noisy,
> Sets up his banners, his standards,
> Far afield he hunts in Ao.
> ....
> My lord on his journeys
> Without clamour wins fame.
> Truly, a gentleman he;
> In very truth, a great achievement.[7]

The majesty of the royal hunter is expressed in a painting of Kublai Khan, heir to the Mongol dynasty in China in the thirteenth century, riding to the hunt with his retinue and falcons. The ruler is responsible for all he surveys, from the nobles riding at his heels to the deer in the forest.

There is a long history of hunting imagery in China, as is illustrated in representations of hunting in the art of the Magao Grottoes in Dunhuang. The Magao Grottoes provide the setting for monumental sculptures and murals that may have been executed over a period of 1500 years, thus providing a visual documentary of the history of hunting in China. While maintaining class distinctions as expressed in dress and bearing, these images typically portray the hunter or group of hunters more vigorously than the stately painting of Kublai Khan. Several murals from the Magao Grottoes represent the thrill of the chase as hunters on horseback bear down on frightened game.

These hunting scenes, though energetic, present an image of an orderly society. Humans and animals both have their place, and there is little evidence of the rapturous romanticism toward unbridled nature expressed in Western art and literature. In Chinese art and literature, the hunt represents a conjunction of heavenly will and social responsibility:

> A lucky day, fifth of the week;
> We have made the sacrifice of propitiation,
>   we have prayed.
> Our hunting chariots so lovely,
> Our four steeds so strong,
> We climb that high hill
> Chasing the herds of game
> ....
> We lead hither all our followers,
> Anxious to please the Son of Heaven.
> We have drawn our bows;
> Our arrows on the bowstring.
> We shoot the little boar,
> We fell the great wild ox,
> So that we have something to offer, for
>   guest, for stranger,
> To go with the heavy wine [*Book of Songs*].[8]

As indicated in Chinese art and poetry, harmony of heaven and earth is not always gentle; sometimes it is manifest in the vigorous pursuit of game.

Defending the Social Order

Whereas the Chinese see the emperor as mediating the natural forces, in a number of traditions the ruler is depicted as being at war with nature. He is portrayed as a mighty hunter battling some prodigious beast. The animal metaphorically

Opposite: **The Chinese emperor Kublai Khan rides to the hunt with his retinue and hawks, expressing the full glory of his office. (National Palace Museum, Taiwan.)**

represents the forces of chaos or evil, and the king or hero upholds the social order against the forces of chaos which threaten to overthrow it. Thus, the hero is cast in the role of protector of his people and guardian of the social order.

The story of the Saxon hero Beowulf battling the sea-monster Grendel symbolizes the triumph of society over unbridled nature. Beowulf kills Grendel to put an end to the monster's intolerable habit of devouring the subjects of the Danish King Hrothgar. But nature is not easily subdued. Grendel's mother avenges her son's death by killing a number of Hrothgar's men, forcing Beowulf to confront her in her infernal lair at the bottom of the sea.

Grendel's mother is a freak of nature that upsets the "natural" order by devouring humans. According to the prevailing view of that time, it is humans who should devour nature. This disturbance of the "natural" order is expressed in Hrothgar's description of the place of untamed evil that is the haunt of the sea-monsters:

> They inhabit uncharted territory, the retreat of wolves: windy cliffs and dangerous fen paths, where a mountain stream goes down under the misty bluffs and the flood runs under the earth. It is not many miles from there that the mere stands. Over it hang frosty groves, the firmly rooted wood shadowing the water.... There is no man alive who knows the bottom of that mere.

As this passage illustrates, Hrothgar's kingdom is on the edge of a fearsome place of uncontrolled danger hidden from the eyes of men. The society of humans stands cheek-by-jowl with chaos. It is a source of terror that defies the more regular laws of nature, in which humans hunt animals. Hrothgar suggests that even animals, the "natural" prey of humans, fear nature's defiance of the social order established by humans:

> Although the antlered hart, when pursued by hounds and driven far over the heath, may seek out the forest, still he will sooner give up his life on the bank than jump in to save his head. That is not a safe place. There surging water rises up dark towards the clouds when wind stirs up hateful storms, until the air becomes gloomy and the heavens weep.

Beowulf, alone among men, dives fully armed into the unsavory waters that hide Grendel's mother. He kills the fearsome mother of uncharted danger, thus saving the Danes from this unnatural manifestation of nature.

Stories depicting the struggle of humans against unbridled nature suggest that heaven, however conceptualized, is on the side of humans. In the story of Beowulf, the heavens weep at the chaotic evil represented by the dwelling place of Grendel and his mother. In this case, the battle between good and evil is depicted in ecological terms. Neither humans nor animals can live in a place characterized by storms, frosty groves, surging water, and floods running under the earth. Heaven weeps, perhaps in the form of dense fog. In stories of the Persian empire, the struggle of humans with nature is depicted in terms of ultimate Good and ultimate Evil.

This struggle is illustrated by an episode in the life of the great Persian warrior Rostam recounted in the *Shah-nama* or *Epic of Kings*, written by the poet Ferdowsi around the end of the eleventh century C.E.[9] The *Shah-nama* gives a virtual genealogy of Persian kings from the creation of the world to the conquest of Persia by Muslim Arabs. The epic poem reflects a Zoroastrian view of the cosmos, in which the universe is divided into two great realms, each headed by a powerful leader, engaged in a ferocious battle for control of the universe. Ahura Mazda is commander of the forces of Good, and Ahriman is personified as the Prince of Darkness, the commander of Evil. In the *Shah-nama*, Persian warriors are linked to the forces of Ahura Mazda, whereas their opponents are often referred to as Ahriman.

The *Shah-nama* clearly links Rostam's many battles on behalf of the Persian social order with the struggle for Good. On one occasion, the Persian king Key Khosrow asks the hero to hunt down an onager (wild ass) that has invaded a tame herd of horses. The onager is the color of the sun, stronger than a horse, and more vicious than either horse or ass. Rostam tries to kill the onager with his bow and arrow, but the animal disappears, revealing it to be supernatural. The wild animal is in fact Akvan the Div, a demonic spirit that lives by a spring near the grazing ground of the horses. Symbolically, it dwells on the edge of society, a dangerous position. The crisis begins when the Div crosses the boundary, invading the tame world of humans and horses.

As the story unfolds, the identity of the onager-demon merges with that of Ahriman, the Zoroastrian Prince of Darkness. Rostam's opponent is variously referred to as Akvan the Div and as Ahriman. In other tales recounted in the *Shah-nama*, this identification is further extended to Afrasiyah, king of the Turks and Key Khosrow's rival in war. The adversary is at the same time the human adversary Afrasiyah; Ahriman, the personification of Evil; and Akvan the Div, who is further transformed into a wild animal. Thus, Evil is represented on three levels in the form of the wild ass: human, cosmic, and Div. Akvan traps Rostam while the hero is sleeping, thus endangering the Persian social order. Rostam bemoans the far-reaching consequences of his carelessness:

> This foul demon has spread a bloody snare for me. Alas now for my courage and strength and these shoulders of mine! Alas also for my swordsmanship and mace-wielding! This happening will bring my world to ruin and everything will foster the ambitions of Afrasiyah. Gudarz will not survive, nor Khosrow nor Tus, nor will throne or crown, elephant or drum. Through my own act evil will descend on the earth, so slack has my market become [1967:148–149].

In essence, Rostam laments, the balance of cosmic forces will be upset and Evil will triumph over Good because the hero has been ensnared by the Div. The most immediate effect is that the Persian King Khosrow will be overthrown and Rostam's warrior comrades Gudarz and Tus will be slain, since they are allied with the forces of Good.

Akvan-Ahriman-Afrasiya-Evil are further associated with uncontrolled forces that impinge upon the civilized world. Just as the wild ass has invaded the tame herd, Evil threatens "throne," "crown," "elephant" and "drum," in other words, those emblems of monarchy and military might that symbolize the social order. In this story, Evil is equated with disorder and untamed wilderness. Fortunately for the fate of the universe, Rostam uses his cunning to escape from Akvan's trap and kills the demon by calling on two great inventions of the civilized world; He lassos the Div and crushes its head with an axe.

King Peroz (457/9–484 C.E.) is shown hunting mofflon or wild sheep in what is considered one of the finest examples of Sassanian silver work. The Sassanian dynasty reigned in Persia from the third to the seventh century. The bowl of silver plate with partial gilding shows King Peroz in full court regalia and wearing a crown. The king would not have dressed this way for the hunt; these emblems were worn only on official occasions. The image links the monarch's prowess in the hunt with his high social rank. The importance of the king is also emphasized by the use of gilding. King Peroz's head, in silver, contrasts with the gold of his crown and the halo that frames his face. The halo represents *Farr*, the essence of royalty. The Persians believed that *Farr* was signified by radiance emanating from the figure of a king or one who was about to become king.

Zal or Dastan was one of the greatest of kings whose careers are recounted in the *Shah-nama*. His hunting skills come to the fore in the story of how he found his queen. While making a survey of his extensive realm, Zal pauses to camp near the palace of King Mahrab of Kabol, who pays tribute to him. Rudaba, King Mahrab's daughter, falls in love with Zal and sets about gently scheming to catch his eye. She sends her serving girls to gather flowers on the bank of a river near his camp. Just as he catches sight of the girls, Zal is aiming his bow and arrow at a duck on the river. He shoots the fowl and sends his servant to retrieve it. The girls engage the servant in flattering conversation, pretending not to know his rank or the name of his lord:

> Warrior, be so agreeable as to tell me who that man is with the arms of
> a lion, that elephant-bodied hero. Of what people is he the king? I mean
> the man who shot the arrow from the bow with such skill. What terrors
> the enemy must suffer who faces him? Never have we beheld a cavalier
> more handsome or anyone so sure with bow and arrow [1967:42].

Zal's servant identifies his lord by rank and genealogy, adding, "The sky revolves over no other knight like him and destiny will never see another man of such renown." Rudaba's serving girl then seizes the opportunity to extol the virtues of her mistress and, as a result of their negotiations, the royal marriage is arranged.

The story presents several evocative images. The description of Zal compares his strength with that of a lion or elephant. The king's hunting skill is equated with his prowess at war. At the same time, Zal's ability to inspire terror in his enemies is linked with his ability to inspire love in the hearts of women.

King Peros, who reigned during the 5th century, is shown hunting moufflon or wild sheep in a crown and full court regalia on a Sassanian silver plate. It is unlikely he would have worn such elaborate dress for hunting (The Metropolitan Museum of Art, Fletcher Fund, 1934).

There is additional symbolism in the description of Zal shooting the duck. The king catches sight of the women as he is aiming at the duck, suggesting an equivalency between the two types of game. Zal sends his servant to retrieve the slain duck; the slave also retrieves the information that leads the king to his future queen. But there is symbolic inversion here. Zal is prey as well as predator. His future queen Rudaba is also a hunter. Just as Agta women of the Philippines send their dogs to sniff out the game, Rudaba sends her serving girls to sniff out her future husband. As the story suggests, the themes of hunting, warfare, and love are often metaphorically linked.

Egyptian pharaohs made sure their subjects were aware of their hunting prowess. Amenophis III (or Amenhotep), who reigned during the fourteenth century B.C.E., sent out scarabs throughout his realm inscribed with stories of his hunting successes. One of them reads: "The total number of lions killed by His Majesty with his own arrows, from the first to the tenth year [of his reign]: 102 wild lions." The royal hunt was also a spectator sport for the Egyptians. Members of the nobility gathered to watch the pharaoh demonstrate his prowess in the hunt.

Hunting appears to have been one of the royal duties of Egyptian monarchs. The historian Vera Olivova suggests that hunting dangerous wild animals became an obligation as well as a recreation when Menes, founder of the first royal dynasty was carried off and killed by a hippopotamus. However, the story of Menes' abduction bears the mark of a creation myth, describing the symbolic origins of the royal hunt, rather than its historical source. It is seldom necessary for monarchs to protect their realm from wild animals since they are almost invariably surrounded by minions who perform this onerous task for them. Pharaohs and kings hunt for entertainment, for physical training, or to display their skills to their subjects — rarely for food or protection. The story of Menes may be viewed as a myth outlining the pharaoh's responsibility for protecting his kingdom and his rule from the ravages of nature.

In the mythology of the Canaanite warrior-god Baal, the forces of nature are personified and battled as though they were human foes. A contest with two of Baal's enemies is described in a text from Ras Shamra, the ancient city of Ugarit in Syria. The account was recorded in cuneiform around 1400 B.C.E.:

> Then soars and swoops the mace in the hand of Baal,
> Even as an eagle in his fingers,
> It smites the head of Prince Sea,
> Between the eyes of Judge River
> Sea collapses and falls to the ground,
> His strength is impaired;
> His dexterity fails.
> Baal drags him away and disperses him,
> He annihilates Judge River.
> ....
> Let Baal reign.

Even Baal's weapon is described in terms of nature, depicted as that great bird of prey, the eagle. But Baal battles the forces of nature on behalf of human beings, who have enlisted his aid through sacrifices to him.

Hunting of deer was important symbolically for the Moche, a pre–Inca culture that dominated the coast of Peru between 100 B.C.E. and 750 C.E. Elaborately dressed individuals are shown spearing the animals or trapping them in nets. Archaeologist Christopher Donnan notes that the figures are not suitably dressed for the hunt. Their paraphernalia indicates their social status, identifying them as members of the elite or gods.

Art and literature of this tradition present nature as a formidable rival threatening the safety of the kingdom, perhaps reflecting the tenuous nature of societies carved out of the wilderness. Rulers, and gods as well, exerted all their might toward ensuring the triumph of the social order over the inchoate forces of nature. By the tenth century C.E., nature had been largely subdued in Europe and England, and hunting became a secular activity organized around royal privilege.

Presiding Over Nature

In his verse "The Hunting of the Hart," the fourteenth-century English poet Geoffrey Chaucer describes the entire day of a hunt, from the moment the hunter learns of it by hearing a hunting horn while still lying in bed:

> Anon-right, whan I herde that,
> How that they woulde on hunting goon,
> I was right glad, and up anoon;

The poet mounts his horse and pursues the hunting party hoping to join them. When he overtakes them he discovers he is in exalted company:

> "Say, felow, who shal hunte [n] here?"
> Quod I; and he answerde ageyn,
> "Sir, th'emperour Octovien,"
> Quod he, "and is heer faste by."

The hart proves to be more clever than the hunting party and the hounds, eluding them at the last. The hunt ends as it begins, with the sound of a horn. Only now the mood has changed:

> Therwith the hunte wonder faste
> Blew a forloyn at the laste.

The hunt was a mark of royal privilege for British kings and queens, who early established their exclusive rights to various forms of game. Saxon kings hunted deer in their own specially designated "royal forests." The Norman king William the Conqueror, who took the English throne in 1066, extended the boundaries of the royal forests and increased penalties for poaching. In fact, some said it was better to be one of the king's deer than one of his subjects, since he seemed to love the animals more.

Members of the nobility could not hunt deer, even on their own land, without the express permission of the king. They could hunt lesser game — such as foxes and hares — on their own land or in the adjacent forests. Similar privileges were granted to abbots and other dignitaries of the Church, giving rise to the term "chase" to describe a tract of land and its associated hunting privileges.

Art depicting hunting among the Moche, who dominated the north coast of Peru from around 100 B.C.E. to 750 C.E., illustrates a form of hunting in which game are driven into a netted area by beaters, known in Europe as the battue. It is a form of hunting characteristic of stratified societies, in which the beaters are of lower rank than those who dispatch the game. The scene on this Moche vase displays a variety of social rank as indicated by the relative size and style of dress of the human figures. The figure barely visible to the extreme left of the photo is of highest rank. Though his noble regalia may have made hunting more difficult, the rigors of the hunt were eased by the use of nets (Peru, North Coast, Moche Culture, Stirrup Spout Vessel, Unknown, Painted stirrup, painted décor of deer hunt, one side warrior figures, 29 × 12 cm., Purchased from "Buckingham Fund, 1955.2250 Image © The Art Institute of Chicago).

King Henry VIII was an ardent hunter, who appeared to use the sport to demonstrate his virility. According to one observer, the king "never takes his diversion without tiring eight or ten horses..." (Courtney 1983:10). To facilitate his passion for hunting, Henry took over large tracts of land, including the area that is now Hyde Park and Regent's Park in London. The king is said to have been hunting in Epping Forest on the morning his second wife Anne Boleyn was executed.

Elizabeth I, the daughter of that ill-fated marriage, was a devoted hunter. She was an excellent shot with a crossbow from horseback — not an easy trick — and her passion for hunting continued into her old age. She is depicted standing regally in full court dress with a hunting knife posed over a stag in George Turberville's *Noble Art of Venerie or Hunting*, published in 1575. It was her royal privilege to administer the coup de grace to the fallen deer.

A similar scene is enacted in a portrait of Henry, Prince of Wales (1594–1612) by Robert Peake. The painting emphasizes the social rank of the young prince, who has just dismounted from his horse to dispatch a stag whose antlers are held by Robert Devereaux, Third Earl of Essex (1591–1646). Though hardly more than a boy, the prince is nevertheless accorded the full measure of his royal status, expressed in his dress, stance, and demeanor. Social rank of the Prince and Earl is explicitly expressed by their respective coats of arms, which are suspended behind them. In the background are an enclosed deer park and view of a town and a castle, further establishing the social importance of the central figures.

Hunting was also a sport of royalty and the nobility in France during the same period. Gaston II (1331–1391), count of Foix and viscount of the Béarn, was an adventurous warrior and devotee of the hunt. Between his ventures on the battlefield, he devoted himself to the life of a gentleman on his estates at Orthez, where he wrote a masterpiece called *The Book of Hunting*. In the book, Gaston discusses attributes of various game animals, from deer to boar, and advises on the mode of hunting suitable for each. He also counsels on the care and training of dogs, including a section on how to treat dogs that are sick from rabies. He also describes the function of each member of the hunt, from the grooms who tend the dogs to the role of the "whipper-in" in beginning the hunt and keeping dogs and hunters on track.

As in England, French noblewomen participated in the hunt. For both men and women, hunting was as much a social event as a chance to find game. *Halte de Chasse*, a painting by the eighteenth-century artist Carle van Loo depicts the elegance of a royal hunting venture. The picnic is set in the forest of Compiègne, where Louis XV exercised his royal prerogative of stag hunting, *la grande vénerie*. The king is in the center wearing a red coat. Madame de Pompadour sits languorously in the foreground. Noblemen wear the royal blue livery required of all members of the king's hunting party, which could only be worn with the king's express permission.

It is perhaps in seventeenth and eighteenth-century England that hunting reached its zenith as an art form. In his book *The Complete Gentleman*, published in 1622, Henry Peacham asserts that a reputation for horsemanship is an attribute "of kings and princes." He argues that "wild beasts were of a purpose created by God that men by chasing and encountering them might be fitted and enabled for warlike exercises."

The proper British gentleman of that era was almost obligated to display a sporting scene in his study. The British art connoisseur Sir Oliver Millar (1974) asserts that the beginning of sporting painting in England dates from this period. He describes *The Grosvenor Hunt*, painted in 1762 by George Stubbs, as "the most sublime of all English sporting pictures, a classic statement as a whole and in its marvellous detail on the very essence of hunting." Stubbs, one of the best-loved of British sporting artists, painted the work for Richard, the first Earl of Grosvenor, who appears just to the right of the tree. The painting may serve the same function as modern society pages. Then as now, it appears, to be seen among the nobility is an important marker of elite status. One's position in the painting reflects one's rank in society.

Coming to Terms with Nature

In the art forms of Europe, the Middle East and Asia, where social roles are clearly defined, the nobility expressed in hunting was almost exclusively a province of the upper classes or of kings and emperors. However, nobility can be viewed as a character trait, an indefinable essence that elevates the individual beyond the ordinary. In this case, hunting and other "noble" sporting activities provide an arena where men can prove their worth. In this type of art and literature, the human

George Stubbs' *The Grosvenor Hunt*, painted in 1762, is virtually a portrait of many members of the English elite of his time (Trustees of Anne, Duchess of Westminster's Settled Life Fund).

hunter contends against a worthy opponent, one who shares his own noble qualities and provides the contest of a lifetime.

Sir Walter Scott's poem "The Stag-Hunt" describes the chase from the perspective of the stag. As the poem begins, the majestic still of the evening is disrupted by the "deep-mouthed bloodhound's heavy bay," signifying the approach of a party of hunters. Scott compares the beleaguered stag to a king whose castle is under siege:

> As Chief, who hears his warder call,
> "To arms! The foemen storm the wall,"
> The antlered monarch of the waste
> Sprang from his heathery couch in haste.

There is just a suggestion that the hunter is less noble than the stag he pursues or the steed he rides:

> The Hunter marked that mountain high,
> The lone lake's western boundary,
> And deemed the stag must turn to bay,
> Where that huge rampart barred the way;
> Already glorying in the prize,
> Measured his antlers with his eyes....

Even as the hunter prepares for the kill, the wily stag eludes the hounds. The frustrated and chase-maddened hunter urges his horse into the rugged terrain:

> Close on the hounds the hunter came,
> To cheer them on the vanished game;
> But, stumbling in the rugged dell,
> The gallant horse exhausted fell.
> The impatient rider strove in vain
> To rouse him with the spur and rein,
> For the good steed, his labours o'er,
> Stretched his stiff limbs, to rise no more.

In this poem, the stag bears the standard of a monarch, and the fallen horse is more noble than the hunter who rides him to his death. The regal bearing of the stag is the subject of *The Monarch of the Glen*, a painting by the nineteenth-century English artist Sir Edwin Landseer.

The transformation of hunter into prey is a pervasive theme in hunting art and literature, even seeming to transcend considerations of social rank. In the epic literature of Japan, the story of Prince Yamato recounts the heroic adventures of a figure considered instrumental in establishing the present line of Japanese emperors. The Yamato clan, which traces its lineage to the sun-goddess Amaterasu, gained ascendancy over other clans by the third or fourth century C.E. The figure of Prince Yamato may be a composite of several early warriors of the clan.

The hero is invited to a stag hunt near Mount Fuji, where he quickly becomes the quarry. The hunters set fire to the long dry grass, aiming either to burn Prince Yamato to death or to drive him into their ambush. The prince refuses to become the prey, however. He uses his famous sword *Ame no murakumo*, or "cloud-cluster," to slash his way through the burning grass to freedom. The perfidy of the hunters is subverted by the prowess of their prey.

Transformation is also involved in the betrayal and death of the Persian hero Rostam. The warrior's jealous half-brother Shaghad connives with a rival king to kill the hero. Shaghad and the king prepare for a hunt by digging a number of pits and lining them with knives and spears. The king then entices Rostam into his trap by inviting him to the hunt, taking great care to describe the abundance of game: "At his speech Rostam's passion was stirred to boiling for the field with its streams, its gazelles and wild asses" Ferdowsi 1976:215).

However, it is Rostam who is to be the game. The hero is sent to hunt in the pit-strewn area. The hero rides out to the hunt on his great horse Rakhsh. The horse smells the newly turned earth and refuses to proceed, but Rostam, seduced by the lure of the chase, urges him on. The poet Ferdowsi supplies this chastening note:

> Fate covered his eyes and he was maddened, so that he brought out a whip of supple leather with which he lashed at the unnerved Rakhsh and roused him to passion. Being hemmed in between two pits, he sought for a way of escape from the clutch of fate, but his hind legs plunged down into one of the pits, where there was no room either to hold fast or to struggle [1967:215].

Rostam learns too late that, on this hunt, he is the prey. He and his horse are mortally wounded by their fall into the blade-lined pit, but before he dies, Rostam kills his treacherous half-brother with his bow and arrow.

The ballad "John Peel," by J. W. Graves, plays on the theme of death, both for the hunter and the prey:

> D'ye ken [know] John Peel with his coat so gray?
> D'ye ken John Peel at the break of day?
> D'ye ken John Peel when he's far, far away,
> With his hounds and his horn in the morning?
>   'Twas the sound of his horn called me from my bed,
>   And the cry of his hounds have me oft-times led,
>   For Peel's view-hallo would awaken the dead,
>   Or a fox from his lair in the morning.
> D'ye ken that bitch whose tongue is death?
> D'ye ken her sons of peerless faith?
> D'ye ken that fox with his last breath
> Cursed them all as he died in the morning?
>   'Twas the sound of his horn called me from my bed,

And the cry of his hounds has me oft-times led,
For Peel's view-hallo would awaken the dead,
Or a fox from his lair in the morning.

Through a process of symbolic association, this song links the mortality of the
hunter with that of his prey. The hunter has been called from his bed by a shout
that would awaken the dead. The same shout summons the fox to his death. The
ballad then switches abruptly to the perspective of the fox who "Cursed them all
as he died in the morning."

A mystical union between hunter and prey is described in William Faulkner's
short story "The Bear." Faulkner builds on the idea that the animal existed as a primordial force long before the boy who provides the focus for the story was born.
The boy sets out to hunt the bear; instead the bear seeks him out. The animal wan-
ders by camp as the boy is excitedly preparing for his first foray into the forest. The
boy is never named. Just as the bear is the primordial animal, the boy is the primordial human initiate. The boy is instructed in the arts of the wild by Sam, who
is part–Indian, part-black. Sam plays the role of the mentor, a common feature of
the hero myth. Sam is also the mediator between the primordial animal and
the primordial human. Sam warns the boy that the bear, if cornered, will seek him
out:

> "You watch close in the morning. Because he's smart. That's how come
> he has lived this long. If he gets hemmed up and has to pick out some-
> body to run over, he will pick out you."
> "How?" the boy said. "How will he know—"He ceased. "You mean he
> already knows me, that I ain't even been here before, ain't had time to
> find out yet whether I—" He ceased again, looking at Sam, the old man
> whose face revealed nothing until it smiled. He said humbly, not even
> amazed. "It was me he was watching…" [Faulkner 1979:285].

Thus begins a quest that lasts through several years of the boy's adolescence. The
boy's fantasies of at last killing the bear define his emerging maturity and sense of
mastery over the forest and himself. The bear is the symbolic focus for the boy's
rite of passage into manhood. Finally the boy confronts the bear at the right time,
with the right gun and the right dog—but does not shoot:

> He could smell it, strong and hot and rank. Sprawling, he looked up to
> where it loomed and towered over him like a cloudburst and colored like
> a thunderclap, quite familiar, peacefully and even lucidly familiar, until
> he remembered: This was the way he used to dream about it [1979:292].

What the boy has sought in the forest, in the form of the bear, is himself. As he
reflects on the encounter in company with his father, he comes to understand that,
through the hunt, he and the bear were joined in a mutual quest. The boy hunted

to test himself; the bear participated in the hunt with him "to put that freedom and liberty in jeopardy in order to savor them, to remind his old strong bones and flesh to keep supple and quick to defend and preserve them" (1979:295).

The hunt is a particularly potent source of symbolism, since it invariably evokes images of the fragility of life and the inevitability of death. The hunt is a quest for death. If the outcome is successful, it is the prey who will die. However, the irony of the chase is that eventually, the hunter must also die. Sir Walter Scott's poem "Huntsman, Rest!" compares life to the hunt and death to the end of the chase:

> Huntsman, rest! Thy chase is done,
> Think not of the rising sun,
> For at dawning to assail ye,
> Here no bugles sound reveille.

The hunting horn that summoned the fox to his death in the ballad of John Peel will never awaken the hunter whose chase is done.

The art record demonstrates that sports are symbolically linked to the struggle for survival, whatever form that contest takes. Perhaps because of its uncertainty, hunting has always held a mystique that extends beyond providing meat for its protein value.

Three

The Hunt Domesticated: Ritual Origins of the Bullfight

If the slayer think that he slays, if the slain think that he is slain, neither of them knows the truth. The Self slays not, nor is he slain.

King of Death, *Katha Upanishad*

The battle between humans and animals does not always take place in the wild. One of the most spectacular contests, combining ritual with blood, is the bullfight. This domesticated replication of the primordial battle between man and beast probably developed from bull sacrifice, which was prevalent in India and Macedonia several thousand years before the current era. Related activities also gave rise to the medieval sports of bear-baiting and bull-baiting.

Domestication of plants and animals becomes part of the archaeological record around 13,000 years ago in the ancient Middle East, in what is now Syria. But the shift to herding animals and planting crops did not entirely replace hunting. As noted in Chapter Two, hunting continued as a recreation for the elite and as an indicator of royal power long after the primary means of subsistence had shifted to agriculture. Even today, hunting continues as a sport alongside herding, and farmers all over the world continue to hunt game where it is available.

As hunting became the province of the elite in Asia and Europe, many elegant lords and ladies abandoned the pursuit of game animals into brambles and thickets in favor of having the game brought to them. In his youth, Henry VIII of England was skilled at the chase. As he grew older and fatter, and was unable to hunt from horseback, he engaged in the *battue*, a form of hunting that relied on beaters to flush out the game. Even that most passionate of sportswomen, Queen Elizabeth I, often preferred the battue to the chase. One such hunt at Windsor was witnessed by the French ambassador, de Castelnau. He wrote to his king, Henry III, that the hunt consisted of "driving a number of deer up and down inside a netted space in front of a well-screened butt or 'feuillade' where the Queen was stationed with her arblast (arbalest or crossbow)" (Courtney 1983:12). In some cases, domestication of the contest against animals was due more to religious ritual than to the ennui of the nobility.

From Sacrifice to Spectacle

The Ainu bear ceremony, described in Chapter Two, may be the last example of a bear sacrifice ritual widely practiced among prehistoric peoples across what is now northern Europe. The most complete record of animal sacrifice in northern Europe comes to us from the Celts of western Europe. The Celts themselves left no written records. As Julius Caesar notes in his account of the conquest of Europe, *The Battle for Gaul,* they had a religious prohibition against maintaining written records. Our knowledge of the Celts comes to us from the archaeological record, descriptions of them by Romans and Greeks, and from their own folktales, recorded much later by Christian monks. Of necessity, the archaeological record is incomplete, and written sources contain omissions or biases aimed at asserting the superiority of the Roman and Christian point of view.

The Celts comprised a language group of people inhabiting much of what is now Europe and England. They inhabited much of northern Europe from 800 B.C.E. to 400 C.E. The name comes from the Greek word *Keltoi,* meaning barbarian. They were also called *Galli* by the Romans and *Galatai* by the Greeks, also names meaning "barbarian." Thus, the terms "Celtic" and "Gaelic," by which these people are now known, were originally pejorative. Romans described both Germanic peoples and Celtic peoples by the same term, but the evidence suggests they comprised two culture groups. Both were ferocious warriors, in aspect and in action. In his *Diodorus Siliculus, History,* the Roman historian Diodorus wrote:

> Their aspect is terrifying.... They are very tall in stature, with rippling muscles under clear white skin. Their hair is blond, but not naturally so: they bleach it, to this day, artificially, washing it in lime and combing it back from their foreheads. They look like wood-demons, their hair thick and shaggy like a horse's mane.[11]

Women as well as men were warriors. Some Celtic warriors wore bronze helmets adorned with horns, which were symbolically linked to the horned god Cernunnos. Though the name Cernunnos appears only once in the archaeological record, in France, the name is applied to all male antlered deities in Celtic iconography. Cernunnos is associated with a number of animals, especially the stag, and with symbols of abundance, such as cornucopiae. He is often portrayed with an erect penis, suggesting an association with male fertility.

Perhaps even more distressing to the Romans, Celts often went into battle, as Diodorus puts it, "content ... with the weapons nature gave them: they go naked into battle."[12] Celtic warriors were not unadorned, however. They were skilled metalworkers and fond of jewelry, especially the decorated neck ring known as the torc. Both men and women engaged in battle wearing this ornamentation — along with designs drawn on their bodies in blue dye — but little else. Men typically wore a belt of chain, and women wore a girdle of the same material. They also blew "weird, discordant" sounds on horns, shouted in chorus with their "deep and harsh voices," and "beat their swords rhythmically against their shields."[13]

The Celts cut off their enemies' heads and slung them on their belts, attached them to the necks of their horses, or gave them to their attendants for safekeeping until after the battle. Later, they would preserve the heads and nail them over the doors of their dwellings. Diodorus writes: "In exactly the same way as hunters do with their skulls of the animals they have slain ... they preserved the heads of their most high-ranking victims in cedar oil, keeping them carefully in wooden boxes."[14]

The human head apparently had ritual significance. Writing in the third century of the current era, the Roman historian Livy writes that Celts customarily carried the heads of enemies killed in battle to their temples, where "they cleaned out the head...and gilded the skull, which thereafter served them as a holy vessel to pour libations from and as a drinking cup for the priest and the temple attendants."[15] Disembodied heads are a frequent motif in Celtic art.

Apparently, nakedness was reserved for the battlefield. In ordinary life, Celts typically wore brightly colored tunics, either striped or plaid. For women, the tunics generally swept the floor; for men, tunics were knee-length. Both men and women wore a rectangular cloak secured by a broach. The Roman poet Virgil was more kindly than Diodorus in his description of the Celts: "Golden is their hair, and golden their garb. They are resplendent in their striped cloaks, and their milk-white necks are circled with gold."[16]

By the time Julius Caesar subjugated Europe and England in the first century B.C.E., Celts in the British Isles had developed three clearly delineated classes: the nobility or warrior class, the Aes Dana, people of learning; and the commoners or churls. The Roman historian Strabo's *Geographica*, written at the end of the first century B.C.E., distinguishes specializations among the Aes Dana:

> Among all the Gallic peoples, generally speaking, there are three sets of [people] who are held in exceptional honour: the Bards, the Vates, and the Druids. The Bards are singers and poets; the Vates, diviners and natural philosophers; while the Druids, in addition to natural philosophy, study also moral philosophy.[17]

According to classical literature and Celtic folklore, women were on a par with men in all three classes of Aes Dana.

Both wild and domesticated animals were sacrificed by the Celts. We may have an image of bull sacrifice in the form of the Gundestrup Cauldron, dating from around 100 B.C.E. It depicts various motifs of Celtic plants, animals, and deities. The bottom of the bowl shows a bull fending off two dogs, while a third dog appears to be dead. A human figure over the bull prepares to stab the animal through its neck. The human figure appears to be wearing a horned headdress. Though scholars agree on the relative date of the work, they disagree on its origin. The motif of the bowl is Celtic, but the style is Thracian, suggesting a Mediterranean origin.

In the British Isles, bulls were symbolically linked to the invention of culture through their association with the god Hu Gadarn, leader of the Cymry or Welsh

The base of the Gundestrup cauldron illustrates the ritual slaying of a bull. The dogs and the figure preparing to stab the animal from above bear striking similarities to images of Mithraic bull sacrifice and the secular activity of bull-baiting (National Museum, Copenhagen).

Celts. Hu Gadarn divided the Cymry into clans, which would suggest that he was regarded as the inventor of social structure. He taught his followers how to plow and invented music and song as a way of maintaining traditions.

The Irish hero Cú Chulainn's greatest battle took place in a dispute over a celebrated bull. The Brown Bull of Ulster and the White-horned Bull of Connaught were originally swineherds of two gods, but they spent most of their time fighting. As they quarreled, they changed themselves into a succession of animals, finally becoming eels. One eel went into the River Cruind in Ulster, where it was swallowed by a cow belonging to the Daire and was born as the Brown Bull of Ulster. The other eel went into the spring of Uaran Garad in Connaught, where it entered a cow belonging to Queen Medb. That cow gave birth to the White-horned Bull of Connaught.

All these transformations failed to improve the irascible personalities of the two swineherds. The White-horned Bull was so proud he refused to belong to a woman, so he left Queen Medb's herds for those of her husband. This produced jealousy between the couple, since Medb had no bull worthy of comparison. Refusing to be less than her husband in anything, Medb sent heralds with gifts and compliments to the Daire of Ulster, asking him to lend her the Brown Bull for a year. When the Daire refused, the queen of Connaught determined to take the Bull by force. She assembled the armies of all the rest of Ireland to do battle against Ulster. She expected an easy victory, since the warriors of Ulster were under a curse that caused them to sleep continuously. However, the queen had not bargained for the strength and cunning of the hero Cú Chulainn.

By a little heroic trickery, Cú Chulainn routed Medb's army. The Brown Bull followed her soldiers into Connaught, where he met his old enemy, now the White-horned Bull. The Brown Bull tore his old rival limb from limb and carried off pieces of its carcass on his horns. The Brown Bull went back to Ulster, where he became mad, killing all who crossed his path. Finally, his heart burst with bellowing, he died (Squire 1975:164–175).

According to some scholars, this story may have originated as an explanation for a ritual in which a bull was slain and eaten by his worshippers. It may also be a mythical account explaining regional rivalries. The Cú Chulainn story is part of the Ulster Cycle of stories chronicling the exploits of the hero and his king, Conor Mac Nessa, in their wars against the king and queen of Connaught. Ulster and Connaught were two of five domains of Ireland. After 300 C.E., both Ulster and a large portion of Connaught were taken over by the ruling family of one of the other five domains, the Uí Néill (sons of Niall) of Mide.

For the Celts, bulls as well as bears may have been totemic animals. Certainly there was abundant symbolism regarding bulls among these early inhabitants of the British Isles. According to Pliny, the Druids sacrificed two white bulls in a mistletoe rite correlated with the lunar cycle. There appears to be some continuity between these early religious festivals and later fairs that formed the setting for bull-baiting and bull-running.

An intervening variable between animal sacrifice and the secular torture of animals appears to be the introduction of Christianity by the fourth century of the current era. Sacrifice continued as a central theme in Christianity, but was shifted from the actual sacrifice of humans and animals to Christ's sacrifice of his own life on behalf of humanity. Bears and bulls continued to be killed in a public display in a manner that closely resembled the sacrificial act, but the killing of animals in a public festival had lost its sacred significance.

The medieval sport of bear-baiting resembles the bear sacrifice to some degree, but the main purpose of bear-baiting was entertainment. The bear was tethered to a stake in a pit or sunken garden and dogs were unleashed on it. Robert Laneham described a bear bait that he observed in 1575:

> It was a sport very pleasant to see the bear, with his pink eyes, learing after his enemies' approach, the nimbleness and wait of the dog to take his advantage; and the force and experience of the bear again to avoid his assaults; if he were bitten in one place, how he would pinch in another

to get free; that if he were taken once, then by what shift with biting, with clawing, with roaring, with tossing and tumbling, he would work and wind himself from them; and when he was loose, to shake his ears twice or thrice, with the blood and the slaver hanging around his physiognomy [Quoted in Cuddon 1979:101].

The object of bear-baiting was not to kill the animal, which was considered too valuable to lose. It was more often the dogs who were victims of the sport. In bull-baiting, on the other hand, the object was to kill the bull, and *bulldogs* were specially bred to resist the thrusts of the bull.

Bulls were usually baited on Sundays, and sportsmen entered their dogs in the contest by paying a small fee for each "run" at the bull. The bull was tethered to a post, and the dogs "pinned" the animal by biting down on its muzzle, genitals, or stomach. The bulldog's low profile made it difficult for the bull to rake its belly with its horns, and the dog's projecting lower jaw enabled it to keep its grip on the bull without hindering its breathing, thus increasing its owner's chance of winning bets. The enraged bull would often break loose, goring dogs, and trampling people. The animal would be chased and eventually beaten to death.

An event at Tutbury in Staffordshire was known as the Minstrels Bull-Running. In the beginning, only minstrels who were part of the guild could chase the bull. In the Middle Ages the event was associated with August 16, the day after the Feast of Assumption, a Catholic holy day commemorating Mary's ascent into heaven. It is difficult to tell whether the mid-summer scheduling of the bull-running is related to earlier Celtic festivals held around the same time of year. These included rites in which bulls were driven through sacrificial fires. However, it would be almost impossible to trace the symbolic permutations, if any, that may have influenced the timing of the Tutbury event.

The Prior of Tutbury provided a bull for the Minstrels. The bull was prepared for the event to make it more difficult to catch and thus increase the "sport." The horns, ears, and tail of the animal were cut off, its body was smeared with soap, and its nostrils were filled with pepper. According to one writer of the time, if the bull escaped its pursuers it remained the property of the lord:

> ...but if the said Minstrells can take him, and hold him so long as to cut off but some small matter of his hair, and bring the same to the Mercat Cross in token they have taken him, the said Bull is then brought to the Bailiff's house in Tutbury, and there collar'd and roap'd and so brought to the Bull-ring in the high-street, and there baited with doggs, the first course being allotted for the King; the second for the honour of the town; and the third for the "King of the Minstrells." Which, after it is done, the said Minstrells are to have him for their owne, and may sell, or kill, and divide amongst them, according as they shal think good [Quoted in Cuddon 1979:180–181].

Rules for the Minstrels Bull-Running set out the rights and responsibilities of all participants and demonstrate the importance of the event for expressing social relationships of the different classes involved. Conduct of the event evinces the symbolic inversion characteristic of a festival. The Minstrels are represented by a "king" and have first rights to the bull, which was formerly the property of the highest-ranking personage of the region. Thus, it inverts the usual social order with the eventual object of reaffirming it. Restoration of normal social relationships take place at the bull-bait, where the first course is reserved for the actual lord, and the "King of the Minstrels" is relegated to third place.

Bull-baiting and bull-running display elements of several ritual traditions, including that of the Celts of the British Isles. Bull-running in England may have been linked to running of bulls among Ibero-Celts, which may have been the precursor to the running of the bulls before present-day bullfights in Pamplona, Spain. Bull-baiting in England was almost certainly influenced by Mithraism, a religion involving bull sacrifice that originated in ancient Persian and was introduced into Britain by Roman soldiers. Mithraism centered on worship of the god Mithra, viewed as the chief warrior in the struggle between Good and Evil, leading the fight against the Prince of Darkness.

Imagery on a marble bas-relief showing Mithra slaying a bull by plunging a knife into its neck is similar to that of the Gundestrup Cauldron. In the bas-relief, as in the Gundestrup Cauldron, dogs aid in dispatching the bull, while Mithra as a human figure atop the bull slits it throat with a knife. The bas-relief also displays symbols associated with Mithrism. The god is accompanied by two youths, and all three of the human figures wear the headgear characteristic of Mithraic imagery.

There are similarities between the religious art and the depiction of medieval bull-baiting. As in the religious ritual, dogs lunge at the bull as the bull charges them in turn. But the heroism of the sacrifice has degenerated into the belligerence of the mob. By the time bull-baiting and bull-running were outlawed, they had become the scene of riots and various forms of disorder. The Minstrels bull-running at Tutbury eventually degenerated into a free-for-all between Staffordshire and Derbyshire. Bull-running no longer reinforced the social order of the town. Rather, it became a raucous rivalry between neighboring shires. The now entirely secularized sport was abolished in 1778 as the result of a special petition from the people of Tutbury.

Bear-baiting and bull-running disappeared in part because they became too far removed from their ritual context. When they were no longer used to ensure game or propitiate the gods, they lost a great deal of their symbolic value. The activities became secularized as Christianity supplanted Mithraism among its Roman adherents in Britain and replaced Druidic religion among the Celts. Still, as long as the sports upheld the social order, bear-baiting and bull-running continued to hold some symbolic worth. Later, when the austerity of Puritanism challenged the voluptuousness of medieval Christianity, bear-baiting, bull-baiting, and bull-running became targets of reform. As the social context shifted, all these activities became relics of the past.

Ironically, bear-baiting, bull-baiting, and bull-running overflowed their symbolic bounds even as they lost their symbolic significance. Both ritual and sport are bounded: ritual by its association with the numinous or transcendent, and sport through being confined by rules and a clearly defined arena. The potential for havoc is contained within these boundaries. As bear-baiting, bull-baiting, and bull-running erupted outside their symbolic and spatial boundaries, they disrupted ordinary reality. When they became too far removed from the ritual and social contexts that gave them meaning, their potential for destruction was no longer tolerated.

The Mythical Origins of Bull Sacrifice

All ritual, including animal sacrifice, is grounded in myths and beliefs about the origins of humans and the relationship of humans to other aspects of the manifest world. Inevitably, these beliefs reflect their social context. As noted in Chapter Two, hunting by elites in the ancient Middle East was symbolically linked to the concept of a battle between Good and Evil, often conceptualized as a battle between the social order and unruly natural forces. The theme is taken a step further in the ritual of bull sacrifice, where the emphasis is on fertility and the emergence of culture. This essentially heroic themes are also symbolically linked to the complexity of the intimate relationship between men and women. These themes are intricately bound up with the rise of agriculture, a dramatic shift in the human way of life that began 13,000 years ago.

The lifestyle of foragers, discussed in Chapter Two, is dependent on the availability of plants and animals in the natural environment. Foragers do not breed the animals or cultivate the plants on which they rely. As human groups settled down to cultivate crops and practice animal husbandry, their survival rested on their ability to stimulate the fertility of the earth and of animals. The fertility of the earth became linked to that of human females, and the virility of the bull became linked to that of human males.

The earliest religions of which we have a record in India and the Middle East appear to involve rites in which the fertility of the land is encouraged by religious rituals based on the sexual union of human females and males, and by sacrifice of bulls. In their later manifestations as Tantra in both the Hindu and Buddhist traditions — and probably in the earlier religions as well — the union of human females and males is linked to beliefs about the essential unity of the universe. In the Hindu tradition the original creative Source underlying the manifest universe is Brahman, which is neither male nor female. Brahman contains within Itself both male and female energies. Being Perfection itself, it cannot be divided into finite quantities:

> [Brahman is the] supreme soul of the universe, self-existent, absolute, and eternal, from which all things emanate, and to which all return. This divine essence is incorporeal, immaterial, invisible, unborn, uncreated, without beginning and without end, illimitable, and inappreciable by the sense until the film of mortal blindness is removed [Dowson 1992:56].

Everything in the manifest or visible universe is produced from the Female Principle, Prakṛti, which is dynamic or active. Prakṛti attracts the Male Principle, which is latent or static, waiting to be awakened by the Female Principle. The Female Principle is also known as Śakti, or in Buddhism as *prajñā* (wisdom), conceived of as an abstract principle or as a goddess. The Male Principle in Hinduism is personified in the form of a god, whose identity varies depending on the particular Hindu tradition. In Tantric Buddhism, the Male Principle is *upāya*, the means by which feminine wisdom is translated into action.

In these traditions, it is believed that humans were originally one, containing both male and female energies, but broke apart in a fall from Paradise. Sexual union of female and male, either in the body or as a meditative practice, is believed to reunite these male and female energies in the form of the *bindu*, a sacred circle or maṇḍala that evokes the essential unity of the universe. N. N. Bhattacharyya writes: "The human body is the abode of both these principles, the static Male and the dynamic Female, and the purpose of Tantric *sādhana* [spiritual exercise] is to get these two principles in a non-dual and absolute union within the body" (1992:25).

Through sexual union enacted in Tantric ritual, females and males emanate Brahman, the unity of male and female energy. On a personal level, the female initiates the male, as possessor of the orifice that defines his being: "...woman is the initiator par excellence: she obviously ushers one into life and, obscurely, into death" (Wayman 1973:170). This concept underlies the story of Gilgamesh, discussed later in this chapter.

Early beliefs and practices aimed at promoting fertility and underscoring the essential unity of the universe provide the source of Hinduism, which later manifested in two distinct paths, Veda and Tantra. The Vedic tradition is based on written scriptures, the Vedas, which represent the earliest exposition of Hindu philosophy, dating from the second millennium B.C.E. Tantrism is based on ritual practice, in which wisdom is acquired through mystical union rather than through verbal exposition.

Bhattacharyya suggests that the Vedic tradition was elitist and intellectualist, underscoring the position of the dominant class. It denied the everyday world as illusion and rejected Tantric rites because they were "much in vogue among the low class people" (1992:3): "Eventually the Vedas came to be looked upon as a symbol of spiritual knowledge, a very sacred and unchallengable tradition not to be approached lightly, and a strong taboo for the ordinary people" (Bhattacharyya 1992:4).

The study and interpretation of the Vedas were monopolized by the dominant class, and a lower-caste person who attempted to acquire knowledge in the Vedas could be punished by death. Bhattacharyya writes:

> This contempt for worldly knowledge was possible only because one section of the community lived on the surplus produced by another and withdrew from the responsibility of labour and hence from the obligation of

acknowledging the reality of the material world. It created the illusion of "pure knowledge"—a form of transcendental wisdom in which world and worldly action had no place, human values no room—and rejected everything that went against it [1992:10].

Tantra continued to exist alongside the Vedas, firmly grounded in the working classes. Tantra did not deny the existence of the ordinary world. Instead, it focused on day-to-day activities: agriculture, breeding cattle, production of wine, iron-smelting, alchemy, and medicine. According to Bhattacharyya, an essential tenet of Tantra is "...that the structures of the microcosm and the macrocosm are identical and that the key to the knowledge of nature is to be found in the body" (1992:1). The word Tantra is derived from the root *tan*, meaning to spread or propagate.

Whereas the dominant classes rejected all forms of work, including agriculture, practitioners of Tantra embraced the corporeal life. The authors of Tantric texts came from all walks of life, and included both men and women. Bhattacharyya writes:

> The main features of this new wave were the revival of primitive beliefs and practices, of course not in their original forms, a simpler and less formal approach to the personal deity, orientation of life by the instructions of the *guru* or preceptor, a liberal and respectful attitude towards women, and denial of the caste system [1992:7].

Tantric practices horrified the more conservative members of the upper classes, especially as later influenced by their British conquerors:

> The use of animal food and spirituous liquors, indulged to in excess, is the rule of these strange ceremonies, in which Śakti is worshipped in the person of a naked woman, and the proceedings terminate with the carnal copulation of the initiated, each couple representing Bhairava and Bhairavī (Śiva and Devī), and becoming thus for the moment identified with them [Wilson 1875: 248–257].

Other British authors marveled at the moral rigor and rejection of inequity evidenced by practitioners of Tantra when not engaged in orgiastic rites:

> ...apart from the ceremonial which they inculcate, the general principles of Tantra breathe a liberal and intelligent spirit. Caste-restrictions are minimized; travelling is permitted; women are honoured; they can act as teachers; the burning of widows is forbidden; girl widows may remarry and the murder of a woman is peculiarly heinous. Prostitution is denounced. Whereas Christianity is sometimes accused of restricting its higher code to Church and Sundays, the opposite may be said of Tantrism. Outside the temple its morality is excellent [Elliot 1957:285].

In spite of their public protestations, the elite of India — whether Hindu, Buddhist, Muslim, or British — relished the release from formalism represented by Tantra. Ultimately, Tantra also became class-oriented, as the poor and uneducated masses did not have access to esoteric texts, and elites used the texts to justify their own licentious lifestyle. As elites gained a monopoly over the Tantric texts, Tantra became divorced from its pragmatic roots.

The Epic of Gilgamesh

Themes represented in the clash between the Vedic intellectualist tradition and the seemingly hedonistic Tantric ritual are presaged in the Epic of Gilgamesh, composed in the third millennium B.C.E. In comparison to the battles of Persian kings described in the *Shah-nama*, the dilemmas of Gilgamesh, king of Uruk, were infinitely more complex. The Persian kings had only to assert the dominion of culture over nature, framed as Good versus Evil. Gilgamesh had to deal with the essence of life itself. How do humans differ from animals, even domesticated ones? What is the purpose of human life? And even the question pondered by the historic Buddha two millennia later: Why were we born to suffer and die?

The Epic of Gilgamesh delineates motifs that consistently underlie the bull sacrifice: fertility, nature transformed into culture, and the quest for immortality. N. K. Sandars writes of the Gilgamesh epic:

> Through the action we are shown a very human concern with mortality,
> the search for knowledge, and for an escape from the common lot of man.
> The gods, who do not die, cannot be tragic. If Gilgamesh is not the first
> human hero, he is the first tragic hero of whom anything is known [1972:7].

We do not have a complete rendition of the story of Gilgamesh. The most complete version comes from the library of King Assurbanipal of Assyria, established in the seventh century B.C.E.

Gilgamesh was king of Uruk, one of the Sumerian city-states arising along the banks of the Tigris and Euphrates Rivers after the great Deluge. He is listed in the "Sumerian King-List" as the fifth ruler of the first dynasty of Uruk after the flood. Scholars have determined that Gilgamesh was a historical figure who lived and reigned in the first half of the third millennium B.C.E. He was known as a just judge and builder of the great city of Uruk, a marvel for its time. The author of the Epic of Gilgamesh describes its wonders: "Look at it still today: the outer wall where the cornice runs, it shines with the brilliance of copper; and the inner wall, it has no equal. Touch the threshold, it is ancient" (Sandars 1972:61). Unfortunately, one can no longer see the walls of Uruk or touch its threshold; the city was destroyed by Sargon, king of the Semites, long after Gilgamesh's death.

Gilgamesh is described as two-thirds god and one-third human. From his mother, a goddess, he inherited beauty, courage, and strength: "Adad the god of the storm endowed him with courage, the great gods made his beauty perfect, surpassing all others, terrifying like a great wild bull" (Sandars 1972:61). From his father he inherited mortality. The tragedy of the Gilgamesh epic is that his attributes are those of a god, but like all humans, he must die.

Gilgamesh's superhuman attributes were both the pride and bane of his subjects. None was his equal in building, in war, or in sexual appetite. Eventually, the people grew restless and asked the gods to create his equal to keep him occupied so they could get some rest. In answer to their prayers, Aruru, the goddess of creation, formed the wild man Enkidu from a lump of clay:

> There was virtue in him of the god of war, of Ninurta himself. His body was rough, he had long hair like a woman's; it waved like the hair of Nisaba, the goddess of corn. His body was covered with matted hair like Samuqan's, the god of cattle. He was innocent of mankind; he knew nothing of the cultivated land [1972: 63].

Enkidu lived with gazelles and ate grass in the hills. Like Gilgamesh, he is a marginal figure, uniting in his being two opposing worlds. Gilgamesh is both god and human, with an aspect like that of a bull. Enkidu has the strength and aspect of a bull, but he is a human who lives like a wild animal.

As is the case with Akvan the Div, described in Chapter Two, trouble arises when the wild invades the tame. Enkidu helps some wild animals escape from the snares of a trapper. The trapper appeals to Gilgamesh, who sends a harlot to tame Enkidu, "to let her woman's power overpower this man" (1972:63).

This phrase evokes the essential premise of Buddhist Tantra that "woman, flesh, and sexual intercourse" are "essential preconditions for the attainment of liberation" (Bhattacharyya 1992:224): "The aspirant has to understand that woman, or her generative organ, is the source of existence and that sexual functioning is the imitation of the process of creation" (Bhattacharyya 1992:225). Thus, as the goddess Aruru "gave birth" to Enkidu by fashioning him from clay, the harlot "gave birth" to him through sexual intercourse.

The word "harlot" may have Tantric associations. The harlot sent to seduce Enkidu is recruited from the "temple of love." From this distance, it is difficult to tell whether this phrase is literal or metaphorical. There was a tradition in the ancient Middle East and in India of women associated with temples and educated in religious ritual, especially as oracles and wives of the god of the temple. In the Buddhist Tantra tradition of ritual, women bring to the sexual union "insight," while males bring "means." Female initiators of male Tantrikas evidence two aspects, one pure, the other dissolute:

> We can only assume it is the same *prajñā*...that is the Perfection of Insight as dissolute as ever, for she consorts as freely with giving, morality, forbearance, striving, and meditation, as her wicked elder sister does with lust, hatred, and delusion. And she discloses the same ultimate truth to all the spiritual heroes [Wayman 1973:170].

The wisdom gained by Enkidu in lying with the woman sent by Gilgamesh forever severs him from the domain of the wild and propels him into the civilized world of humans. Enkidu returns to the wild, but the animals, his former comrades, reject him: "Enkidu was grown weak, for wisdom was in him, and the thoughts of a man were in his heart. So he returned and sat down at the woman's feet, and listened intently to what she said" (Sandars 1972:65). The woman teaches Enkidu to eat bread instead of grass, to drink wine, and to wear clothes. In short, she domesticates the wild man. This may be the oldest surviving written description of Tantric initiation.

The Gilgamesh epic is also regarded as recording the mythical origins of bull sacrifice, eventually transformed into the bullfight. Gilgamesh and Enkidu are drawn into battle with the Bull of Heaven when the king rejects the advances of Ishtar, the goddess of love. Infuriated by his coldness, Ishtar sends the Bull to destroy him. Although Gilgamesh strikes the killing blow, Enkidu instructs him and leads the way. The wild man prepares the animal for the *coup de grace* when he "dodged aside and leapt on the Bull and seized it by its horns" (Sandars 1972:88). Enkidu then cries to Gilgamesh: "My friend, we boasted that we would leave enduring names behind us. Now thrust in your sword between the nape and the horns." Gilgamesh does as he is told, thereby killing the Bull. He and Enkidu then cut out the animal's heart and give it to Shamash, the sun god. The method of killing the bull and the sacrifice to the sun god anticipate bull sacrifice in Mithraism, while Enkidu's vault over the animal suggests later Cretan ritual.

In punishment for the cosmic misdeed, the gods decree that Enkidu must die. Gilgamesh is spared out of respect for his divine mother. Here the Gilgamesh epic reflects class differences later expressed in the dichotomy between the Vedas and the Tantras. The Hindu sacred scripture *Baudhāyana Dharmasūtra* states that the Vedas and agriculture are destructive of each other (I.5.101). The Laws of Manu, which translate Hindu scripture into social code, states that members of the two upper castes, the Brāhmaṇas (priests) and Kṣatriyas (warriors) "must avoid agriculture because it is slavish and involves injury" (Bhattacharyya 1992:11). Just as the labor of those engaged in agriculture support the privilege of elites to reject such mundane but life-sustaining pursuits, the clay-born Enkidu must pay the price from which the divine-born Gilgamesh is exempt.

But the king's grief over the death of his friend leads him to become obsessed by thoughts of his own death. He sets off on a great journey to find the secret of immortality. As he travels, he puts off his kingly robes and begins wearing the skins of animals. Symbolic transformation is evident here. Enkidu leaves the wilderness and enters the world of civilization, where his dies. Because of Enkidu's death, Gilgamesh leaves civilization and goes out in the wilderness seeking immortality. On his journey, the hero meets Siduri, the woman of the vine, who chides him for attempting to escape the fate of men:

> Gilgamesh, where are you hurrying to? You will never find that for which
> you are looking. When the gods created man they allotted him death,

> but life they retained in their own keeping. As for you, Gilgamesh, fill
> your belly with good things; day and night, night and day, dance and be
> merry, feast and rejoice. Let your clothes be fresh, bathe yourself in water,
> cherish the little child that holds your hand, and make your wife happy
> in your embrace; for this too is the lot of man [Sanders 1972:102].

Gilgamesh's meeting with the woman of the vine reflects symbolism found else-
where in the Mediterranean area, as well as in what was then Persia and Arabia.
The hero, repeatedly compared to a bull, is instructed in culture by the woman of
the vine, the maker of wine. Cultivation of the vine and the conversion of grapes
into wine are symbolically associated with the invention of culture. Wine is also
associated with the blood of the bull in ritual sacrifice and later in the bull-fight.
The dancing and feasting Siduri recommends for Gilgamesh suggest associations
with later Dionyssos cults in Greece, Rome, and Egypt.

Dionyssos was the god of fertility and wine. He was often represented as an
erect phallus, and phallic symbols were used in the orgiastic rituals devoted to the
god. Worshippers danced and drank themselves into a state of ecstasy or frenzy, in
which they tore apart some animal — preferably a bull — and ate it raw. The ritual
reenacted a scene in the myth of Dionyssos, who sought to escape his enemies, the
jealous Titans, by changing his form. In his flight, the god transformed himself
successively into a lion, a horse, and a serpent. When he took on the form of a bull,
he was dismembered by the Titans. In their ecstasy, worshippers of the god believed
they were calling back his spirit. Thus, Dionyssos is associated with a form of
immortality.

Similar beliefs and rituals were associated with the Apis bull in Ptolemaic
Egypt about 2300 years ago. As an incarnation of divine procreativity, the Apis
Bull was worshipped at Memphis from early times. When it died, the bull was
given full funeral rites and buried in catacombs of the Serapaeum at Sakkara. The
Apis bull was believed to emerge as Osiris in the afterlife and to be immediately
reincarnated as another bull in the earthly realm. Osiris was the son of Nut, the
goddess whose body makes up the sky. Osiris became a mighty king, civilizing his
people and teaching them agriculture and animal husbandry. He also showed them
the way to worship the gods. Osiris was killed by his jealous brother Seth, but
became the king of the dead in the underworld. The Apis Bull was viewed as a savior and god associated with the afterlife, fertility, and oracles.

In the Sumerian epic, Gilgamesh is instructed in culture by the woman of the
vine, just as Enkidu had earlier been instructed in culture by the harlot. Rejecting
the advice of the woman of the vine, Gilgamesh refuses to give up his quest for
immortality. Later in his journey, he is ferried across the sea to Utnapishtim, a man
who has gained a form of immortality by saving himself, his family, and the animals from a great flood the gods had sent to destroy humanity. Utnapistim chas-
tises the ferryman for bringing the hero to him, saying:

> But this man before whom you walked, bringing him here, whose body
> is covered with foulness and the grace of whose limbs has been spoiled

by wild skins, take him to the washing-place. There he shall wash his long hair clean as snow in the water, he shall throw off his skins and let the sea carry them away, and the beauty of his body shall be shown, the fillet (headband) on his forehead shall be renewed, and he shall be given clothes to cover his nakedness.

Thus Gilgamesh once again acquires the emblems of civilization, but he is not given immortality. Now resigned to his fate, Gilgamesh returns to rule his kingdom. Upon his death, the epic poem summarizes the fate of the hero: "You were given the kingship, such was your destiny, everlasting life was not your destiny" (Sandars 1972:118). Gilgamesh was given unparalleled supremacy over the people and victory in battle. He left a monument for generations to come, but of Gilgamesh himself: "The king has laid himself down and will not rise again..." (Sandars 1972:118).

There is some ambiguity in the lamenting over Gilgamesh's death. The lament itself suggests a link to the origins of Tantrism:

> On the bed of fate he lies, he will not rise again,
> From the couch of many colours he will not come again.

Bhattacharyya suggests that early Tantrics did not encourage belief in existence of the soul apart from the body, and the epic of Gilgamesh offers no hope that the hero will ever return in any form. At the same time, the king is provided with grave offerings to take to the gods, suggesting a link to similar practices among Egyptians, and to beliefs that Osiris among the Egyptians and Dionyssos among the Greeks continue to exist in another realm. In all cases, there is a clear link between agriculture and civilization, and between the heroes and beliefs about immortality.

The epic of Gilgamesh can be viewed as a creation myth defining the relationship of human beings to ultimate reality, to the gods, and to each other. It also contains a social charter for bull sacrifice, describing the genesis of beliefs and rituals that eventually spread throughout the Middle East and the Mediterranean.

Cattle and Caste

There is evidence for an exchange of ideas between the early civilizations of the Tigris-Euphrates, where Sumerian civilization flourished, and populations of the Indus Valley. Excavations at Mohenjo-Daro indicate that people had settled there by about 3000 B.C.E., or even earlier. Excavations by Jonathan Mark Kenoyer of the University of Wisconsin and Richard Meadow of Harvard at Harappa indicate that, between 3300 and 2800 B.C.E., trade networks linked Indus Valley sites to sources of raw materials in areas farther west.[18] Thus, emerging civilizations in the Indus Valley were contemporaneous with those of the Tigris Euphrates and may have shared trade networks with them.

Bull and cow symbolism permeates the Rg Veda, composed between 1500 and 1000 B.C.E. and the earliest of the Vedic sacred writings that form the nucleus of Hindu belief. The Rg Veda traces the origin of religious ritual to the bull sacrifice: "The heroes roasted the dappled bull. These were the first ritual laws."

In Hindu tradition, the bull symbolizes strength and fertility; the milk of the cow represents nurturance. Together they make up "sky-and-earth," a kind of interlocking entity that encircles the sun. "Sky-and-earth" are seen as the "two world-halves." The sky is represented by the bull, who fertilizes the earth, a cow who gives birth to the sun, depicted as a charioteer. As described in the Rg Veda:

> Wide and roomy, strong and inexhaustible, the father and mother protect the universe.... The son of these parents, their clever charioteer with the power to make things clear, purifies the universe by magic. From the dappled milk-cow [the earth] and the bull with good seed [the sky], every day he milks the milk that is his seed.

The semen of the bull is conceptually interwoven with the milk of the cow. The fertility metaphor is often extended so that the semen of the bull is equated with rain, the precious liquid that allows the earth to bring forth sustenance. The cow is often used as a metaphor for the "milk of immortality." In chariot races described in the Rg Veda, the prize is often a cow, and the symbolism is stated explicitly. By winning the race, the victor also wins immortality.

Mithraism and other forms of cattle sacrifice were practiced in India. And, though cattle sacrifice is a prominent feature of the Rg Veda, later Vedic scriptures reject the practice. By about 2000 years ago, a ban on sacrifice of cattle had become widespread, and the penalties for killing a cow were about the same as for killing a high-caste person. The ban on sacrifice of cattle may have paralleled the split between the Vedic and Tantra traditions of Hinduism, since the ban on cattle sacrifice undercuts the power of the traditional priests and reinforces the importance of the caste system. Ironically, however, the Hindu concept of the sacred cow and the ban on killing of animals have their origins in early veneration of the animal expressed in bull sacrifice.

The *Bhagavad-Gita* or *Song of God*, written between the fifth and second centuries B.C.E., reflects a transitional phase in the conceptualization of cattle sacrifice. The *Bhagavad-Gita* is part of the *Mahabharata*, said to be the longest poem in the world, which chronicles the adventures of the descendents of King Bharata (*maha* means great) and of ancient India, where the Bharatas lived and ruled.[19] Stories of the *Mahabharata* are still dramatized in Hindu festivals. The *Bhagavad-Gita* recounts a dialogue between Arjuna, a member of the Kṣatriya or warrior caste and a descendent of King Bharata, and the god Krishna, who is serving as Arjuna's charioteer in an upcoming battle between factions of the Bharata clan. As the two sides prepare for battle, Krishna instructs Arjuna in the true nature of Brahman and the yogas, or paths leading to liberation from the wheel of death and rebirth. Krishna tells Arjuna that, ultimately, the actions of the liberated man *are* Brahman:

When the bonds are broken
His illumined heart
Beats in Brahman:
His every action
Is worship of Brahman:
Can such acts bring evil?
Brahman is the ritual,
Brahman is the offering,
Brahman is he who offers
To the fire that is Brahman.

Krishna then reveals himself to Arjuna as Brahman:

Rites that the Vedas ordain, and the rituals
taught by the scriptures:
All these am I, and the offering made to the
ghosts of the fathers,
Herbs of healing and food, the mantram, the
clarified butter:
I the oblation and I the flame into which it is
offered.

Krishna's list of offerings omits any reference to cattle, a form of offering that may have already fallen into disrepute. Instead, the sacrifice offered to the gods includes herbs, food, mantra (sacred syllables including the syllable OM), and clarified butter or ghee, which is considered a pure, distilled essence of the milk of a cow. These are still offered to the gods in Hindu ceremonies. Above all, Krishna asserts that the true offering underlying all other offerings is devotion:

Give me your whole heart,
Love and adore me,
Worship me always,
Bow to me only,
And you shall find me:
This is my promise
Who love you dearly.

Krishna affirmed the caste system as his own invention and links devotion to the performance of duties associated with one's caste. As a warrior, Arjuna's duty was to do battle; he was not to engage in trade, cultivation, or breeding of cattle:

The leader's duty,
Ordained by his nature,
Is to be bold,
Unflinching and fearless,
Subtle of skill

> And open-handed,
> Great-hearted in battle,
> A resolute ruler.
> Others are born
> To the tasks of providing:
> These are the traders,
> The cultivators,
> The breeders of cattle.

With this document, the division between ruler and the ruled, those who provision the ruler, is sealed.

The Divine Warrior

Class was also a factor in Mithraism, but this differed from the Hindu concept of caste. Mithra was revered as "The Great King" by the nobility and monarchs of Persia, who looked upon him as their protector. Like Arjuna, Mithra was a warrior. However, whereas Arjuna was a human, Mithra was a god. The symbolism of Mithra was closer to that of Christianity, which developed later, than to Hinduism.

Mithra became associated with Shamash, the sun god to whom Gilgamesh and Enkidu offered the heart of the Bull of Heaven. Mithra was viewed as a sun-god who drove across the skies in his chariot, which symbolically links him to Apollo of the Greeks and Surya of the Hindus. The ancient Persians viewed Mithra as the god of light. When Romans captured Persia and adopted Mithraism, they referred to the god as "Sol invictus," or "the invincible sun." The sun itself was referred to as "the eye of Mithras." The Persian crown, the model for present day crowns, was designed to represent the golden sun-disc sacred to Mithra.[20] As commander of the cosmic army of Good, Mithra became a favorite deity of Roman soldiers.

The central act of worship in Mithraism was the sacrifice of the bull, the prototype of which was the slaying of the bull by Mithra himself, represented in relief in every Mithraic sanctuary. In later Greek-influenced images, which provide much of what is known about the religion, Mithra is pictured as a young man, typically in the act of thrusting a knife into the neck of a sacrificial bull. In some representations, a scorpion fastens onto the testicles of the dying bull, while a dog, and usually also a serpent, drink the blood that flows from the sacrificial wound. Either the tail of the bull terminates in ears of grain or the grain grows from the wound.

The ritual sacrifice reenacts an event in the life of Mithra. According to legend, Mithra was born from a stone and was worshipped by the shepherds who witnessed the birth. The shepherds offered the new-born hero the first fruits of their flock and their harvests. Mithra was viewed by Persian Magi as the intermediary between "the unapproachable and unknowable god that reigned in the ethereal spheres and the human race that struggled and suffered here below" (Cumont 1956[1903]:128).

The life of Mithra was marked by extraordinary accomplishments, crowned by his combat with a wild bull, the first living creature created by Ormazd, the origin of all that is light, good and productive. At first, Mithra captured the animal and imprisoned it in a cave, but the bull escaped. The Sun then ordered Mithra to slay the animal, which Mithra only reluctantly agreed to do. Aided by his dog, Mithra overtook the bull, seized it by the nostrils with one hand, and plunged his hunting-knife into the animal's flank. The death of the bull brought forth all the benificent things of the earth:

> From the body of the moribund victim sprang all the useful herbs and plants that cover the earth with their verdure. From the spinal cord of the animal sprang the wheat that gives us our bread, and from its blood the vine that produces the sacred drink of the Mysteries [Cumont 1956[1092]:136-137].

Ahriman, the force of evil, sent all the horrendous beings that he had created against the dying bull, to poison the good things the animal had produced: "The scorpion, the ant, the serpent, strove in vain to consume the genital parts and to drink the blood of the prolific quadruped; but they were powerless to impede the miracle that was happening" (Cumont 1956[1903]:137).

This story and the Mithraic sacrifice reflect imagery in the *Bundahishn*, a book describing Zoroastrianism cosmology, including the creation of the universe and of earthly creatures by Ohrmazd. Ohrmazd dwelled in light, whereas the evil one Ahriman dwelled in darkness. Becoming aware of Ohrmazd's grandeur, Ahriman sought to destroy him, but sank defeated into gloomy darkness, where he formed demons and fiends to fight on his behalf. Ormazd produced creatures of light, beginning with Vohuman, "good thought." Ormazd also produced the creatures of the world, beginning with the sky, water, earth, plants, animals, and humans. The ox was the first animal to be created, and Gayomard was the primordial human.

Seeing the might and splendor of Ormazd's creation, Ahriman despaired of conquering the Kingdom of Light until the evil woman Jeh arrived and convinced him that she could cast a blight on the creation. In his delight, Ahriman kissed Jeh on the head, "and the pollution which they call menstruation became apparent in Jeh."[21] "What is thy wish," Ahriman asked, "so that I may give it to thee?" Jeh asked that he give her a man. Ahriman changed his form from that of a crocodile-like creature into that of a fifteen-year-old man, with whom she promptly fell in love.

Encouraged by Jeh, Ahriman blighted all of Ohrmazd's creation and sent out noxious creatures, including the snake, scorpion, frog, and lizard. Vegetation withered away, and avarice, want, pain, hunger, disease, lust, and lethargy were unleashed upon the world. Ormazd concocted a healing balm to ease the pain of the ox as it died and formed a youthful man from the sweat of Gayomard. When Garyomard died, he fell to the left, and the primeval ox died it fell to the right. The death of the ox gave birth to vegetable life on earth. Fifty-five species of grain and 12 species of medicinal herbs grew from its spinal marrow. Its semen was carried up to the moon, where it was purified and produced various species of animals. From its blood came "the grapevine from which they make the wine." The idea that the death of the bull was the source of life is a recurring theme in bull sacrifice. The worship of Mithras focuses on themes of fertility, death, and rebirth.

The principal agent in the diffusion of Mithraism was the Roman army. As the Romans subjugated other groups of people, they inducted the conquered armies into their own ranks. To prevent trouble among its legions, the Romans stationed soldiers as far as possible from their homes. Thus, auxiliaries recruited in Persia were sent to serve along the borders of the Roman Empire, in Germany and the British Isles, where Mithraic ritual merged with Celtic cattle rites.

The symbolic significance of cattle is widespread: from India to western Europe, to the Mediterranean and ancient Middle East, to Africa. However, the cattle ritual complex that seems to have had the greatest influence on the bullfight comes from the area around the Mediterranean. The golden calf is believed to have been a central object of worship for the Canaanites for about one thousand years. The calf may not itself have been revered as a deity, but as a mount for the gods, much as the bull Nandi is still revered in Hinduism as the mount of the god Śiva. According to Satguru Sivaya Subramuniyaswami, Nandi is a symbol of the powerful instinctive force tamed by Śiva: "Nandi is the perfect devotee, the soul of man, kneeling humbly before God Śiva, ever concentrated on Him" (1993:768).

The chief deity of the Canaanites was El, whose name means "god." He was known as the father of the gods, "the father of mankind," the Bull, and the "creator of creatures."[22] With reference to El, the epithet "Bull" is metaphorical. The god is typically depicted in human form, seated and wearing bull's horns to signify strength. Canaanite worship centered around the sacrifice of sheep and cattle, including an act of communion that involved ritual eating of part of the sacrificed animal by devotees.

The golden calf was a symbol of idolatry to the Israelites, who saw it as being in opposition to their own supreme deity Yahweh. After their flight from Egypt, when Moses was on the mountain receiving the Covenant from God, the people beseeched his brother Aaron to make gods to help them. Aaron melted down their golden earrings and formed the metal into a calf. He built an altar before the calf and proclaimed it to be the god of Israel. He also proclaimed the following day to be a "feast to the LORD" (*Exodus* 32:5): "And they rose up early on the morrow, and offered burnt offerings, and brought peace offerings; and the people sat down to eat and to drink, and rose up to play." (Exodus 32:6)

This provocative statement suggests that religious festivals involving cattle sacrifice may also have included organized games, as well as other types of play events. Bull sacrifice in Crete between 3000 and 1470 B.C.E. included acrobatic performances that may have been part of a fertility rite or initiation ceremony.

All the religions involving bull sacrifice eventually gave way before the might and power of the Roman empire as it began promoting Christianity, and the later Arab sweep across the Middle East and Africa under the banner of Islam. As noted earlier, the medieval sports of bear-baiting and bull-running eventually died out because they became too far removed from their symbolic context. Conversely, Mithraism and other Mediterranean bull rites were displaced because they remained too closely linked to their ritual roots. This brought them into competition with more powerful monotheistic religions. Only the bullfight, which bridges the gap between sacred and secular, has survived and flourished, uniting the symbolic themes of fertility, culture, death, and rebirth associated with bull sacrifice.

The Sacrifice as Pageant

It is difficult to trace the origins of the bullfight with any certainty, perhaps because it is the product of a number of traditions, both religious and secular. There appears to have been an element of sport in rituals connected with bull worship, possibly from their beginnings.

Bull sacrifice at the height of Cretan culture, between 3000 and 1470 B.C.E., combined religious ritual with secular display. Bulls were sacrificed in Crete both by stabbing them and allowing them to bleed to death, and as part of an acrobatic performance that may have been part of a fertility rite or initiation ceremony. Young men and women seized the horns of a charging bull and somersaulted over the back of the animal, landing either on its back or on the ground beyond. The event is depicted in a fresco on the walls of the place at Knossos. It is also represented in a number of figurines and seals found at both Knossos and Hagia Triada. It is significant that the vault was performed in front of an audience, since this may mark a transition from ritual to sport.

The ritual performance may have been linked to the myth of the Minotaur, killed by the Greek hero Theseus. According to legend, King Minos of Crete asked Poseidon to send a bull worthy to be sacrificed in the sea god's honor. However, the bull provided by Poseidon was so magnificent, Minos kept it for himself and sacrificed a bull from his own herd instead. To punish him, Poseidon inspired Minos' wife Pasiphae with an unnatural passion for the bull. Pasiphae gave birth to a man with the head and tail of a bull, and Minos ordered the master craftsman Daedalus to build a labyrinth to house the monster.

To make matters worse, the bull that had excited Pasiphae's passion became violent. One of the labors of Herakles was to capture the bull and take it to the Peloponnesian peninsula of Greece. Then bull then wandered to Marathon where it ravaged the country.

Minos was to suffer even greater tragedy from his betrayal of Poseidon. His son Androgeos journeyed to Athens and humiliated the townspeople by defeating all opponents in the athletic games. King Aegeus then challenged the youth to fight the Marathon bull, which killed him. Minos went to war against Athens, and as a condition of peace, demanded that the Athenians send seven youths and seven maidens every year to be devoured by the Minotaur.

At this point, Theseus arrived in Athens, where he learned that King Aegeus was his father. Theseus was conceived when Aegeus became drunk on a visit to King

Pittheus of Troezen and lay with his host's daughter. The paternity of Theseus is uncertain, however, since Poseidon had also lain with the woman on the same night. Theseus captured the Marathon bull and offered himself as a sacrifice to the Minotaur. When the hero landed in Crete, King Minos' daughter Ariadne fell in love with him and provided him with the secret to the labyrinth, on condition that he take her back with him to Athens. Theseus killed the Minotaur, then made his way out of the labyrinth by following a thread supplied by Ariadne. According to one report, Theseus sacrificed the Minotaur to Poseidon, bringing the episode full circle.

The contest between man and bull, a common feature of Mediterranean and the cultures of the Ancient Middle East, is illustrated in the story of Theseus and the Minotaur, here captured on a Greek vase (British Museum).

Theseus left Crete with Ariadne, who bore him two sons, but abandoned her on the island of Naxos, one of the Cyclades islands. Theseus later married Phaedra, another daughter of King Minos, who fell in love with Hippolytus, Theseus' son by an Amazon. When Hippolytus rejected her, Phaedra falsely accused him of rape. Theseus beseeched Poseidon to kill Hippolytus, and Poseidon did so by sending a bull up from the surf when Hippolytus was driving his chariot by the sea. The bull frightened Hippolytus' horses, and they dragged him to his death. According to some versions of the story, Hippolytus was raised from the dead by the half-divine surgeon Asclepius and became king of Italy under the name of Virbius I.[23] The story of Hippolytus' Roman reincarnation has the mark of a later addition aimed at validating the reign of Virbius I, but it does illustrate the prevalence of death-and-rebirth themes in Mediterranean mythology.

The story of Theseus contains, in a more elaborate form, many of the same elements introduced in the Epic of Gilgamesh. Like Gilgamesh, Theseus may have been born of a union between a god and a human, though in Theseus' case, the link to divinity is uncertain. There is also a symbolic link between the strength and virility of bulls and human males in both stories. Theseus' offspring provide additional links between the two stories. Hippolytus conquers death after being treated by Aesclepius, and Theseus is ancestor to the Winegrowers through one of the sons borne to him by Ariadne. The Winegrowers, Elias, Oeno and Spermo, were given by Dionyssos the power of producing oil, wine, and corn from anything they touched.

Various forms of encounters with bulls were widespread in the centuries leading up to and around the beginning of the current era. Thessalonians fought bulls that were roused to fury with red cloths in religious ceremonies known as *taurokathapsiai*. The bullfighters fought on foot or on horseback. They leaped onto the animal's back, caught it by the horns, and brought it to the ground before killing it.

The Imperial Romans fought a variety of animals in their amphitheaters, bulls among them, and it is probable they introduced a form of the bullfight into the Iberian Peninsula. After the conversion of the emperor Constantine to Christianity during the fourth century C.E., limitations were gradually placed on Roman athletic games. The gladiatorial contests were the primary targets for reform, perhaps in recognition of Christians killed in the arena. Gladiatorial games ended in the fifth century, but contests with animal continued for about another hundred years.

The bull sacrifice of Mithraism never really flourished in Iberia as it did in other parts of Europe, but the bullfight in amphitheaters certainly did. Iberia, now Spain and Portugal, was a fertile ground for the bullfight, since the Celtiberians hunted ferocious cattle in their forests and contended with them in a form of contest. They were said to have used an animal skin or cloak to baffle and distract charging bulls.

When the Moors conquered Spain in the eighth century, they introduced a note of elegance both to the art of the country and to the sport of bullfighting. As was the case in other parts of Europe, life in Spain was marked by squalor and superstition at the time of the Moorish invasion. Dean Derhak writes that the Moors brought Spain out of the Dark Ages of Medieval Europe and transformed it into "a place of humanistic beauty":

> Not only was it artistic, scientific and commercial, but it also exhibited incredible tolerance, imagination and poetry. Moors, as the Spaniards called the Muslims, populated Spain for nearly 700 years ... it was their civilization that enlightened Europe and brought it out of the dark ages to usher in the renaissance.[24]

Within 200 years of their arrival, the Muslim invaders had transformed Andalusia into "a bastion of culture, commerce and beauty."[25] The Muslims also introduced into Spain their fine Arabian horses, originally bred by the Bedouins, and the technique of bullfighting on horseback. Under Muslim rule, Moorish chieftains competed against Iberian knights in great tournaments. After the Muslims were driven out of Iberia in the fifteenth century, bullfighting continued as a pursuit of aristocrats and was an integral part of life at the Spanish royal court (Mackay-Smith et al: 1984:55).

As the sport evolved, bulls were no longer lanced from the back of a horse, and the tradition of the matador fighting on foot was established. In his series of etchings called *Tauromachia*, the Spanish artist Francisco Goya recorded an earlier time when bulls were fought from horseback.

As in the ancient Middle East, bullfighting is associated with virility and fertility in Iberian custom and folklore. During the thirteenth century, in what is now Portugal, marriage customs included ritual killing of a bull. The bridegroom and his friends would obtain a bull from the slaughterhouse. They would then run the animal through the village, agitating it with jackets and wounding it to ensure a flow of blood. Symbolically, this is associated with opening the womb through piercing the hymen. The flow of blood may also symbolize the menstrual flow, which signifies the ability to conceive. The bull was led to the bride's house, where the groom would place in the animal's withers two *banderillas* or darts that had been decorated by the bride. The bull was then killed by a butcher (McCormick and Sevilla 1967).

A Spanish folktale about a bull with golden horns also links the bull with fertility and sexuality. A young girl is loved by two men, but she loves only one of them. When the man she favors is killed by his jealous rival, she takes revenge by killing him and one of his friends. To escape punishment, she dresses as a man, takes the name of Carlos and finds work in a shop in a town where she is unknown. The daughter of the shopkeeper falls in love with Carlos, who is coerced into marrying her. On their wedding night, Carlos confesses the whole story to her bride, who promises not to betray her.

When the couple fails to produce children, the wife's father begins to suspect that Carlos is a woman. He and other men of the town challenge her to a hunt followed by a swim in the river. Carlos evades her companions and goes upstream where she encounters a magnificent bull with golden horns. The bull commands

El Cid Campeado is one of a series of etchings depicting bullfight scenes from Francisco Jose Goya's Tauromachia. This etching documents an earlier form of bullfighting from horseback introduced when Muslim's occupied Spain in the eighth century (The Metropolitan Museum of Art, Rogers Fund, 1921).

her to undress, makes a cross on her pelvis with his golden horn and Carlos becomes, in fact, a man (McCormick and Sevilla 1967).

The modern bullfight continues the symbolic association between the blood of the bull, of men and of wine, as indicated in a poem by Ignacio Aldecoa:

> Blood of the toro,
> Fire of the rockets
> Power of men's muscles,
> Rhythm of the dance.
> Blood of men,
> Fire of the *banderillas.*
> Power of the toro,
> Rhythm of the *veronica.*
> Blood of wine,
> Fire of the sun,
> Power of fire,
> Rhythm of the blood.

The poem also links the strength of men and bulls with fire, rockets and the sun. The symbolism can be extended even further into Christian imagery. The *veronica* is a two-handed pass with the cape. Its name comes from St. Veronica, who wiped the face of Christ with her veil as he carried his cross to Calvary for his crucifixion. In Roman Catholic ritual, the blood of Christ is symbolized by wine.

At the Last Supper, Christ links his own identity with the culture of the vine: "I am the true vine, and my Father is the husbandman. Every branch in me that beareth not fruit he taketh away: and every *branch* that beareth fruit, he purgeth it, that it may bring forth more fruit" (John 15:1-2). Christ further compares his blood with wine:

> And he took the cup, and when he had given thanks, he gave *it* to them: and they drank all of it. And he said unto them: This is my blood of the new testament, which is shed for many. Verily I say unto you, I will drink no more of the fruit of the vine, until that day that I drink it new in the kingdom of God [Matthew 26:27–29].

There are no *corridas* during Holy Week in Spain, but there are many important ones on Easter Sunday. That Christian holy day initiates the bullfight season, which takes place during spring and summer. The timing may indicate a connection to early festivals marking the planting and cultivation season.

Whether deliberately or by chance, Ernest Hemingway's novel *The Sun Also Rises* reiterates the time-honored association of bull sacrifice, fertility, the course of the sun-god through the sky, death and rebirth, and the transformative powers of the grape. The book's title is taken from Ecclesiastes: "*One* generation passeth away, and *another* generation cometh: but the earth abideth for ever.... The sun also ariseth, and the sun goeth down, and hasteth to the place where he arose" (1:1). Those sentiments could have come straight from Gilgamesh, whose quest for immortality was initiated by killing the Bull of Heaven. Other verses from Ecclesiastes evoke the words of the woman of the vine in advising Gilgamesh to be content with his earthly portion:

> Go thy way, eat thy bread with joy, and drink thy wine with a merry heart; for God now accepteth thy works. Let thy garments be always white; and let thy head lack no ointment. Live joyfully with the wife whom thou lovest all the days of the life of thy vanity, which he has given thee under the sun, all the days of thy vanity: for that *is* thy portion in *this* life, and in thy labour which thou takest under the sun [Ecclesiastes 9:7–9].

The words of Ecclesiastes also evoke Mithraism and other religions of the region in referring to the sun as "he," giving it a male personna.

Jake, the hero of Hemingway's novel, is symbolically a steer, unable to physically consummate his love for the female hero Brett because of a war injury. Brett, on the other hand, is fascinated with all forms of virility. On a trip to see the bullfights in Pamplona, Jake, who seems to know everything that matters, gives Brett her first look at fighting bulls. Using Jake's voice, Hemingway describes that initial encounter:

> I leaned way over the wall and tried to see into the cage. It was dark. Some one rapped on the cage with an iron bar. Inside something seemed to explode. The bull, striking into the wood from side to side with his horns, made a great noise. Then I saw a dark muzzle and the shadow of horns, and then, with a clattering on the wood in the hollow box, the bull charged and came out into the corral, skidding with his forefeet in the straw as he stopped, his head up, the great hump of muscle on his neck swollen tight, his body muscles quivering as he looked up at the crowd on the stone walls.

The bull charges two steers in the ring, who seem to serve little purpose but to draw the thrusts of the bull. Like Jake, they are sexually impotent. The woman is fascinated by the virility of the bull: "My God, isn't he beautiful?" Brett says.

On the day of the bullfight that is pivotal to the novel's plot, Jake and Brett take part in a ceremonial observance which symbolically links wine with fertility, virility, death and rebirth. After the Roman Catholic religious procession and the running of the bulls through the streets of Pamplona, Brett is seated on a wine-cask in a wine-shop, and the people of the town cluster around her singing and drinking wine. She, the object of their songs and toasts, is not allowed to drink. Jake, who has been de-sexed in the fiercely masculine contest of war, later introduces Brett to the sexuality of the bullring and to the bullfighter Romero:

> Romero was the whole show. I do not think Brett saw any other bull-fighter. No one else did either, except the hard-shelled technicians. It was all Romero. There were two other matadors, but they did not count. I sat beside Brett and explained to Brett what it was all about.

The symbolism of the quandrant composed of Jake, Brett, Romero, and the bull is not entirely derived from Mediterranean lore, though it is rooted in these traditions. Brett is an experienced woman in matters of sexuality, evoking the harlot in the Gilgamesh epic. She also evokes Ishtar, the goddess whose passion for Gilgamesh results in killing the Bull of Heaven. Brett is encircled by three symbols of male power: Jake the knower, Romero the slayer of bulls, and Bocanegra (Blackmouth) the bull. But the feminine power of Brett conquers all three.

The Hemingway story diverges from the ancient Middle Eastern tradition — but not the Mediterranean tradition — in separating the mind (Jake) from the body (Romero). The view of the mind as being allied to God and the body being allied to animals is integral to the western European philosophical tradition — generally traced to Aristotle. In Asian philosophical traditions, mind and body are emanations of the same essential Being. As one Buddhist philosopher expressed it, "The Buddha *is* the body, and whoever doesn't know that doesn't know anything."

Hemingway has constructed a kind of trinity, in which male power is compartmentalized, but female power is represented in one entity: Brett. Brett has a brief but intense affair with Romero, a youth not yet out of his teens. Hemingway gives a typically terse account of the encounter between love and death:

> The bull who killed Vicente Girones was named Bocanegra, was Number 118 of the bull-breeding establishment of Sanchez Taberno, and was killed by Pedro Romero as the third bull of that same afternoon. His ear was cut by popular acclamation and given to Pedro Romero, who, in turn, gave it to Brett, who wrapped it in a handkerchief belonging to myself, and left both ear and handkerchief, along with a number of Muratti cigarette-stubs, shoved far back in the drawer of the bed-table that stood beside her bed in the Hotel Montoya, in Pamplona.

With this cryptic rendering, Hemingway suggests that the life and death of men and bulls, as well as the trophies and scars of their hard-fought battles, are a matter of casual indifference to women. Women are the prize; men pay the price. Or, in the words of a French folk saying: Women are expensive; men are cheap. Hemingway has come a long way from the Middle Eastern and Hindu view of the complementarity of male and female power, while maintaining their essential symbolism.

The Spanish artist Pablo Picasso provides a different insight into the contest between man and bull, or human and animal. Picasso evinced a lifelong fascination with the bullfight and its associated Minotaur legend. As a youth, he attended bullfights with his father, who also provided the boy with his early instruction in art. Significantly, Picasso's first painting, *Picador*, expresses a bullfight motif.

During the summer of 1934, Picasso completed a series of bullfight paintings, drawings and etchings. The bullfight takes on a monumental quality in his work from that period. In one work the bull clearly dominates the canvas. The writhing horse is contrasted with the massive strength and sexuality of the bull.

The association of the bullfight with sensuality is more explicit in Picasso's drawing of a female toreador. In this work, the voluptuousness of the woman contrasts with the vigorous sensuality of the bull. The woman has lured the bull with her cape, but appears to be less hunter than prey, as the contest is transformed into a scene of sexuality.

In Picasso's etching *Vanquished Minotaur*, the bullfight is merged with the Minotaur myth. The contest takes place in the bullring, but the defeated one is half-man, half-beast. The figure standing over him in the ring is that of a Greek hero. He and the spectators appear to be grieving, rather than celebrating the triumph of man over beast. And a woman leans forward from the stands to caress the creature's shoulder, much as a woman might comfort her despondent lover. In this work, the bull is fully mythologized, transformed from the quarry of the ring into the half-bull, half-man of legend. Thus the identity of man and beast is complete. And the image of woman as seducer is merged with that of woman the nurturer and giver of the promise of life.

Perhaps none other than Federico García Lorca better expresses the interplay of triumph and death in the bullring, in his poetic tribute to the great bullfighter Ignacio Sanchez Mejias. To accommodate a friend, Sanchez Mejias set aside his own misgivings — and his retirement from the ring — to fight his last bull:

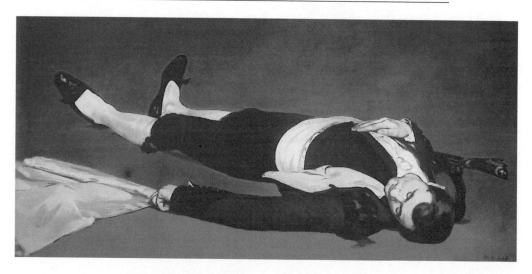

The stillness of Edouard Manet's *The Dead Toreador* provides a stark contrast to the color and frenzied activity of the bullfight. In the bull sacrifice it is the bull who provides fertility by his death. Here, the matador has been sacrificed (National Gallery of Art, Washington, Widener Collection).

> At five in the afternoon.
> It was exactly five in the afternoon.
> A boy brought the white sheet
> at five in the afternoon.
> A basketful of lime ready prepared
> at five in the afternoon.
> The rest was death, and death alone
> at five in the afternoon.
> ....
> When the bull ring was covered with iodine
> at five in the afternoon.
> Death laid eggs in the wound
> at five in the afternoon.
> At five in the afternoon.
> At five o'clock in the afternoon.
> ....
> A coffin on wheels is his bed
> at five in the afternoon.

Lorca does not romanticize the death of his friend in the bullring. Instead, he dwells on the biological decay of death: the lime prepared to decompose the body, the flies circling above the body to lay their eggs and generate a new form of life. As in Gilgamesh, Lorca celebrates the heroism of his friend and laments his eternal end:

> The air of Andalusian Rome
> gilded his head

where his smile was a spikenard
of wit and intelligence.
What a great torero in the ring!
What a good peasant in the sierra!
How gentle with the sheaves!
How hard with the spurs!
How tender with the dew!
How dazzling the fiesta!
How tremendous with the final
banderillas of darkness!

But now he sleeps without end.
Now the moss and the grass
open with sure fingers
the flower of his skull.

Ah, Gilgamesh! How long you sleep, and how long you live in our memories!

Ignacio Sanchez Mejias, the bullfighter celebrated by Lorca, had survived the tests of youth and returned to the ring after his retirement in loyalty to a friend. Lorca mourns greatness reduced to biological decay. In her poem Pamplona,[28] Karen Eilene Saenz returns to bullfight themes associated with youth, of fertility and romance, of manhood's flowering quickly cut short by death:

Blood dries dark upon red sands
Where white camellias bloom

               In summer

The streets are thick with bulls
Braying rivers of hoof and horn
Trampling ghosts of future lovers
While patrons framed in tavern doors
Anoint themselves with olive wine.

Horn to bone, rivers run red
And boys bloom quickly to men
Before expiring upon white stones.

Today, bullfighting is variously viewed as spectacle, theater, barbaric butchery, sport and art. Along with sacred cow reverence in India, it may represent the last vestige of cattle religions that were widespread from India through the ancient Middle East to the Mediterranean. The historian John Armitage suggests that the modern bullfight strikes a necessary balance between ritual and spectacle:

Rome made the mistake of feeding a love of violence by offering bigger and bigger spectacles of bestial horror. Modern Spain might be said to have gauged correctly the needs of individuals and society by providing entertainment which has as its climax the ritual killing of the bull, the bull being both victim and idol. Because the majority is not in need of such spectacles it does not necessarily follow that they have no value to the community. Some believe that outlets for passionate feelings have been badly neglected in most Western countries and that some compensation for the law and order of urban living should be made available [1977:12–13].

Ironically, it may have been the secularization of the bullfight by the Romans that allowed the former religious ritual to survive the onslaught of Christianity. Consider the fate of the Olympics: The great athletic festivals were outlawed under the Romans at the end of the fourth century by Christian emperors who thought the Games were pagan. The Roman emperor Theodosius banned all pagan cults, and the last Olympiad was held in 393 C.E. The Olympics were not revived until 1896, fifteen centuries later, long after the Games had lost their association with religion.

PART 3. THE HUMAN ADVERSARY

Four

Combat Sports:
The Socialization of Conflict

We can call [war] the most intense, the most energetic form of play and
at the same time the most palpable and primitive.
                                        Johan Huizinga, *Homo Ludens*

In the Biblical story of Jacob, God tests the moral and physical courage of the
progenitor of the Israelites. As he journeys to seek the favor of his estranged brother
Esau, Jacob is fearful that Esau will intercept him and kill his followers. He sends
away his retinue and prepares to meet his fate alone.

But Jacob's battle is not with his brother's army. Instead, he wrestles all night
with a stranger. As dawn arrives, the unknown visitor tries to escape from Jacob's
grasp, but Jacob refuses to release him without learning the name of his opponent
and receiving his blessing. Jacob's enigmatic opponent then provides a clue to his
identity, not by giving his own name, but by the power of his blessing, which shapes
the fate of Jacob and all his descendents. The stranger tells him, "Your name shall
no more be called Jacob, but Israel, for you have striven with God and with men,
and have prevailed." Israel means "He who strives with God" or "God strives"
(Genesis 32:1–30).

In this story, the hero proves his social responsibility in a test of moral and
physical courage. Symbolic battle in the spiritual realm can also represent a battle
between conflicting elements of the moral order, a concept reflected in the Zoroastrian belief that the opposing armies of Good and Evil are locked in a great battle
for control of the universe. This is also the theme underlying the ritual defense of
God and his wife by the Raramuri, described in Chapter One. Ritual warfare sometimes dramatizes an encounter between competing forces of nature. During their
summer festivals, the Celts enacted a ceremonial battle between winter and summer in the belief that it was necessary for the verdant and productive season of summer to wrest its domain from the chilly grasp of winter.

Combat sports are closely linked to these religious concepts and practices. On
the one hand, ethical and philosophical conflicts provide the context for the development of sport as a part of religious ritual. At the same time, sport promotes the

values of courage and direct response to a challenge. Combat sports, especially wrestling, provide a metaphor for "coming to grips" with a problem. The eighteenth-century British statesman and orator Edmund Burke argued for the value of meeting opposition: "He that wrestles with us strengthens our nerves, and sharpens our skill. Our antagonist is our helper."[27]

The human opponent is often the visible symbol of more terrifying and abstract powers. As Paul expressed it in his Epistle to the Ephesians (6:11): "...we wrestle not against flesh and blood, but against principalities, against powers, against the rulers of the darkness of this world, against spiritual wickedness in high places."

Combat sports enact a number of symbolic themes, the chief of which is social responsibility. This is often expressed indirectly in the Asian martial arts, where the emphasis is on spiritual striving. Social and mythological themes were acted out for the benefit of spectators in the Roman gladiatorial ring and in medieval jousting tournaments. Modern boxers and amateur wrestlers often compete on behalf of their countries or other political entities. Historically, wrestling linked the power of the athlete to strength, beauty and sexuality. Modern professional wrestling matches are enacted in the form of dramas pitting Good against Evil in a limited arena.

War as Ritual—The Asian Martial Arts

> Although you see the sword that moves to strike you, if your mind is not detained by it and you meet the rhythm of the advancing sword; if you do not think of striking your opponent and no thoughts or judgments remain; if the instant you see the swinging sword your mind is not the least bit detained and you move straight in and wrench the sword away from him; the sword that was going to cut you down will become your own, and, contrarily, will be the sword that cuts down your opponent [Takuan Sōhō 1986:19].

With these words, the seventeenth-century Japanese Zen master Takuan Sōhō explains how Buddhist detachment from worldly desires aids the samurai in engaging his opponent. His instruction is contained in a letter to Yagyu Munenori, head of the Yagyu Shinkage school of swordsmanship. Yagyu Munenori was sword master to Tokugawa Ieyasu, founder of the Tokugawa shogunate, which ruled Japan from 1603 to 1867 from its capital at Edo, now Tokyo. Takuan Sōhō's philosophy reconciles religious aspiration with the practical necessity of survival in an often violent world. The resolution of this seeming contradiction is central to a long tradition of Asian martial arts.

According to legend, the tradition began in China in the sixth century C.E., with a Buddhist monk known as the Bodhidharma. The Bodhidharma is said to have established both the Ch'an school of Buddhism, precursor to Japanese Zen, and the *kung fu* tradition of martial arts. The Bodhidharma is reputed to have been a missionary from India, a monk named Da Mo, who settled at the Shaolin Monastery in Henan province in 520 or 526 C.E. During his nine years of meditation in a cave on a mountainside near the monastery, Da Mo often became physically and spiritually exhausted. To relieve his fatigue, he developed a program of regular exercise, now known as *kung fu*. His techniques are recorded in three treatises attributed to him: the *Book of the transformation of muscles and tendons*, the *Book on the cleansing of the marrow*, and a collection on spiritual exercises.

The Bodhidharma taught his exercises to the monks of the Shaolin Monastery, drawing upon an analogy to nature, as in the Taoist tradition. According to The Shaolin Wing Chun Nam Anh School of kung fu, the techniques improved both the physical and spiritual conditioning of the monks:

> They now had enough strength to do their day's work and were vigorous enough to perform their spiritual exercises. Learning combat techniques allowed them to be able to defend themselves against assaults on their monasteries in times of war, and against thieves on the roads.[28]

The monks became famous for their fighting skills. According to legend, thirteen monks from the monastery safeguarded the Tang dynasty by rescuing the emperor Li Shimin after he had been captured by a rival emperor Wang Shichong. The decision of the monks to rescue Li owes its logic less to Buddhist detachment than to the Chinese doctrine of the Mandate of Heaven:

> They all agreed that the Tang king, Li Yuan, and his son ruled in harmony with the heavens, and were sensitive to the feelings of the people. The harvests were always bountiful and their troops were highly disciplined and did not encroach in any way on the interests of the people. Wang Shichong on the other hand, after proclaiming himself emperor, disrupted the country and hurt the people and was nothing more than a simple bandit [Wang 1988:35].

Stories describing the exploits of the monks of the Shaolin Monastery incorporate recurring themes in the Asian martial arts. The monks gain their power by combining spiritual with physical discipline, and they use this power on behalf of the common good. The sources for this unique blend of warfare and transcendence can be traced to the philosophical traditions of China and India, as well as to Chinese religious rituals based in regional rivalries. In fact, the tradition of ritualized warfare in China predates the Bodhidharma. At least one form of *kung fu* dates from around 2600 B.C.E., when peasants wearing headdresses of horns practiced a kind of simulated combat.

Under the favor of emperors during the Tang, Yuan and Ming dynasties, the Shaolin monastery became a prosperous and renowned center of learning. With the ascendancy of the Ching dynasty, the Shaolin monastery became a center of resistance on behalf of the Ming dynasty. Emperor Kan Shi, grandson of the founder of the Ching dynasty, destroyed the temple at the monastery and massacred almost all the monks and nuns residing there. "Only five great masters survived the butchery...."[29] They were known as the "Five Invincibles." Among them was a nun named Ng Mui, who fled to the south, where she moved from monastery to monastery.

Ng Mui met a beautiful village girl named Yim Wing Chun, which means "to sing spring." The girl's father was imprisoned after she resisted the advances of an officer who wanted to marry her. The girl fled to Ng Mui, who taught her some kung fu techniques. The girl returned to her village and announced that she would marry only a man who could match her in combat. Certain of victory, the officer accepted her challenge. When he was defeated, the officer exacted revenge against her father, and Yim Wing Chun fled to take further instruction from Ng Mui. After several years of study, Yim Wing Chun became a famous warrior, raising armies to fight against the Ching dynasty. Eventually, she married a former student of the Shaolin monastery, Leung Bok Chau, and taught him her martial arts techniques. Leung Bok Chau preserved, developed and taught the Wing Chun style of kung fu in honor of his bride.[30]

Techniques of Wing Chung Kung Fu are known as "Sticking hands," which is based on deflecting, controlling and trapping an opponent's hands.[31] Film star Bruce Lee popularized Wing Chun and combined it with other styles to develop his own *Jeet Kune Do*, "the Philosophical Way of the Intercepting Fist." Six months before his death, Bruce Lee ordered his three schools of Jeet Kune Do closed, with instructions that no further teaching of his art was to take place.[32] As a result, there are no authorized teachers of Jeet Kune Do, but there are numerous adaptations of the Jeet Kune Do technique, according to the World Jeet Kune Do Federation.[33]

Some schools in this tradition still teach by analogy, in the kung fu tradition, though not with reference to nature. For example, the Oakland school of Jeet Kune Do conveys the concept of power by analogy to the force of water through a hose. Speed is compared to the motion of a whip. Speed and economy of motion are described as:

> The less you move the better.
> Clean and sharp as a two edged sword, pure Chinese Kung-Fu.

An organization called The Buddhist Way of Wing Chun Kung Fu, based in England, stresses its connection to Buddhist meditation techniques. The group describes its purpose as "researching, preserving, developing and furthering the practice of Wing Chun Kung Fu according to its original Buddhist principles"[34]:

> What we practise and advocate is a set of dynamic Buddhist meditational practices in movement — a Buddhist yoga. The constituent practices of Wing Chun (as we practise them and as our research indicates they originally were practiced) are extensions of traditional Buddhist seated meditational practices into movement, which allow the expression, communication and experience of Buddhist concepts and principles in movement. These are enjoyable, liberating practices, which encapsulate

the eightfold path of traditional Buddhism, project it into the physical realm and develop its constituent elements in the practitioner.[35]

The Buddhist Way of Wing Chun Kung Fu specifically distances itself from practices associated with other forms of martial arts: "We *do not*: break iron bars over our heads, or break boards, or break bricks, or scream/shout when practising (though we have been known to give in to bouts of laughter), or posture for the sake of it. Our practice *is not* a martial (military) art, but it is a Buddhist Practice."[36]

The contribution of the Bodhidharma to martial arts, which may be more mythological than historical, represents a synthesis rather than a departure from previous traditions. Philosophically, Ch'an or Zen unites the Mahayana form of Buddhism developed in India with Chinese Taoism, which emphasizes balance and non-resistance. The system of physical training attributed to the Bodhidharma combines Indian yoga breathing techniques and a form of Chinese unarmed combat called *kempo*, or "way of the fist."

Kempo is related to the healing art of acupuncture, which consists of using needles to balance the body's flow of energy. Kempo applies the techniques of acupuncture by making use of weak points in the body of one's opponent. The Taoist concept of balance of *yin* and *yang* forces is expressed directly in the Asian martial arts in the many moves aimed at throwing the opponent off balance. Various kung fu schools also apply the Taoist belief that human beings should take their cues for appropriate attitudes and behavior from nature. Names for techniques of the Shaolin monks are taken from the movements of animals, such as "Wild tiger leaps the ravine" and "Sparrow hawk spins in the air." These may have evolved out of earlier martial arts traditions. During the Han dynasty (207 B.C.E. to C.E. 220) a famous medical practitioner named Hua To worked out a system of physical exercises based on his observation of animal movements.

A perhaps related form of ritualized warfare is preserved in the *Song Jiang zhen*, or ceremonial martial arts performances still held in some regions of Taiwan. Sponsored by Buddhist temples as part of religious festivals, the *Song Jiang zhen* is named after the hero of the *Shiubu zhauan (The Water Margin)*, an epic tale about various forms of ethical and physical conflict. *The Water Margin* was written by Shih Nai-An possibly in the thirteenth century The tales are similar to the story of Robin Hood, in that the 108 heroes of the Water Margin lived as outlaws, fighting against an unjust emperor to help the people. The episodes all involve pairs engaged in some form of physical contest or struggling with some type of ethical dilemma.

The number 108 has sacred significance in Buddhism. Prayer beads or mala carried by Buddhist monks usually consist of 108 beads and are used to keep track of the number of mantras chanted by the devotee. In Buddhist mythology, the practice is traced to instructions given by Buddha Sakyamuni, the founder of Buddhism, to King Vaidunya. Historically, the mala originated in early Hindu ritual, and 108 is the number of beads on malas used in worship of the Hindu gods Siva and Vishnu. As in Buddhism, Hindu worshippers use the mala to keep track of the number of mantra chanted.

In Buddhism, the 108 beads symbolize the number of attachments preventing the devotee from attaining enlightenment. The number 108 also provides a means of purification. The devotee attains freedom from attachment by marking off mantra on a mala. In Thai Buddhism, statues of Buddha Sakyamuni are sacramentalized through rituals conducted by 108 monks. There is a symbolic link between the 108 heroes of the Water Margin and the 108 beads of the mala. Just as devotees subdue their attachments through the 108 beads of the mala, the 108 heroes of the Water Margin subdue forces that threaten the well-being of the social order.

This theme is ritually enacted in the modern performance of the Song Jiang Zhen in Taiwan, which involves fighting with fists or with weapons and takes place as part of an elaborate religious parade. According to historian Donald S. Sutton, the combatants represent local communities and are fiercely competitive: "When two troupes pass each other on the streets or on a country road, the leaders salute each other with a vigorous dance that is as much ritualized confrontation as a formal greeting. Even the salutations at temples, a shout at temples with fists upraised, convey militance" (1990:547).

Sutton suggests the troupes may have grown out of the need for villagers in earlier times to form small militia to protect themselves against bandits or in feuds against neighboring villages. He notes that the real hero of these displays is the social group demonstrating its solidarity against outsiders.

From Warrior to Athlete

In China, martial arts moved from the monastery to the battlefield. In the Japanese tradition, combat moved from the battlefield to the more limited arena of the martial arts. In both cases, these ritualistic forms of warfare reconcile the life-and-death intensity of the battlefield with the contemplative detachment of meditation. In both traditions, the actions of the warrior blend social responsibility with a quest for spiritual enlightenment.

Jujutsu and other martial arts of Japan are sometimes traced to a mythological origin. However, the historical origins of jujutsu are much more down-to-earth. This combat sport grew out of grappling techniques developed by samurai in combat. Mounted warriors fighting at close quarters pulled their opponents from their horses to better administer the *coup de grace*.

The transition from war to sport is in large part due to the triumph of the Tokugawa shogunate. After attaining power as shogun in 1603 and uniting all of Japan under his rule at Edo, Tokugawa Ieyasu quickly moved to dismantle the war machines of his rivals. Ieyasu decreed that makers of swords must be licensed by his own government, thus preventing subjugated daimyos (landowners) from arming themselves against him. Visitors were not allowed to visit the emperor in his residence at Kyoto, thus preventing potential rivals from gaining the symbolic advantage of the emperor's support. He also required every daimyo to spend every second year in Edo. This imposed a great financial burden on the daimyo, weakening his power in his own province, and virtually made him a hostage, thus undercutting the ability of the daimyos to mount an offensive against the Tokugawa shogunate.

By the beginning of the eighteenth century, the domination of the Tokugawa clan was so entrenched, samurai of rival clans had little hope of prevailing against them. The martial arts gradually shifted from training for warfare to sport, part of the entertainment for the bored nobility in the capital at Edo. Stephen Turnbull (1990), a student of Japanese combat history, describes the warriors of the Edo period as "armchair samurai" who expended their energies on practicing the techniques of warfare, with little opportunity for actual combat.

Traditionally, two Japanese terms commonly used for martial arts are *bugei*, which refers to actual combat, and *budo*, which substitutes friendly combat for life-or-death duels. Forms of bugei are distinguished by the suffix *–jutsu*, which means technique. Forms of budo are signified by the suffix *–do*. Bugei was designed as training for combat, whereas budo is an activity engaged in for its own sake. Thus *ju-jutsu* is a form of warfare and *judo* is a sport. The bugei forms were largely restricted to the elite ranks of the samurai, but the budo forms were open to the non-samurai classes.

Whether engaged in for warfare or sport, the Asian martial arts integrate philosophy with physical activity. Thus, they reconcile two axes of oppositions characteristic of Western philosophy. The first and most obvious is the resolution of mind-body duality. In Western thought, especially as expressed in the United States, athletes develop their bodies at the expense of their minds. This association may have emerged historically out of Christian opposition to Greek and Roman public performances, which were allied in Christian minds with paganism. Many medieval saints sought union with the divine through mortification of the body.

Eastern religious traditions, on the other hand, have often aimed at locating and harnessing the life force in the body to promote spiritual growth. This is based on concepts about the flow of vital energy. In Hindu thought, this energy is called *prana*. One controls it primarily through breathing techniques. Energy can also be directed through meditation and other forms of yoga. Hatha yoga involves a system of postures and physical exercises, which combined with proper breathing and meditation, direct prana through the seven *chakras* or points of power located along the human spine and culminating in the brain.

In China, vital energy is known as *chi*; in Japan, it is called *ki*. According to these two traditions, energy flows throughout the universe and harmony can be attained through a balance of the male and female principles. In popular Taoism, harmony and balance are often equated with Good or "good luck"; uncontrolled energy or energy that is blocked is associated with the demonic. In all three traditions — Indian, Chinese and Japanese — physical activity is seen as a way of directing and aligning the flow of energy. The energy of one's own body must be aligned with that of one's immediate surroundings and of the universe as a whole. The martial arts are a means of achieving control over one's energy and are, therefore, a form of meditation.

In both China and Japan, the development of spiritual and physical prowess is viewed as an act of social responsibility. The fighting monks of both countries battled on behalf of the social order. The monks of the Shaolin monastery fought to preserve the reign of a righteous emperor and to overthrow the reign of one they viewed as a usurper. They fought on behalf of the social order, as defined by their interpretation of the Mandate of Heaven.

In medieval Japan, Buddhist monks fought on behalf of the earthly representative of the social order. They did not risk their lives for their own glory, though fame often followed their deeds. Their purpose was to serve a worthy master. The twelfth-century warrior-monk Benkei is said to have joined the Minamoto in their fight against the Taira after his defeat by the legendary boy-warrior Minamoto Yoshitsune. Benkei was a rogue monk who took possession of a bridge and charged a toll to anyone who sought passage. He was contemptuous of samurai, having defeated many at the bridge. When Yoshitsune fought him to a draw, Benkei decided he had finally found a master worthy of his loyalty. According to legend, Yoshitsune was instructed in martial arts and swordfighting by the *tengu*, mythological beings who were half men and half birds inhabiting the mountains around the monastery where Yoshitsune spent his youth.

Buddhist monks also influenced the Japanese tradition of warfare by training the samurai. *Samurai* means "one who serves." The Zen master Takuan Sōhō advised the warriors of his day: "Nothing is more precious than life. Yet, at the moment when we must throw away this valued life and stand on right-mindedness, there is nothing more highly esteemed than right-mindedness." To Takuan, there is only one context in which the death of a samurai would result from right-mindedness, and that is in the service of his lord or daimyo:

> In regard to this, from the time one has been taken into a daimyo's service, of the clothes on his back, the sword he wears at his side, his foot-gear, his palanquin, his horse and all of his materiel, there is no single item that is not due to the favor of his lord. Family, wife, child and his own retainers — all of them and their relations — not one can be said not to receive the lord's favor. Having these favors well impressed on his mind, a man will face his lord's opponents on the battlefield and cast away his one life. This is dying for right-mindedness [1986:49–50].

For the Chinese and Japanese, being a warrior or a warrior-monk meant fighting on behalf of the social order. To the modern Western mind, cognizant of the possibility of total annihilation, war represents the ultimate in disorder. In the Asian tradition, conflict is controlled in an elaborate social and conceptual system that balances order and disorder, individual and society, body and mind in an all-encompassing quest for spiritual transcendence.

War as Spectacle

The Romans of Imperial times achieved perhaps the ultimate in death as entertainment. Roman emperors staged an array of encounters — man against man, man against beast, and beast against beast—in their amphitheaters. There appears to be almost no combination of such contests unknown to the Imperial Romans. Yet even for the Romans, the public display of violence as sport upheld the social order. Early gladiators were usually prisoners of war or those who were deemed outlaws. In addition, those who controlled the contests also controlled society. Thus, there was congruence between the values and social relationships of the amphitheater and those of the society as a whole.

The origin of gladiatorial contests can be traced to the Etruscans, whose domination of the Apennine peninsula predates that of the Romans. Prisoners of war were sacrificed during large religious festivals that also included chariot races, wrestling and boxing matches, running, pole-vaulting, high-jumping, and other forms of sporting activities. The contests were presided over by a judge, whose authority was symbolized by the same curved stick used by priests, the *lituo*[37]: "Great honours were showered on to the winners of the contests, who received prizes proving their athletic worth before the magistrates of the city."[38]

Not so fortunate were participants in the gladiatorial contests, who were generally slaves captured in warfare. Originally, prisoners of war were publicly sacrificed. Eventually, the sacrifice of prisoners evolved into armed combat performed before an audience consisting of both men and women and members of all classes. As the games developed, gladiators were trained in special schools and used a variety of arms. Not only did men fight each other, they also fought wild animals in the gladiatorial ring.

When Romans displaced the Etruscans on the Apennine peninsula, in the sixth century B.C.E., they adapted Etruscan arts and customs, including gladiatorial contests, to their own tastes. In Roman Imperial times, from about the third century B.C.E., gladiatorial contests took the form of theatrical performances. The contests began with a ceremonial procession, in which the gladiators addressed the Emperor with the words, *Morituri te salutant*, which means "Those who go to their death, greet thee." A number of these performances acted out mythological themes. One favorite was the story of Orpheus. According to myth, Orpheus enchanted all of Nature with his lyre; trees and cliffs bent down to him, and birds and beasts gathered around him. However, the musician was torn apart by followers of Dionysus for failing to pay homage to the god. In the theatrical performance enacted in the Roman gladiatorial ring, the climax came when a bear was released into the ring to tear the musician playing Orpheus to pieces.

Most gladiatorial fights were to the death. A wounded man could ask for mercy by laying down his arms and raising his right index finger. The crowd would vote for life or death by signaling thumbs up or thumbs down. If the vote was for death, the doomed gladiator then received the *coup de grace* from the winner of the contest. Figures dressed up as the god of the underworld made certain of the gladiator's death with red-hot irons, and representatives of the Etruscan Phersu or his Greek counterpart Charon carried the body off by the "Gate of the Goddess of Death."

Gladiatorial contests were arranged and financed by politicians and military leaders who were trying to gain popular support. Victorious military leaders staged such contests in honor of their ancestors. As the games became more elaborate, performers were professionals trained in gladiatorial schools. Candidates for the schools were often slaves or war prisoners. The most famous was the rebellious slave Spartacus, from the gladiator school of Capua. The schools were often owned by military leaders, who thus were able to maintain a private guard of gladiators in addition to their mercenary armies. In the first century C.E., the schools were brought under state control to avert any possibility they would be used for training personal armies to fight against the emperor.

Not all combat performances among the Imperial Romans were contests to the death. Young men of the nobility also performed the *lusus Troiae*, a ceremonial form of combat that appears as a form of training for warfare among Greek elites and may have developed among the Etruscans. According to Virgil's description in the *Aeneid*, the graceful military dance on horseback was performed by noble Trojan youths who bound their hair with wreathes of leaves and carried wooden javelins tipped with iron. The youths performed at ceremonial funeral games for Aeneas' father:

> After the boys had joyfully paraded
> The length of the whole gathering, under the gaze
> Of their families, Epytides' voice of command
> Rang out across the arena to where they were ready,
> And he gave his whip a crack. They galloped away
> In equal bands, then broke up into threes
> As if for a figure of a dance, and then
> At the next command they wheeled and charged each other
> With lances couched. Then they engaged in a series
> Of matching evolutions as the two
> Companies faced each other, and then they rode
> In interlocking circles left and right
> And finally engaged in a mock battle,
> Now with their backs exposed to flight, and now
> Turning to the attack with lances poised,
> Now making peace and riding side by side.

Virgil's description of the *lusus Troiae* suggests that it had the formal quality of a mounted ballet. Not so the jousting tournaments of medieval Europe. The origins of that sporting form appear to be somewhat disreputable. According to historian John Armitage, young knights engaged in a disorderly form of jousting as early as the twelfth and thirteenth centuries. Armitage notes that these are "not to be confused with the later gentlemanly combats between two heavily armed figures in the lists" (1977:19).

Even later tournaments could be far from elegant. Sports historian J. A. Cuddon notes the general battle at a tournament was called a *melee* and was fairly confusing. It was sometimes difficult to determine who had actually won. Attempts to bring order into the contest led to the development of the joust, a contest between two knights. Some combatants were virtually professionals, traveling throughout Europe and England, making a living by capturing knights in the tournament and holding them and their equipment for ransom.

Medieval tournaments reflected class differences, since competition was restricted to the aristocracy. Before a tournament, heralds inspected banners of the contestants to make sure no one had entered the lists illegally by masquerading as a knight. The day before a tournament the knights attended a ceremony at which they swore to keep the peace. This was an attempt, often unsuccessful, to keep the the occasion from being used to settle old scores. Aristocratic ladies then chose a "knight of honor" to open the tournament.

The tournament was training for warfare, but on a social level, it also provided aristocratic males with an arena in which to impress women by demonstrating their manly skills. In a sixteenth-century poem by Sir Philip Sidney, "The Tournament," the victorious knight attributes his success not to skill in horsemanship nor to his strength, nor to cheating, nor to good luck, nor even to fortunate heritage, but to the fact that the woman he loves is watching the competition:

> Having this day my horse, my hand, my lance
> Guided so well that I obtained the prize,
> Both by the judgement of the English eyes
> And of some sent from that sweet enemy France;
> Horsemen my skill in horsemanship advance,
> Town-folks my strength; a daintier judge applies
> His praise to sleight which from good use doth rise;
> Some lucky wits impute it but to chance;
> Others, because of both sides I do take
> My blood from them who did excel in this,
> Think Nature me a man-at-arms did make.
> How far they shot awry! the true cause is
> Stella looked on, and from her heavenly face
> Sent forth the beams which made so fair my race.

In Europe, a theatrical element was introduced by René, duke of Anjou and Naples, who staged elaborate tournaments on his estates. The knights played different roles and the plot of the "play" was organized so that it culminated in a tournament. In England, tournament as theater was used to flatter Queen Elizabeth I. This custom appears to have started with a particularly spectacular tournament held in 1581, the 23rd anniversary of her accession to the throne. It was such a success it became an annual event. These tournaments had plots affirming the majesty of the queen ("Oriana" and the "Virgin Queen") and continued long after her death.

As the heyday of the tournament neared its end, it was often viewed nostalgically as a time when men were guided by knightly honor and love for their ladies. This view is reflected in a parody by Miguel de Cervantes, who wrote his classic work *Don Quixote* near the end of the sixteenth century. The hero of this novel presents an absurd figure by trying to live according to the ideals of a fading era, slaughtering dragons for his lady. Alas for Don Quixote, since there are no more dragons, he is reduced to tilting at windmills.

The romantic view of jousting is also the subject of a gentle parody in a song from the 20th-century play "Camelot." On her way to marry King Arthur, a man she has never met, Guinevere sings wistfully of the pleasures she has missed by taking part in an arranged marriage at an early age: "Oh, where are the simple joys of maidenhood?" she sings. Where is the knight who will fight and die for me?

A jousting tournament of more modern origins, the *Sinkska Alka* has traditionally been held annually in the township of Sinj, Croatia, inland from Split on the Adriatic coast. The tournament commemorates a battle fought between the people of the town and invading Turks in 1716. The Turks attempted to take the town of Sinj, but were driven back in an intense two-day conflict. A website maintained by the town of Sinj describes the importance of the tournament:

> For centuries the Alka tournament had a commemorative function that also offered the people of Sinj — who have known the blessings of peace only in the most recent times — an opportunity to engage in contests of strength and skill. These formerly impoverished peasants and shepherds, exploited by the Venetian Republic mostly as soldiers to protect its trade with the Turkish hinterland, embraced the Alka tournament as the focus of their dreams and aspirations. One might even say that the Alka gave these people, who had come from different parts of the former Turkish Empire, something in common, helped them develop their own identity. Exposed to the perils of life along the border, accustomed to taking care of them-selves, the people of Sinj and the Cetina district were always ready to take arms, unwilling to let anyone else decide their fate.[39]

Only the citizens of Sinj and the surrounding area are eligible for the jousting, which today is entirely symbolic. Knights do not compete directly against each other in combat, but instead the elaborately costumed contestants joust against rings and are judged on a point system. The contest is preceded by a procession through the streets of the town. The Sinj website notes:

> The Alka tournament has survived with few interruptions until the present day, adapted in conformity with regional characteristics, yet making a vital contribution to the formation of the ethics of heroism and self-sacrifice that have always guided the people of the Cetina district.[40]

The Sinj website adds that the Sinjska Alka combines the traditions of European and "oriental" chivalry with the local ethnographic heritage.

Medieval tournaments and Roman gladiatorial contests dramatize some of the same themes expressed in Asian martial arts. They uphold the solidarity of the group and act out principles of honor and courage. However, their emphasis is different. The Asian martial arts emphasize the sacred over the secular and the participant over the spectator, whereas the emphasis is reversed in the martial spectacles of western Europe.

The Asian martial arts stress personal discipline and social responsibility on the part of the participants. They provide a context in which philosophical and religious principles can be tested and demonstrated. In this sense, the audience is irrelevant. Asian warfare, whether conducted on the battlefield or in the smaller arena of the martial arts, were not intended as a spectator sport.

The implications of the Asian martial arts extend far beyond the participants, however. Moral lessons exemplified by the conduct of martial arts specialists are conveyed to a broader audience as they are translated into art and literature. The audience is instructed in ethical and social values through vicarious participation in the danger and intensity of ritualized combat. In the *Song Jiang zhen*, or other martial arts performances, the audience assumes greater importance. In this case, the contests are not only a spiritual practice for participants, they provide instruction and entertainment for spectators.

Roman gladiatorial contests and medieval tournaments were secular events staged for the benefit of spectators. They often took the form of morality plays designed to instruct and entertain the public while, at the same time, reaffirming the social status of those who organized them. The tournament at Sinj in Croatia integrates the audience into the performance through the ceremonial procession. Designated warriors then symbolically defend the town, demonstrating their prowess against inanimate objects. The entire drama emphasizes the solidarity of the township, and outsiders — like invaders — are excluded.

War as Sport

Wrestling could be called the simplest and most basic form of combat. Its symbolic value may owe a great deal to the fact that it takes place on a level playing field. The outcome cannot be blamed on wind, faulty weapons or an advantageous draw. Wrestling, quite literally, is *mano a mano*.[41]

Wrestling has long played an important role in human social life and continues to express social values in many societies. The Nuba of the lower Sudan conduct annual wrestling festivals known as *lebolo*. The object of the event is to demonstrate bravery and endurance, rather than to establish the dominance of a single champion. At some contests, there are several victors; at others, there are none. According to a description by anthropologist Siegfried Nadel:

> When a wrestler has been successful in several fights or defeated a powerful opponent, [the older men] rush into the arena and form a solid ring around him, yelling and singing. He kneels down, a sheep skin with a slit in the middle is dropped over his head, the coveted wrestler's trophy, and he is lifted on the shoulders of one of the senior boys and carried in triumph around the arena [1947:232].

Prowess in the wrestling arena is associated with prowess and virtue in the social arena. The Nuba are cattle herders, and cattle are both a means of survival and an important marker of masculine identity. A Sudanese song links a man's prowess at wrestling with the productivity of his cattle and his social responsibilities:

> You are strong. You can throw ten men. But some time ago you weakened. You threw two men only, or you were sitting idle. Your cattle are strong and give plenty of milk. You have great strength. But now you dress up, you go to the village to be with the girls. Thus you can no longer throw ten men. You throw only three, or sit idle [Nadel 1947:136–137].

Wrestling is often linked to religious ritual, as in the case of the Raramuri defense of God in the Easter festival, discussed in Chapter One. Hand-to-hand combat has also been used to represent the most elemental of human striving. Kings and heroes — from Jacob to Gilgamesh — have taken on opposing forces with their bare hands.

Japanese legend traces the ceremonial wrestling events called *sumo* to the beginnings of human society and assigns the contest a role in shaping the class system. The *Koziki*, or "Records of Ancient Matters," describes a dispute between the people of divine lineage and those of a common race. The divine ones demanded that the common people surrender their land. Takeminakata-no-Kami, who spoke on behalf of the common people, challenged Takemikazuchi-no-Kami, representative of the divine ones, to settle the dispute by wrestling. The divine combatant won the match and, with it, control over Japan for those of divine birth. The victory of Takemikazuchi-no-Kami fulfilled the oracle of Amaterasu-Omikami, the mythological ancestor of the Japanese emperor, who said that Japan must be ruled over by members of the imperial clan.

Sumo was associated with the military arts and was sometimes used to settle disputes. In the early days of the sport, combatants fought to the death. This practice was discontinued under the reign of Emperor Syomu in the first half of the eighth century, and the Wrestling Festival was established as one of three important sporting ceremonies at the royal court. The Wrestling Festival was discontinued near the end of the twelfth century, but sumo events are still part of Shinto religious festivals. Shinto, the state religion of Japan, combines reverence for *kami* (nature spirits) with mythology and ritual that support the country's social order.

Modern sumo, which pits two massive combatants clad only in loincloths against each other, retains many classically symbolic elements. The four columns that support the roof of the ring represent both the referees of the ancient Wrestling Festival and the four seasons. Cloth draped around the columns just below the eaves of the roof represents the rotation of the seasons. Matches are preceded by a Shinto ceremony in which prayers are offered to the deities of heaven and earth and of the four seasons. The emphasis on the four seasons suggests the importance of sumo as an agricultural ritual. Though reports of very early sumo events are sketchy, there is some evidence that sumo began as an agricultural ritual.

The competition takes place in a circle marked off by half buried rice bales on a raised square platform. The object is to force one's opponent out of the circle.

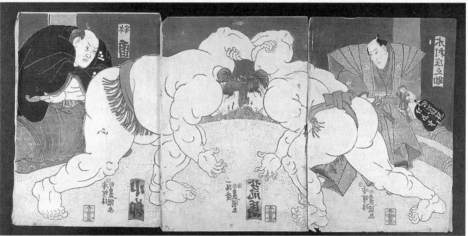

Top: Sumo wrestling is considered one of the oldest of the Japanese martial arts. The eighth century chronicle Nihon-Sho-ki refers to a sumo contest of 23 B.C. Early sumo contests were staged to propitiate the gods and they became a way of resolving disputes as an alternative to warfare. By the time of this work sumo had become a spectator sport. The drawing from the Kamakura period (1185–1333) probably was part of a hand scroll that recorded the episodes of a bout (Seattle Art Museum, gift of Mrs. John C. Atwood, Jr.). *Bottom:* Two sumo wrestlers square off against each other as officials anxiously observe them in this drawing from the late Edo period by the famed artist Kunisada (Victoria and Albert Museum, London).

Competition begins with a ceremonial procession led by the *yokuzuna* (grand champion) wearing a ceremonial apron. The *rikishi* (wrestlers), also clad in ceremonial aprons file in as the announcer makes the introductions and form a circle around the ring:

> After all the rikishi have mounted the *dohyo* [square platform supporting the ring], they turn inward and face each other. In unison they clap their hands to summon the gods. They lift their aprons to signify foot stomping which drives the demons from the dohyo. Finally, they all lift their arms to show that they carry no concealed weapons.[42]

The ceremonial foot stomping may date back to early matches in which the wrestler vanquished and often killed his opponent by trampling him. Before the matches begin, combatants return to their dressing room where they exchange their ceremonial aprons for fighting gear, which consists of silk loin cloths.

Before a match, each combatant rinses his mouth with water and wipes his mouth with a piece of paper. He then throws a handful of salt across the ring. These are purification rites, which are also found in Shinto religious ritual. For sumo combatants, the water is viewed as a source of strength. Salt, which is used to control evil spirits, is believed to prevent injury in wrestling.

Just before the match, the combatants take positions facing each other from the eastern and western side of the ring, squat down, and purify themselves further by rubbing their hands together, ending with the palms upward. They then enact another series of foot-stomping rituals before facing each other in the center of the ring. There they squat down, rest their fists on the ground in front of them and crouch, staring each other in the eye. This moment, called *sikiri* or "get-set," allows each wrestler to arrive at the appropriate state for combat. If they fail to reach the ideal condition simultaneously, they must begin the purification rituals again.

Sumo is closely associated with Japanese national pride. Sigetake Sugiura, tutor to Emperor Hirohito when he was Crown Prince, included sumo in his instruction on morals: "Of all sports in Japan, Sumo is the most unique, the like of which is not found anywhere in the world. It is for this reason that the sport is called a national sport" (quoted in Hikoyama 1940:9–10).

Wrestling and Sensuality

Wrestling has provided an enduring source of material for artists, who seem fascinated by the power and form of the grappling human body. Japanese artists focused on the massive bulk of sumo combatants. European artists seemed to use the contorted human figure as a test of their drawing skills or as a metaphor for male sensuality. Even the seventeenth-century Flemish artist Peter Paul Rubens, better known for his portrayals of voluptuous women, tested his drawing skills in *Two naked youths wrestling*. In this work, the contortions of the human body display rippling musculature, producing an image that is in some ways more sensuous than

The massive power of the sumo wrestler, as well as his ceremonial loincloth, is represented in this life-size wooden sculpture by Hy Farber (reproduced by permission of the artist).

other types of nudes. On the other hand, American artist Paul Manship relies on the power and energy of the athlete in his bronze *Wrestlers*.

In ancient Greece, boxing was viewed as a disfiguring sport and boxers were often depicted with signs of their trauma. Wrestlers, on the other hand, were considered

Opposite, bottom: Though Paul Manship deals with a subject matter and composition similar to that of Rubens, Manship's 1914 bronze *Wrestlers* is more sharply defined and graceful than Rubens' pen-and-ink drawing. Both works of art emphasize the musculature and sensuality of the wrestler (The Dayton Art Institute, Bequest of Hon. Jefferson Patterson).

Top: *Two Naked Youths Wrestling*, by the 17th-century Flemish artist Peter Paul Rubens, appears to be an experiment by the artist to explore his command of the human form (Fitzwilliam Museum, Cambridge).

The grace and beauty of wrestlers is emphasized in this Greek vase adorned with two pairs of wrestlers and an interested female onlooker (Antikensammlung, Staatliche Museen zu Berlin-Preussischer Kulturbesitz-).

to epitomize the beauty of the athlete. The inscription on the victor's monument of Theognetos of Aegina compares the grace of his form with that of his art:

> Recognize when looking at Theognetos, boy victor
> at Olympia, a master of the wrestler's art.
> Most beautiful to see, at contest no less blessed,
> he has crowned the city of his goodly kin [quoted in Poliakoff 1987:10].

Greek symbolism links wrestling with sexuality. The god Hermes was credited with having invented wrestling, and his statue traditionally presided over the *palaestra*, a facility where athletes practiced combat sports. The statue often took the form of a *herm*, a sculpted head on a rectangular marble base, unadorned except for an erect phallus. Hermes is said to have been the father of Palaestra, the goddess of wrestling.

    Hermes is an enigmatic god, who symbolically unites attributes not usually associated with each other in Western tradition. He was at the same time god of commerce and of thieves, of athletes and intellectuals. He is associated with the Egyptian god Thoth, who was recorder of the gods and the principal pleader for the soul at the judgment of the dead. Thoth was the inventor of writing and author of ancient texts including the *Book of Breathings*, which taught humans how to become gods.[43] In his Greek form, Hermes was associated with a similar form of mysticism and is believed to be the author, or at least the inspirational source, of the "books of Hermes," which formed the basis for mystical writings similar to gnosticism, which emphasized secret knowledge of ancient mysteries. According to the British scholar R. F. Willetts, "in many ways, Hermes is the most sympathetic, the most baffling, the most confusing, the most complex, and therefore the most Greek of all the Olympian gods" (1970:1289).

Symbolism associated with Hermes is no doubt baffling primarily to some philosophers in the Western tradition, in which success in commerce can be viewed as a mark of God's favor. According to the German sociologist Max Weber, in his book *The Protestant Ethic and the Spirit of Capitalism* (1958), the rise of Protestantism in Western Europe coincides with and promotes the ethic of capitalism, which is based on the pursuit of profit as an economic goal. According to this ethic, an association between commerce and thievery would seem to be a contradiction in terms.

Similarly, philosophical and religious traditions of Western Europe embrace the concept of a mind-body dichotomy. Though the formulation of a mind-body dichotomy is generally attributed to the seventeenth-century French philosopher René Descartes, the concept of an irreconcilable chasm between the mind and the body dates from much earlier. The Christian mystic Meister Eckhart (1260–1327) asserted that God created man to prove that, for Him, nothing was impossible, including combining the divine spirit with the material body. Conversely, the Greek athletic tradition linked excellence in athletics with excellence in other aspects of human life. Vitruvius, the first century architect and engineer, indicated that in their design of the palaestra Greeks took care to consider both the comfort of athletes and the convenience of intellectuals:

> Three of the sides are single colonnades; the fourth, which faces south, should be double, so that when gales occur, the rain is not blown into the inner part. In each of the three single sides there should be a large recess with seats, in which philosophers, littérateurs and other members of the intelligentsia may sit and argue [quoted in Harris 1964:146].

Wrestling is associated with sexuality in the epic of Gilgamesh, king of Uruk. Enkidu, the wild man from the mountains, is created to be the hero's companion by the goddess Aruru, who fashions him from clay. Aruru creates Enkidu in response to an appeal from Gilgamesh's subjects, whose resources are being exhausted by his kingly passions. No rival could resist his army, no woman his sexual appetites. The people beseech the gods, who in turn supplicate Aruru, the goddess of creation: "You made him, O Aruru, now create his equal; let it be as like him as his own reflection, his second self, stormy heart for stormy heart. Let them contend together and leave Uruk in quiet."

Gilgamesh learns of Enkidu's existence in a dream interpreted by his mother Ninsun, a goddess. She describes what will be their first meeting: "When you see

him you will be glad; you will love him as a woman and he will never forsake you."
Gilgamesh meets Enkidu when the wild man bars the king's way to his marriage
bed. While his bride awaits him, Gilgamesh wrestles with Enkidu:

> ...they snorted like bulls locked together. They shattered the doorposts
> and the walls shook. Gilgamesh bent his knee with his foot planted on
> the ground and with a turn Enkidu was thrown. Then immediately his
> fury died. When Enkidu was thrown he said to Gilgamesh, "There is not
> another like you in the world. Ninsun, who is as strong as a wild ox in
> the byre, she was the mother who bore you, and now you are raised above
> all men, and Enlil has given you the kingship, for your strength surpasses
> the strength of men." So Enkidu and Gilgamesh embraced and their
> friendship was sealed.

The friendship between King Gilgamesh and the wild man Enkidu unites the social
world of men with untamed nature. The partnership symbolizes a necessary balance between the extremes of the wilderness and the excesses of civilization. Enkidu
is tamed through the offices of Gilgamesh, whose kingly passions have become
destructive and must be offset by a worthy opponent.

Athletes as Gods

Greek legend unites the prowess of athletes with the power of gods, and this
theme is reflected in their biographies. Theogenes of Thasos was the son of a priest
at a temple of Herakles. The athlete's name means "god-born," and Theogenes
claimed he was not the son of the priest, but of the god. Theogenes's statue was
believed to have the power to cure illness.

Theogenes was a victor in all four of the major Greek Games. He won the
boxing and pankratian events at Olympia. The pankratian combined boxing with
wrestling, but was more violent than either. Though biting and gouging were illegal, contestants often did both. Theogenes was also three times victor in boxing at
the Pythian Games. At the Isthmian Games, he won the boxing event nine times
and the pankration once. Theogenes won the boxing event nine times at Nemea
and the long-distance race at Argos. An inscription at Delphi states that he won
1300 victories in other meetings, a claim that seems unlikely, since as the British
sports historian H. A. Harris notes, these feats "would have required 649 years to
complete" (1964:20). Evidently, American business executives did not invent the
practice of padding their resumes.

In spite of his claim to divine origins and heroic status, Theogenes appears to
have been an unpleasant character. The first century Greek biographer and moral-
ist Plutarch dismisses most of Theogenes' victories as being unworthy of note and
"records a scene of hooliganism at a ritual feast at which Theogenes thought he was
not being accorded proper treatment" (Harris 1964:117). During his lifetime, Theogenes' enemies were powerless against him, but after his death, one of his townsmen

The pankratian was a particularly aggressive Greek sport, in which relatively few holds were barred. Though eye-gouging was barred, the pankratiast on the center right has resorted to this device even though an official keeps close watch. At left are two boxers. The boxer on the right displays the disfiguring marks of his sport, one of several indicators that he is the older of the two (British Museum).

at Thasos flogged his statue under cover of darkness. Even this proved to be perilous. The statue fell on the man and killed him. By law, the statue had to be punished, so it was taken out to sea in a ship and thrown overboard.

Soon afterward Thasos was devastated by a severe famine. Leaders of the city consulted the oracle at Delphi, which ordered them to recall their political exiles. They did so, but the famine continued. The oracle then told them they had forgotten Theogenes. The statue was retrieved from the sea and restored to its base in the marketplace. As soon as the statue was replaced on its base, the famine ended (Harris 1964:115–118).

A similar cult grew up around Theogenes' chief opponent, Euthymus. In Euthymus' time, Temesa, a city on the west coast of Italy, was being terrorized by the ghost of one of Odysseus' companions, Polites, who had been killed by the city's inhabitants. In retaliation, Polites' ghost demanded the annual tribute of a maiden. Euthymus arrived at Temesa one year just as the sacrificial offering was about to take place. He fell in love with the woman, and after defeating the ghost in combat, married her. Euthymus did not die, but was taken from the mortal plane by the river god Caecinus, said to be his father (Harris 1964:119).

A number of Greek athletes claimed deities for their family trees, either literally or by association. Pindar's victory ode for Diagoras of Rhodes, winner of the Olympic gold medal for boxing in 464 B.C.E. suggests that the athlete and compatriots are descendants of Helios, the sun god:

> I have come with Diagoras, singing
> Aphrodite's sea-child, the bride of Helios,
> Rhodes,
> that I might glorify him for his boxing —
> a man prodigious, eager for the fray.

The origins of the four great Games — the Olympian, the Nemean, the Isthmian and the Pythian — are shrouded in mystery and mysticism. According to legend, the Pythian Games resulted from a contest between Apollo and Python. The youthful Apollo killed Python because of a slight to Apollo's mother. Apollo was then ordered to establish the Pythian Games in honor of the great serpent. The Pythian Games were held at Delphi at the festivals of Apollo, and the victors of games were awarded the laurel, sacred to Apollo. The Olympics were said to have been started by Herakles, and were held at Olympia in honor of Zeus.

The scholar Labib Boutros suggests that the Olympic Games may have developed out of seasonal wrestling contests in which the Phoenician god Baal is pitted against the forces of nature. Baal's battle against *Prince Sea* is described in Chapter Three. Baal's contest with *Mot* on Mt. Cassios is more clearly a wrestling match:

> They shake *each other like gmr*— beasts
>   Mot is strong, Baal is strong.
> They gore like buffaloes
>   Mot is strong, Baal is strong.
> They bite like serpents
>   Mot is strong, Baal is strong.
> They kick like steeds
>   Mot is down, Baal is down [Boutros 1981:28].

Baal emerged the winner because he fell on top of Mot. Boutros suggests the battle could be the prototype for the Greek pankration, a particularly rough combat sport. At Tyre, Baal was known as Melkart. There appears to be agreement among scholars that Melkart became the Greek Herakles. Like Herakles, Baal is sometimes depicted with a lion.

Boxing, Wrestling, and the Uncommon Man

Although boxing and wrestling in the English and American traditions are rarely depicted in such exalted contexts, they continue to express similar symbolic themes. At fairs and rural markets in medieval England, wrestling provided a way for young men to prove their strength, with a ram as a prize. In his *Canterbury Tales*, Chaucer describes the miller as just such a man:

> The millere was a stout carl for the nones;
> Ful byg he was of brawn, and eek of bones.
> That proved wel, for over al there he cam,
> At wrastlynge he wold have always the ram.

Wrestling was not restricted to such rustic entertainments. Some English kings and nobles maintained court wrestlers, as indicated in Shakespeare's description of Duke Frederick's court in *As You Like It*. In this account, the noble youth Orlando displays his worth by engaging in combat with Charles, the personal wrestler of Ferdinand, who has usurped his brother's position as Duke. The strength of Orlando's opponent is established in a previous match described by Le Beau, courtier to Ferdinand:

> The eldest of the three [brothers] wrestled with Charles, the duke's wrestler; which Charles in a moment threw him, and broke three of his ribs, that there is little hope of life in him: so he served the second, and so the third. Yonder they lie; the poor old man, their father, making such pitiful dole over them that all the beholders take his part with weeping.

Ferdinand's daughter Celia and Rosalind, daughter of the rightful Duke, plead with Orlando not to wrestle with the fearsome Charles:

> *Celia:* Young gentleman, your spirits are too bold for your years. You have seen cruel proof of this man's strength: if you saw yourself with your eyes, or knew yourself with your judgment, the fear of your adventure would counsel you to a more equal enterprise. We pray you, for your own sake, to embrace your own safety, and give over this attempt.
> *Rosalind:* Do, young sir; your reputation shall not therefore be misprised: we will make it our suit to the duke that the wrestling might not go forward.

Orlando's response to the young noblewomen demonstrates his courage and his modesty, both essential qualities for the hero I call the Paragon:

> I beseech you, punish me not with your hard thoughts: wherein I confess me much guilty, to deny so fair and excellent ladies anything. But let your fair eyes and gentle wishes go with me to my trial: wherein if I be foiled, there is but one shamed that was never gracious; if killed, but one dead that is willing to be so: I shall do my friends no wrong, for I have none to lament me: the world no injury, for in it I have nothing; only in the world I fill up a place, which may be better supplied when I have made it empty.

Charles and Orlando wrestle, and Orlando quickly throws his brutish opponent. In Shakespeare's play, Orlando wins both the wrestling match and the fair Rosalind for his bride.

Fist-fighting was introduced into England by the Romans, but other forms of combat sports indigenous to England continued alongside the more elegant Roman sport. The indigenous tradition was a rustic sport fought with various types of weapons, including the broadsword and quarterstaff. A quarterstaff was a pole six and a half feet long, held by combatants with one hand in the middle and the other hand between the middle and end, which allowed the combatant to exercise a great amount of thrust while maintaining control over his weapon.

English combat sports took on a measure of refinement under the influence of the eighteenth-century fighter James Figg. Figg was a boxer, a fencer and an expert with the cudgel, sword and staff. Combatants of Figg's time shaved their heads to display battle scars gained in bouts involving backswords, sticks and cudgels. The sport historian J. A. Cuddon describes Figg's defense of his self-declared title of champion in the 1720s against Ned Sutton, a pipe-maker: "Figg cut Sutton across the shoulder with a broadsword, knocked him out, and finally broke his knee with a quarterstaff" (1979:132). Figg's battle with Sutton inspired one observer, John Byrom, to compare the fighters favorably to classical Greek and Roman heroes:

> Now after such Men, who can bear to be told
> Of your Roman and Greek puny Heroes of old?
> To compare such poor dogs as Alcides and Theseus
> To Sutton and Figg would be very facetious.
> Were Hector himself, with Apollo to back him,
> To encounter with Sutton,—zooks! how he would thack him!
> Or Achilles, tho' old Mother Thetis had dipt him,
> With Figg—odds my life, how he would have unript him
> [Quoted in Cuddon 1979:132]!

Byrom's enthusiasm is clearly more impressive than his syntax. And it is possible that, given the weapons wielded by British combatants, similarly armed Greek pankrationists might well have emerged the victors.

Perhaps James Figg's greatest contribution to combat sports was organizing them so they were more appealing both to the public and the aristocracy. He established a martial arts academy and advertised himself as a "Master of the Noble Science of Defence." His patron was the Earl of Peterborough and his academy attracted members of the nobility, as well as professional fighters.

Figg trained a number of boxers and fighters, among them Jack Broughton, who also influenced the modern martial arts. After one of his opponents died from injuries, Broughton drew up a code of rules that governed boxing for nearly a century. Broughton also introduced the use of padded gloves, which at first were used only in practice. Keith P. Myers considers that Broughton's introduction of the gloves was "an effort to attract to his gym the richer and more genteel classes of society that didn't relish the idea of broken noses and black eyes. But these gloves were meant purely as a training aid, with actual fights still being fought bare-fisted for a long time to come."[44]

The careers of Figg and Broughton echo themes of social class distinctions prevalent in all stratified societies, where combat sports are not simply slug fests engaged in to settle disputes between the combatants. They involve complex relationships among participants, patrons and the public. In the case of Roman amphitheaters, Japanese sumo, and boxing discussed in this chapter, the contests are staged and combatants are sponsored by members of the ruling or elite classes. Combatants are from lower ranking or disenfranchised classes. Members of the elite and the fighters they sponsor may both enhance their status through the arrangement. Just as elites gain status from their patronage of skillful artists and musical performers, elite males may also gain status from their skill in picking and sponsoring successful fighters. Fighters gain status both from their performance in combat and from their association with an elite sponsor.

In the U.S. South of the nineteenth century, wealthy plantation owners staged matches between slaves, betting high stakes on the outcome. One slave from Virginia, Tom Molineaux, was so successful in the ring, his grateful owner granted him his freedom. Molineaux left the South for New York, where he was trained by another freed slave who had become a noted prize fighter in England. In 1810, Molineaux traveled to England to fight Tom Cribb, one of that country's greatest champions, in a match that aroused nationalistic fervor on both sides of the Atlantic. After 39 rounds of intense fighting, Molineaux collapsed from exhaustion. In describing that fight, Pierce Egan, author of the book *Life in London*, extolled the virtues of Molineaux, whom he called "The Tremendous Man of Colour": "Molineaux proved himself as courageous a man as ever an adversary contended with ... [Molineaux] astonished everyone, not only by his extraordinary power of hitting and his gigantic strength, but also by his acquaintance with the science, which was far greater than any had given him credit for."[45]

In a rematch with Cribb, Molineaux lost by a knockout. This reaffirmed the faith of the English in their champion, and Molineaux became a celebrity in England, where he continued to reside until his death in 1818.

In Molineaux's career, issues of social class included the issue of ethnicity. In the U.S. South, Molineaux's ethnic identity automatically consigned him to a disenfranchised social caste. He was able to transcend this social status through his prowess in the ring. In his bouts in England, his ethnicity was a marginal issue, whereas his nationality was a central issue. Ultimately, Molineaux's skill as a fighter allowed him to transcend barriers of both ethnicity and nationality.

Fifty years later, the national pride of England and the United States got a chance at a rematch when the American giant John C. Heenan met the British marvel Tom Sayers. It would have appeared to be a mismatch. At five-foot-eight and 155 pounds, Sayers was forty pounds slighter and nine years older than the six-foot-two American fighter, referred to by the British as "The Immense Invader." However, it proved to be a monumental bare-knuckles battle. Before an audience that included the aristocracy and members of Parliament, the two men fought for two hours and twenty minutes. Sayers lost the use of his right arm, and Heenan was practically blinded (Cuddon 1979:135; Durant and Bettman 1952:32–35). The match, which was declared a draw, ended in accordance with the best of sporting traditions. Sayers retained the championship belt, but offered to share it with Heenan in the name of fair play. The American refused it on the same grounds, and the two fighters became good friends.

In the United States, the boxing ring later became the arena for a battle over ethnic pride. In the first decade of the twentieth century, the ring was dominated by a black boxer from Texas, Jack Johnson. Johnson's seeming invincibility touched off a search for a "White Hope" to defend the honor of "the Caucasian race." That dubious honor went to a Kansas cowboy named Jess Willard, who knew little about boxing but qualified by virtue of sheer size: He was six feet, seven inches tall and weighed 260 pounds. On April 5, 1915, Willard defeated an aging, overweight Jack Johnson in a fight staged in Havana, Cuba. In the end, Johnson was defeated by that most intractable of opponents — time.

In *The Sun Also Rises*, Ernest Hemingway uses a boxing event as the vehicle for a sarcastic comment on ethnic injustice in his account of a black American fighter in Vienna. When the American knocks down the local hero in the ring, the spectators start a riot aimed at killing the American victor. Describing his attempts during a four-day drunken binge to help the black boxer escape from the city, the character Bill Gorton muses:

> Injustice everywhere. Promoter claimed nigger promised let local boy stay. Claimed nigger violated contract. Can't knock out Vienna boy in Vienna. "My God, Mister Gorton," said nigger, "I didn't do nothing in there for forty minutes but try and let him stay. That white boy musta ruptured himself swinging at me. I never did hit him."

This account challenges the idea that sport is simply a showcase for physical prowess. It is also a showcase for national and regional loyalties. This is an ironic twist on the sporting adage, "Let the best man win." In the eyes of the Viennese sports fans, Hemingway suggests, the "best man" is the local hero, their champion. The incident provides a symbolic contrast to Hemingway's representation in the same novel of bullfighting as an epic contest in which the "best man" is the one who displays purity of form and spirit. Thus, the experience of the black boxer who is held in check and cheated by the prejudices of officials and spectators underscores the later triumph of the bullfighter Romero, who is allowed to display his full artistry for an appreciative audience.

Modern fighters are still symbolic warriors, though they do not all represent the same cultural imagery. Conceptually, there is a distinction between professional

Opposite: Boxer is considered one of Richmond Barthé's finest sculptures, combining dignity with emotional power (The Metropolitan Museum of Art, Rogers Fund, 1942).

fighters and those who compete in the modern Olympics, the context for the most idealized form of Western combat sports. Olympic wrestling is modeled on the aesthetics of the Greco-Roman style and has little in common with professional wrestling, which is aimed at enacting moralistic dramas for an audience. Modern Olympic boxers wear protective headgear and are scored on defense as well as offense. Since scoring is based on style rather than impact, there is no need to batter the opponent senseless.

Olympic athletes compete for their countries, reflecting earlier traditions of warfare. Their symbolic value is enhanced because they participate as amateurs. Like soldiers who fight for their country's autonomy, Olympic athletes fight for their country's honor. Professional athletes are respected for their expertise rather than for their loyalties. Whereas professionals are assumed to compete for gain, high-level amateur athletes are respected because their participation in sports appears to be selfless. To draw further on the metaphor of war, amateurs are like volunteer soldiers[46] who risk their lives for the good of their country, whereas professional athletes are viewed as mercenaries.

The image of the amateur contender is idealistic, but the symbolism of the mercenary is not altogether negative. Mercenaries exude some of the cachet of professional soldiers or hired killers, or even of Roman gladiators who are expected to fight to the death. Their image contains elements of sophistication, sensuality and danger.

The symbolic imagery of the U.S. boxer Muhammad Ali is enhanced by all these associations and more, as he played a variety of heroic roles for generations of Americans. As an amateur, he fought on behalf of his country in the 1960 Olympics, winning the light-heavyweight title. As a professional, he refused to fight as a soldier in the Vietnam War, drawing criticism from some quarters, and giving him the heroic role of Outlaw. His refusal later became a symbol of patriotism, as American sentiment turned against the war. In the popular view, the Rebel-hero fought the agents of injustice and won. Ali later won greater appeal in his career as a Rogue, when his impish poems added wit and intelligence to the sport of boxing. Ultimately, when his health prevented him from returning to the ring, Ali assumed the exalted heroic status of Paragon, a senior statesman for sport and for the United States in general.

Sport as Theater

Sport is often a morality tale. Nowhere is this more apparent than in professional wrestling, which may more appropriately understood as theater. It is almost always possible to predict the outcome of a wrestling match. The combatant who cheats blatantly and draws the ire of the audience nearly always loses. The metaphoric realms of Good and Evil are drawn in heavy symbolism. According to the French sociologist Roland Barthes, "The virtue of all-in wrestling is that it is the spectacle of excess. Here we find the grandiloquence which must have been that of ancient theatres" (1972:15). Wrestlers dramatize, in extravagant form, themes of everyday life:

Alexander Archipenko takes an abstract approach to the contest against a human opponent in his bronze *Struggle (La Lutte)*, also called *The Boxers* (Milwaukee Art
Museum).

> What is thus displayed for the public is the great spectacle of Suffering,
> Defeat, and Justice. Wrestling presents man's suffering with all the
> amplification of tragic masks. The wrestler who suffers in a hold which
> is reputedly cruel (an arm-lock, a twisted leg) offers an excessive portrayal
> of Suffering; like a primitive Pietà, he exhibits for all to see his face, exag-
> geratedly contorted by an intolerable affliction [Barthes 1972:19].

Wrestlers play different roles for the benefit of a moral drama. Evil is pitted against
Good, Arrogance against Humility, and Duplicity against Honor. Barthes writes:

> But what wrestling is above all meant to portray is a purely moral concept: that of justice. The idea of "paying" is essential to wrestling, and the crowd's "Give it to him" means above all else "Make him pay." This is therefore, needless to say, an immanent justice. The baser the action of the "bastard," the more delighted the public is by the blow which he justly receives in return [1972:21].

Barthes adds that the "bastard" is one who operates outside the rules of society: "Essentially someone unstable, who accepts the rules only when they are useful to him and transgresses the formal continuity of attitudes. He is unpredictable, therefore asocial" (1972:24). Thus, the "good" wrestler is one whose behavior conforms to social norms, whereas the "bad" wrestler challenges them. According to Barthes, the metaphorical roles enacted by wrestlers are skillfully drawn:

> Wrestlers, who are very experienced, know perfectly how to direct the spontaneous episodes of the fight so as to make them conform to the image which the public has of the great legendary themes of its mythology. A wrestler can irritate or disgust, he never disappoints, for he always accomplishes completely, by a progressive solidification of signs, what the public expects of him [1972:24].

The metaphorical role of wrestling is expressed in the public personae of the combatants, as reflected in their names, such as Hulk Hogan, Andre the Giant and The Ultimate Warrior.

Only the most naïve of fans would bet on the outcome of a wrestling match. However, the public is not being tricked by the enactment of a wrestling event, nor is it cheated if the outcome is predetermined. As Barthes indicates, this aspect of professional wrestling underscores its relationship to theater. Sport and theater are both marked off from "real life," but they provide different dynamic contexts for the symbolic enactment of conflict.

In watching a theatrical performance, we may suspend belief for the duration of the play and become thoroughly involved in the dramatized adventures, but we know that the outcome has already been plotted according to some socially acceptable formula. When the play ends, we will come back to reality, leave the theater, and barring some real-life adventure, return to our homes.

Typically, in wrestling as in theater, the resolution of conflict upholds the social order and affirms cultural values. Good vanquishes Evil, Arrogance surrenders to Humility, and Duplicity is ousted by Honor. The oversimplification of heroic themes in the limited arena of wrestling is reassuring, because in our daily lives, we can never be sure justice will prevail. The drama of everyday life takes place on a grander scale, the issues are less clearly drawn, and the outcome is uncertain.

In sport, other than professional wrestling, the moral themes are less clearly delineated than in theater. The contest need not pit Good against Evil. Instead, it may pit one nation, town, or district against another. Unlike theater and like real-life, the outcome of a sporting event is uncertain. Ideally, the officials should be

Fletcher Martin's *The Glory* captures the moment of victory. In this oil painting, the contestant is anonymous, as are the officials and spectators. The reporter in front mediates between the viewer and the event, just as real-life sports writers mediate between athletes and their audiences (Edwin A. Ulrich Museum of Art, The Wichita State University, Endowment Association Art Collection).

fair and knowledgeable, just as real-life officials should be just and knowledgeable. Theoretically, the best man should win and the moral order should be reinforced. However, there are corrupt, incompetent officials in sport just as there are corrupt, incompetent officials in real life. In sport as in life, there is always a danger that evil will, in fact, triumph over good. That would be an unsatisfactory ending, but it is the possibility of the overthrow of the moral order that lends sport its dramatic tension.

Sport is half-way between theater and real-life. Though sport is defined as not-real and the conflict is confined to a limited arena, the dramatic effect is not contrived, as in theater. In sport, the effort is real, the emotion is real, and the injuries are real. The blood is not greasepaint. It is real.

Five

War Games

"This is not war, but it is magnificent."
> General George S. Patton, in a letter to his wife
> written as he was awaiting permission to cross the
> Rhine and invade Germany during World War II.[47]

Ball games combine the intensity of warfare with the exuberance of children's games. Alfred, Lord Tennyson uses this juxtaposition to dramatic effect in his translation of the Old English poem "The Battle of Brunanburh." The poem commemorates an actual fight of 937 B.C.E., when two Saxon brothers, King Athelstan and Prince Edmund, routed a party of invading Vikings. Punning on the fact that Athelstan and Edmund were sons of Edward, Tennyson describes the bloody battle:

> On places of slaughter —
> The struggle of standards,
> The rush of the javelins,
> The crash of the charges,
> The wielding of weapons —
> The play that they played with
> The children of Edward.[48]

Though the "play" is that of "children," the battle is lethal. On the other hand, Brazilian soccer coach Luiz Felipe Scolari used battle metaphors to describe the team he coached to victory in the finals of the 2002 World Cup: "I think this Brazil team is the ideal image of modern football [soccer]. In addition to our [other] qualities, we have fighting spirit."[49]

Sport has been described as "war without weapons," suggesting that sport is a non-lethal form of conflict resolution. P. Goodhart and C. Chataway (1968) describe the modern Olympics as a substitute for armed conflict, a form of sport that nations can engage in without doing material damage to themselves or others. The view of sport as war without weapons may be an optimistic assessment since the weapons of sport can be lethal. Further, sports competition may be an impetus to armed conflict. Eric Anderson, a coach at the University of California, Irvine, notes that sport is "much more likely to increase international tensions"[50] than to reduce them. Certainly, sporting contests have led to war, especially between nations already in conflict with each other. In 1969, El Salvador invaded Honduras after three hotly contested soccer games in the qualifying rounds for the World Cup. The anthropologist William H. Durham writes:

> The attack began a war that lasted only 100 hours, but left several thousand dead on both sides, turned 100,000 people into homeless and jobless refugees, destroyed half of El Salvador's oil refining and storage facilities, and paralyzed the nine-year-old Central American Common Market [1979:1].

The "Soccer War" ended when the Organization of American States (OAS) arranged a cease-fire and threatened economic sanctions. Durham rejects conventional descriptions of the conflict as a "Soccer War," suggesting instead that the "more important' causes of the outbreak of violence were economic and population pressures. However, these broader issues were mirrored and galvanized in the on-the-field soccer conflict.

Sport strained diplomatic ties between Australia and New Zealand following an "unsportsmanlike" act in a cricket match between the two countries in 1981. The incident occurred at the end of the match when only one ball remained to be bowled and New Zealand needed six runs to even the score, a possible outcome if the New Zealand batter could hit a fly ball over the boundary. New Zealand's chance to tie the game was spoiled when Australia's captain Greg Chappell instructed the bowler, his brother Trevor, to roll the ball along the ground. The maneuver makes a powerful stroke impossible and, though it is "legal," it is not "cricket."

An angry New Zealand fan demanded a declaration of war against Australia and radio stations played "Waltzing Matilda," Australia's national song, at half speed. Two busloads of Australian and New Zealand tourists got into a fist fight, and New Zealand's Prime Minister called on war terminology in denouncing Chappell's winning play as "an act of cowardice." Order was restored when the Australian Prime Minister called the play "a very serious mistake," and Greg Chappell, one of Australia's leading cricketeers, was forced to make a public apology (Womack 1982:25; reported in *Newsweek*, February 16, 1981).

The distinction between war and sport is not based on the degree of danger or level of violence. Allen Guttman notes that, "At the Battle of Brémule in 1119, three men were killed; at the tournament at Neuss in 1240, sixty died" (1978:7). War differs from sport in that sport takes place in a limited arena that is specifically designated as "not real" or "not serious." Thus, it provides a "safe" context for acting out potentially lethal conflicts. Anderson writes:

> Few other venues bring people together to cheer for their nation's representatives in such a public, political, and entertaining way. Citizens cheer for their nation (represented by the team or individual) against the threat of a common enemy (another nation's team or individual athletes) at a

fraction of the expense of war. And unlike war, sport possesses clear rules and boundaries that all can understand. The outcome is clear, easily understood, and quantifiable. This enables a nation to say, "we beat them by this much" or "we won more medals than any other nation." Sport also provides a unique combination of action, drama, and uncertainty for spectators from all social categories.[51]

Like combat sports, ball games are an enactment of conflict, but in the case of ball games, aggression is displaced onto control of the ball. In many ball games the formation of armies is retained. Allen Guttman writes of football, "It is, like chess, 'a crazy miniature war,' a playful war waged for its own sake" (1978:121).[52]

Women and War

In ball games, the opposing forces are arrayed as teams, and this is a significant part of the symbolism. Like warfare, and unlike one-on-one hand-to-hand combat, most ball games allow the individual to join with others in a communal effort. There is often a cooperative ethic associated with team sports, as expressed to me by a Hungarian water polo player: "Water polo is a better sport than swimming or diving, for one thing, because it's a team sport." Although swimmers and divers would perhaps dispute this point, John Armitage, author of *Man at Play*, concurs:

> Team games offer major satisfactions beyond the competitiveness of the match. There is pleasure in acting in unison with others, of weaving a purposeful pattern leading to a goal or a try; the communal bath and the visit to the pub are part of the ritual, which if removed would lack ingredients that have long been regarded as essential to the play [1977:12].

Armitage's inclusion of post-game activities as essential to the dynamics of the team helps to explain a number of gender issues relating to team sports in North America. As already noted, the dynamics of sports reflect the dynamics of social life overall and participation in sports is considered part of an individual's socialization into appropriate adult roles.

Traditionally, in North America, males are socialized into group interaction appropriate for the boardroom, the battlefield and the locker room. Cooperation and competition are balanced against each other. Females, on the other hand, are socialized into centering their lives on the nuclear family, consisting of husband and children. Females compete with other females for males, who are expected to provide for the economic needs of women and their children.

These economic realities are reflected in sports, in that males are encouraged to participate in team sports, whereas females are encouraged to participate in activities that emphasize individual excellence and petite beauty, such as ballet and gymnastics. This has traditionally been explained as due to biological differences between males and females: (1) males are stronger and therefore can take the rough interaction of team sports; (2) the reproductive capacities of females can be compromised by the body contact characteristic of team sports; and (3) females do not have the physical strength required in team sports.

None of these arguments can be supported by biology. Ballet requires greater physical strength than team sports, and the extreme thinness required by ballet and gymnastics compromises female reproductive potential because of the reduction in body fat. Males do have greater upper body strength, one measure of strength, but women have greater endurance. An endurance race conducted across California's Death Valley and other rugged terrain in the height of summer was handily won in 2002 by a woman. She attributed her win to her ability to maintain a constant speed without stopping for rest.

The ability of women to aggressively play team contact sports received a boost in the last decade of the twentieth century when formation of the Women's National Basketball Association provided a chance for women to play basketball professionally and the World Cup win of the U.S. women's soccer team in 1999 proved that female players could draw strong fan support. The United States was late coming to this realization, and the dichotomy between "male" team sports and "female" individual sports that emphasize grace and agility appears unique to North America.

In ancient Greece, both girls and boys played a ball game in which a ball handler rode on the back of another player, a game that continued to be played in Northern Greece until the nineteenth century. In ancient Sparta, both sexes played nude, "but girls reportedly took greater pleasure in watching males play than vice-versa. They were also much more vocal, making endless quips of every sort."[53]

Participation of women in vigorous sports in the Mediterranean is traditionally traced to Lycurgus, the founder of the Spartan constitution, who believed that physical training for women prepared them to become mothers of Spartan soldiers (Harris 1964:181). The Greek philosopher Plato similarly favored vigorous exercise for women. In his Laws (ca. 350 B.C.E.), Plato recommended physical instruction for both boys and girls, beginning in the womb. He felt that a pregnant woman should keep the fetus in constant motion. From birth until the age of three, the child should be supervised in carefully regulated play, and systematic instruction for both boys and girls should begin at the age of six. Unlike Lycurgus, Plato rejected combat sports such as wrestling and the pankration for women, but did recommend fencing for them.

A fresco from the Piazza Armesina in Sicily, dating from the first half of the fourth century C.E., shows girls engaging in a variety of physical exercises, including volleying a ball. The small size of the ball indicates the game may be *harpastum*, a vigorous game in which players on one team try to snatch the ball away from the other team.[54]

In nineteenth-century England, field hockey gained favor as a form of physical training for males in the elite public schools. Throughout much of this period, the aggressive sport was considered unsuitable for women. By the 1880s, however, university women were playing field hockey in secret. Lady Margaret Hall, Oxford, popularized the sport, and in 1887, the first women's hockey club was founded. By the end of the nineteenth century, English women were also playing ice hockey (Cudden 1979).

The British humorist of the early twentieth century P. G. Wodehouse captured the essence of the upper class female field hockey player in his fictional character Gertrude Butterwick. Gertrude combines all the feminine graces with a fierce intensity honed by excelling at field hockey. In his 1925 novel *The Luck of the Bodkins*, Wodehouse describes a tense moment when Gertrude's cousin Reggie Tennyson, still hung over from a night with his friends at the Drone's Club, urges her to reconcile with a suitor she has rejected:

> One of these days you will wake up in the cold gray dawn kicking yourself because you were such a chump as to let Monty get away from you. What's the matter with Monty? Good-looking, amiable, kind to animals, wealthy to the bursting point — you couldn't have a better bet. And, in the friendliest spirit, may I inquire who the dickens you think you are? Greta Garbo, or somebody? Don't you be a goat, young Gertrude. You take my advice and run after him and give him a nice big kiss and tell him you're sorry that you were such a mug and that it's all on again."
>
> An all–England centre-forward can be very terrible when roused, and the levin flash in Gertrude Butterwick's handsome eyes seemed to suggest that Reginald Tennyson was about to be snubbed with a ferocity which in his enfeebled state could not but have the worst effects. That hard stare was back on her face. She looked at him as if he were a referee who had just penalized her for sticks in the game of the season.
>
> Fortunately, before she could give utterance to her thoughts, bells began to ring and whistles to blow, and the panic fear of being left behind by a parting train sank the hockey player in the woman. With a shrill and purely feminine squeak, Gertrude bounded off.

Gender roles expressed in ball play reflect the overall gender roles and social organization of the group. In stratified societies, social class is reflected in sports participation. Robert S. Santley, et al, suggest that the Aztec ballgame, called tlachtli was "a vehicle to increase the power, prestige, and wealth of the elite" (1991:15). Elites both bet large sums of wealth on the outcomes of the games and demonstrated their prowess as players.

Fernando de Alva Ixtlilxochitl (1952) recounts a Toltec legend in which Topiltzin, the Toltec king, played the game against three rivals. The winner of the game also won the right to rule the others. S. Jeffrey K. Wilkerson describes a similar match engaged in by Moctezuma II a few years before the arrival of the Spanish. Nezahualpili, the ruler of Texcoco, had interpreted the appearance of a comet in the east as a harbinger of the Triple Alliance, which included Texcoco and the Aztec capital of Tenochtitlán, now Mexico City. Moctezuma decided to test the prediction by challenging Nezahualpili to a ball game. "As predicted, Moctezuma lost the game, and eventually his empire" (Wilkerson 1991:45) Wilkerson notes: "In general playing *tlachtli* was a prerogative of the elite. Although played by mortals, the outcome was thought to be controlled by the gods alone" (1991:45).

The association of ball games with male social status and military prowess shapes the nature of female as participants, as spectators, or as support players. Mary Kay Duffié notes that Māori and women and men of New Zealand traditionally supported their warriors, and now their rugby players, with a *haka* performance involving songs, musical instruments and dance: "The most impressive dance of the Māori was, and still is, the haka, which would be used for either welcoming guests or defying enemies" (2001:21). The haka was composed by a war chief, and lyrics of its songs stress the prowess of the warrior in crucial matters of life and death:

> *Ka mate, ka mate,* Death, Death,
> *Ka ora, ka ora,* Life, life,
> *Ka mate, ka mate,* Death, death,
> *Ka ora, Ka ora,* Life, life
> *Tenei te tangata puhuruhuru,* This is the hairy man
> *Nana i tiki mai i whakawhiti te roa,* Who causes the sun to shine
> *Upane, kaupane,* Up and up,
> *Upane, kaupane,* Up and up
> *Whiti te ra,* The sun to shine [Duffié 2001:22]

Haka is designed to inspire one's own warriors and intimidate one's opponent. Performers eject their tongues vigorously to the rhythm of the chant. *Haka* also expresses the close cooperation required in warfare and participation in team sports: "The most striking features of the haka are the distortions of the face and the incredibly good timing of song with actions. A skilled haka party moves and sounds as one man" (Duffié 2001:22).

War Games and Ball Games

Just as warriors fight on behalf of tribes and nations, sports teams typically play on behalf of some social group. In ball games, school plays against school, town against town, and nation against nation.

Ball games are often seen as training grounds for war, as expressed in the statement attributed to the Duke of Wellington: "The battle of Waterloo was won on the playing fields of Eton." And heroes often presage their future prowess in their childhood games. The Celtic hero Cú Chulainn earned his name when he was six years old, as the unintended result of playing a game of hurling, a traditional Celtic sport similar to field hockey and one of the fastest of all stick-and-ball games. As a child, the hero played the game single-handedly against all the other boys and defeated them. One day he was playing outside the castle of the Ulster king Conchobar when the king rode by with his nobles on the way to a banquet given by Culann, the chief smith of the clan. Conchobar called to the boy and invited him to go with them. The boy replied that he would join the banquet after the game was finished.

When the Ulster warriors were in Culann's hall, the host asked the king's permission to let loose his ferocious watchdog, which was a strong as a hundred hounds, to guard them from attack while they were feasting. Forgetting his invitation to the boy, Conchobar gave his permission. When the boy arrived, the hound rushed at him, ready to tear him apart, but the boy hero flung his playing-ball into the hound's mouth, seized it by its hind legs and dashed it against a rock until it was dead. Culann was furious at the death of his watchdog, so the boy promised to guard the smith's house himself until he could find and train another watchdog as fierce and strong as the hound he had killed. That is how the hero came to be known as Cú Chulainn, or "Culann's Hound."

In this story, Cú Chulainn demonstrates many of the desirable attributes of the athletic hero. He is strong, he is courageous, he is not deterred by barriers, and he takes responsibility for his own actions. These attributes are also desirable in military heroes. U.S. General Douglas MacArthur exhibited these attributes in his determination to recapture the Philippines during World War II. When forced to leave Corregidor Island in 1942, he declared, "I shall return." After U.S. troops secured a foothold in the Philippines on October 20, 1944, MacArthur declared, "I have returned." When the 403rd Regimental Combat Team recaptured Corregidor under the command of Colonel George M. Jones five months later, MacArthur said, "I see the old flagpole still stands. Have your troops hoist the colors to its peak, and let no enemy ever haul them down." In the end, it was a friendly nation who hauled down the U.S. flag, when the Philippines gained independence from the United States.

When Adolf Hitler wrote in *Mein Kampf,* "Give me an athlete and I'll give you and army,"[55] he reflected a view that many others have held: Good athletes make good soldiers. Not only are athletes physically fit, they have *esprit de corps,* courage, idealism, and the ability to commit themselves totally to an elusive goal.

Many ball games mirror the form of warfare and call on the same skills. In the following pages, I focus on three types of military encounters as expressed in the sports that recreate their dynamics. Some of these sports developed as a training ground for a particular form of warfare. The *raid* calls for swift, decisive action. It is not aimed at capturing and holding territory. Instead, the object is to move in quickly, grab as much booty as possible, and flee. This form of warfare is most apparent in games played on horseback, such as polo. The *battle* pits two armies against each other in a prolonged and concerted effort. In general, the object is to capture and hold territory. American football and rugby epitomize this form of combat. The *duel* consists of a face-off between opponents that often involves a war of nerves. It is represented here in the sports of baseball and cricket.

The Raid

Sports played on horseback are most evocative of a form of warfare that apparently developed on the Mongolian steppes and spread through other parts of Asia. The violence and awful grandeur of battle is underscored by the powerful image of vigorous men mounted on magnificent animals. It is not surprising that warfare on horseback is depicted in art traditions ranging from China to Europe, wherever in fact, the horse has been known.

The origins of the Afghan sport of buzkashi can be traced to the tradition of warfare conducted on the Central Asian steppe from at least the first millennium B.C.E.. The name of the sport translates as "goat-grabbing" and the object of the game is to grab the headless carcass of a goat or calf and ride as fast as one can to score a goal. In the more traditional form of the game, *tudabarai*, there are no boundaries and no teams. The object is to gain control of the carcass and ride off in any direction, fending off the attempts of hundreds of opponents to snatch it away. A more formal version of the game was developed by Afghan governments in an attempt to popularize it outside Afghanistan. Called *qarajai*, this version is played by teams of ten players each and with clearly demarcated goals. A player scores by snatching up the carcass and depositing it in the team's goal, which is known as the *hallal* or circle of justice. A player can also score by riding around a flag at the far end of the field while carrying the calf. Both versions of buzkashi retain much that evokes traditional warfare in the region.

Afghanis trace buzkashi to Alexander the Great of Macedonia, of the fourth century B.C.E., who conquered Egypt, Persia and the Indus region of India, extending his empire into present-day Tajikistan. Historically, however, the origins of buzkashi predate Alexander. The practice of riding horses may have appeared on the Ukrainian steppes as early 4000 B.C.E., and the warfare-on-horseback tradition can be traced with some certainty to the Scythians, the best-known of whom is Attila the Hun (406–453 C.E.). Long before Attila exerted his might over settled populations to the south and east, Scythians invaded the area now occupied by Afghanistan, then spread into Iran and the Punjab by around 1500 B.C.E.

Though the Scythians were considered to be ruthless and unyielding on the battlefield and in diplomacy, Atilla was described as "temperate" in his behavior at a feast given by the Hun and attended by the Roman diplomat Priscus:

> A luxurious meal, served on silver plate, had been made ready for us and the barbarian guests, but Atilla ate nothing but meat on a wooden trencher. In everything else, too, he showed himself temperate; his cup was of wood, while to the guests were given goblets of gold and silver. His dress, too, was quite simple, affecting only to be clean. The sword he carried at his side, the latchets of his Scythian shoes, the bridle of his horse were not adorned, like those of the other Scythians, with gold or gems or anything costly.[56]

Both men and women Scythians fought on horseback using swords, knives, and a double-curved bow. They were skilled at shooting backwards over their horses rumps as they turned away from the enemy.[57] Many wore bronze helmets and chain-mail jerkins lined with red felt. Their shields and weapons were decorated with gold, ivory and gems. Their horses wore ornate costumes, and many Scythians had full body tattoos with intricate designs.[58]

Buzkashi, as it is still played in Afghanistan, is believed to have derived from the aggressive maneuvers of horsemen who made swift raids on enemy encampments, snatching up sheep, goats and other goods without dismounting. The modern game is played with a stuffed goatskin or calfskin. The animal is ritually slaughtered and gutted, then filled with sand and sewn up. It is then soaked in cold water and the feet are cut off to make it harder to get a grip on it. Players, or *chapadazan* try to snatch up the carcass, which may weigh from 60 to 150 pounds, from the ground without dismounting. All the while, the horseman must fend off opponents who try to steal the prize away, drawing on the same skills that allowed mounted warriors to successfully execute their raids.

Riders carry whips with short wooden handles which they can use to whip their opponents. However, they are not allowed to whip their opponent's mounts. This is a clear expression of the idea that war is between men, not animals. It may reflect the idea that superb beast is to be respected at all times, and may also evoke a time when the opponent's horse was part of the booty of warfare.

Buzkashi still duplicates the frenzy of war and can be just as deadly. Eric Slater, a journalist with the *Los Angeles Times*, describes a game held in Kabul in January 2002, after Afghanistan's even more deadly encounter with U.S. military personnel:

> Somehow, amid the thrash of whips and hail of hooves, the team from Parwan discovered an interloper, an extra rider who had sneaked onto the field to aid the losing Kabul side. In an instant, the Parwan team set upon him, lashing and pummeling the man as he spurred his horse desperately to get away.[59]

At this point, the war metaphor becomes even more pronounced, as spectators from the Kabul side rushed to aid their beleaguered comrade: "The would-be savior's soldiers leaped from the bleachers and began running to the aid of their commander, their AK-47s at the ready, spectators dropping to the ground, taking cover."[60]

The *Los Angeles Times* reporter calls buzkashi "a ritual that appears little more than unadulterated mayhem." In the aftermath of a form of warfare conducted by the United States, in which machinery takes the place of man-to-man combat enacted on horseback, buzkashi seemed chaotic to this reporter. To the Afghanis, the horseback sport of buzkashi may make more sense than the spectacle of invaders encased in steel dropping megatons of explosives. Indeed, the journalist describes buzkashi as a demonstration of the "power that is physical, political and endlessly metaphorical in its parallels to Afghan life": "The game is also a chance for everyone from powerful commanders to lowly tribesmen to demonstrate their bravery. *Chapandazan*, or riders, seldom go home without having shed blood, and sometimes lose their lives beneath the horses' hooves."[61]

Buzkashi is similar in concept to polo, and may be similar in origin as well. Polo probably developed in Central Asia, perhaps as early as 525 B.C.E. It was almost certainly related to warfare, as a context for practicing skills important in battle, and perhaps as a way of expressing traditional rivalries as well. The origins of polo are often traced to the Mongol warrior Temuchin, who later became known as Genghis Khan (Universal Ruler) after uniting the previously disunited Mongols under his command and extending his empire from the Korean peninsula almost to Kiev, in what is now Russia, and from the Mongol steppes south to the Indus Valley.

Polo, like buzkashi, is based on the snatch-and-grab style of warfare pursued by steppe horsemen. It also reflects similar values of daring and bravery. Genghis Khan never aspired to amassing material wealth, though his warfare was aimed at taking booty. He was tolerant of the religious beliefs of others, but was intolerant of disloyalty, either among his own followers or the followers of others. He would put to death a warrior who betrayed his commander, even to him, but would reward those who fought loyally to their commanders, even against him.

Though Genghis Khan is often credited with developing the sport of polo, in fact it arrived in China long before that legendary leader. Genghis Khan's reign took place in the twelfth century. The first recorded polo match in China dates from 709 and the reign of the Emperor Chung Tsung. The word "polo" comes from *pulu*, the Tibetan term for a willow root from which the balls are made, suggesting the game may have had Tibetan origins. A polo game was part of the festivities celebrating the marriage of the Chinese emperor's daughter to the king of Tibet.

During imperial times, the Chinese game of polo appears to have been attended by a great deal of ceremony. The sticks ended in a crescent point and were known as "moon sticks." The ball was painted red, and the horses were decorated with bells, mirrors, tassels and pheasant feathers.

Polo became something of a national sport in Korea during the Koryo period, when the country acquired its modern name. On the other hand, Stephen Turnbull (1990) says the sport was never very popular in Japan, even though it was considered one of the eighteen forms of martial arts. It was played during the Edo period in a variant form, called *dakyu*. Each team of seven men was identified by red or white badges and each player carried a ball of his team's color in his racket, which terminated in a net like a lacrosse racket, rather than a mallet. During the first stage of the game, each player tried to throw his ball into a goal — a net bag inside a wooden screen. When one side got all seven balls into the goal, the second stage began, in which each team tried to gain possession of a banded ball and put it into the net. Dakyu appears to be a mounted version of billiards, and indeed, the origins of the two games may have been similar.

It is clear that the Japanese version of the game is less vivid than polo in its usual form, since chucking a ball into a net is less dramatic than the spectacle of men on horseback vying with each other to control a ball, or even more vivid, the carcass of a calf. The failure of polo or *dakyu* to win the allegiance of samurai in Japan may have been because they had an alternate sport that filled the same niche — dog shooting. A dog was released within concentric circles, and a mounted archer tried to shoot it before it escaped the "target." Dog shooting originally provided a means of training for warfare, but by the Edo period, the sport of warfare had been suppressed by the shogun.

Ancient Persians clearly recognized polo's potential for practicing battle skills. For centuries polo was a kind of national sport in Persia. The game is referred to a number of times in the writings of Ferdowsi, author of the *Shah-Nama*. In one episode of the epic history, the youthful hero Siyavosh demonstrates his skill at polo in the camp of Afrasiyah, king of the Turks, the traditional enemy of the Persians. At the time of the game, Siyavosh had married Afrasiyah's daughter, and his relations with his father-in-law were amicable. Still, the polo field appears to be a microcosm of the battlefield as Siyavosh's compatriots are arrayed against Afrasiyah's men:

> The sound of kettle-drums spread about the ground, from which the dust arose as high as the sky. You would have said that with the clash of the cymbals and the blare of the trumpets the whole area moved from its place. The commander [Afrasiyah] made the first stroke on the meydan [playing field], hitting the ball magnificently high so that it rose into the clouds, but then Siyavosh put spurs to his horse and, when the ball fell within reach, did not let it reach the dust. Instead, he took aim at it as it neared the ground and smote it so high that it disappeared from sight. At that the great king commanded that another ball should be brought to Siyavosh, who placed it to his lips to the accompaniment of a salvo from the bugles and the drums [1967:97].

Siyavosh's second foray onto the field was even more spectacular than his first:

> He then mounted a fresh horse, threw the ball up out of his hand and struck it with his mallet until it appeared to come alongside the moon. You would have said the sky had sucked it up. Afrasiyah laughed aloud at the play, and, when nobles had recovered from their amazement, with one voice they declared that they had never seen so notable a horseman in the saddle [1967: 97–98].

Afrasiyah then commanded his own men to take the field against the Persian team led by Siyavosh, thus providing a context in which the Persians proved their superior skill against the Turks: "There ensued between the two teams a tussle so fierce that the dust rose up to the sun. This way and that, with much talk, the ball passed from one side to the other. Each time the Turks attacked for a goal the Iranians beat them to the ball and frustrated the Turks" (1967:98).

In keeping with his royal nature, Siyavosh demonstrated his generosity in dealing with his outmatched opponent and his command over his own followers: "Siyavosh was angered and said to the Iranians in the Pahlavi tongue, 'Is this a ground where games are played, or is it a battle-field? Give way and let the Turks have the ball for once'" (Ferdowsi 1985:98).

Such amiability between two deadly enemies could not last and Siyavosh was later betrayed and killed by his father-in-law.

Persian women of the nobility were allowed the privilege of playing polo, and there are several accounts of them doing so. The poet Nizami (1126–1200) describes

Commissioned by the Shah Ismáil for his son, this manuscript illustration was painted in Persia during the Safavid dynasty (1501–1726 C.E.). It represents an episode from the epic Shah-nama (Book of Kings), written by the poet Ferdowsi in the tenth century. The artwork depicts the game of polo played by the hero Siyavosh before the Turkish King Afrasiyah. Afrasiyah was an enemy of the Persian monarchs and was often equated with Ahriman, the personification of Evil. Afrasiyah later betrayed and killed Siyavosh. The polo game in which Siyavosh demonstrated his prowess represents the moral and physical superiority of the Persians versus the duplicity and physical inferiority of the Turks (The Metropolitan Museum of Art, Gift of Arthur A. Houghton, Jr., 1970).

a game in which a queen with six ladies-in-waiting play against the king and his courtiers. The Persian word for polo is *chaugan*, which denotes the stick or mallet for hitting the ball, but it also means the game itself. The *chaugan* and the *meydan* provided Persian writers with a plentiful source of imagery. The fifteenth-century poet Mahmud Arifi wrote an allegorical poem in which the ball and the polo stick personified forms of mystic love (Cuddon 1979).

Arabs learned polo from the Persians around 800 B.C.E. and quickly became ardent participants. The game was an exclusively royal and aristocratic privilege, and Arabs, like the Persians, viewed it as excellent training for war. One sultan, Nur-ed-din, is reported to have been such an enthusiast he played the game at night by torchlight (Cuddon 1979).

Polo was introduced into India by Islamic conquerors in the thirteenth century and quickly became a fashionable sport at the court of the Moghul emperors. Polo was on the wane in India when the British cavalry adopted the sport during their occupation of that country. Appropriately enough, the first match played in England, in 1871, was between two military units: The Tenth Hussars beat the Ninth Lancers on Hounslow Heath, a suburb of London. The game continued to be associated with the military well into the twentieth century. Lord Louis Mountbatten, founder of the Royal Navy Polo Association, compared the *chukka*, or playing period of polo, to a naval engagement, stating that both need "leadership, decisiveness, speed, communication, maneuverability and good fast shooting."

From its early days, polo must have been a sport of the elite, however status is defined. When it was still an essential component of training for warfare, skilled players must also have been respected warriors who were able to amass booty. Now, when war is largely a matter of men and machines, polo is no longer so closely linked to warfare. It is still a sport of elites, however. At the very least, players must be able to outfit their mounts, and enthusiasts should ideally be able to support a string of polo ponies.

Polo remains a favorite sport of the British Royal family, including among its dedicated players, Prince Philip and his son, Prince Charles. Prince Philip's injuries eventually forced him to give up the game, and Prince Charles took a number of noted spills. According to Nicholas Courtney (1983), author of *Sporting Royals: Past and Present*, a tribute to polo is carved on a wooden board high in the foothills of the Himalayas, close to one of the earliest polo fields:

> Let other men do other things,
> The King of Sports is still the Sport of Kings.

The Battle

Kings, by and large, do not meet the enemy on foot, and they are seldom found among the rank and file of the army. There is seldom room for individual glory in the daily business of warfare. The battle pits group against group, rather than man against man. For the most part, battle is a communal effort in which participants are encouraged to commit themselves totally to the good of the group. And, as a rule, glory goes to group action rather than to individual heroism. For example, the image of soldiers raising the flag over Iwo Jima during World War II has become an American icon, but few Americans remember the soldiers' names.

Similarly, when the scene was duplicated in clearing the wreckage of the Twin Towers of the World Trade Center in New York more than fifty years later, the names of the individual firefighters and police officers were less memorable than the heroism of the group effort. Firefighters, especially, were viewed as restoring the honor of the United States as a whole by risking their own lives in saving people trapped in the rubble.

Just as spectacular moments of individual daring seldom win wars, so too they rarely win football or soccer games. The strategy of battle is not based on a dramatic race to seize the prize followed by a speedy retreat. Rather, participants in battle work to win ground and hold it. As in warfare, so it is in team sports such as football, basketball, rugby and soccer. It is not enough to score; the team must also hold the line against the other side. Prior to the 2002 World Cup soccer finals pitting the offensively outstanding Brazilian team against the "tough-as-nails German defenders," the German coach Rudi Voeller emphasized the importance of the team effort: "I am realistic and aware of our limitations. We are a bit below teams like Brazil and England, who have more class than we have, but with our team spirit and a collective effort, we can beat any side."[62]

This is not to say there are no moments of spectacular daring in these team sports. The occasional fast break can create a moment as exciting as any raid, but the game does not depend on these dynamics alone. A single brilliant play enlivens the game, but it takes more than that to win it. In testimony before the Committee on Armed Services of the U.S. House of Representatives in 1949, General Omar Bradley suggests the same is true of military engagements:

> Our military forces are one team — in the game to win regardless of who carries the ball. This is no time for "fancy dans" who won't hit the line with all they have on every play, unless they can call the signals. Each player on this team — whether he shines in the spotlight of the backfield or eats dirt in the line — must be an All-American.

In art, American football is often depicted as a communal effort organized around force. This concept is expressed in a 1942 painting by John S. Curry. The individual players are not identified, nor are the teams. The faces of the players are obscured and team insignia are not visible. The only markers of identity are the numbers on the players' jerseys. Both teams are engaged in what appears to be a headlong rush down the field. The similarity to war is emphasized by the massive, but lightly sketched background, which evokes images of castle ramparts and territory to be conquered. In R. Tait McKenzie's bronze *Onslaught*, the athletes appear to emerge from the earth to become locked in a cosmic struggle.

The football players in John S. Curry's canvas *End Run*, painted at the beginning of
World War II, surge forward like an army beseiging a vaguely defined fortress. (John
Steuart Currey, *End Run*, 1942–46, Oil on canvas, 38" × 59.5" Collection of The But-
ler Institute of American Art, Youngstown, Ohio).

Massive force is expressed in a wood sculpture portraying an American football player by Hy Farber. Again, this work focuses on the controlled strength of the
athlete rather than his individual personality. The theme of forceful action is
expressed by Theodore Roosevelt in his work *The American Boy* (1900): "In life, as
in a football game, the principle to follow is: Hit the line hard."

Roosevelt also cautioned that the strength of the man, the soldier, and the
athlete should be used on behalf of society:

> He cannot do good work if he is not strong and does not try with his
> whole heart and soul to count in any contest; and his strength will be a
> curse to himself and to every one else if he does not have thorough com-
> mand over himself and over his own evil passions, and if he does not use
> his strength on the side of decency, justice, and fair dealing.[63]

The aggressiveness of football is well-orchestrated and controlled, usually
reflecting regional loyalties. The association with territorial boundaries and group
loyalties is long-standing. The annual Thanksgiving Day game between Yale and
Princeton, held in New York in the 1890s, has been described as "the most glam-
orous sporting event in the country" (Durant and Bettman 1952:67). On the morning of the game, fans decked themselves out with banners and beribboned canes,
and paraded up and down Fifth Avenue in their vehicles.[64]

As depicted in this wood sculpture by Hy Farber, the football player is a massive but anonymous figure. The strength of his shoulders dominates this view of the athlete, as though presenting an invincible force to the opposing team (reproduced by permission of the artist).

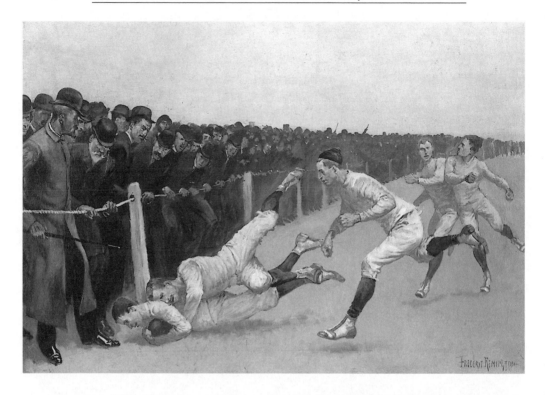

Ivy League football in the nineteenth century was a gentlemen's affair, which meant that only young men of the upper classes could compete. But the action on the field was anything but gentle, as players strived to embody Theodore Roosevelt's dictum "Hit the line hard." Frederic Remington's painting *Touchdown, Yale vs. Princeton, Thanksgiving Day, Nov. 27, 1890, Yale 32, Princeton 0* commemorates a famous game in an annual rivalry between the two Ivy League universities (Yale University Art Gallery, Whitney Collections of Sporting Art, given in memory of Harry Payne Whitney, B.A. 1894, Payne Whitney, B.A. 1898, by Francis P. Garvan, B.A. 1897).

The nineteenth century Ivy League games reflected class differences. The schools drew on the nation's elite for students and, as in the British tradition, young men of the upper classes had to prove their valor through participation in what Roosevelt called "rough pastimes and field-sports." The annual game between freshmen and sophomores played at Harvard in the nineteenth century, which may be viewed as a rite of passage, was brutal. The dropping of the ball for the kickoff was usually a signal for mayhem. The even, held on the first Monday of the fall term, was known as Bloody Monday.

Similar imagery of strength is represented in Robert W. Jensen's pen-and-ink drawing of an ice hockey player bearing down on his opponent. The explosive power of ice hockey is expressed in his composition of athletes converging on the point of play.

Not all team sports of the battle genre are organized around the model of power or massive strength. In fact, grace and speed are essential even for those

An anonymous player bears down on his opponent in the sport of ice hockey, which is associated in the minds of the public with massive force (reproduced by permission of the artist, Robert W. Jensen).

sports that connote massive strength and power in the public mind. A football player darting his way through the opposing line is relying on speed and strategy rather than strength, and ice hockey viewed from the upper rows exudes grace evocative of ballet. In dealing with symbols, however, one is dealing with collective representations, the way sport is viewed by the public or interested observers, including artists.

Robert W. Jensen captures an explosive moment in ice hockey as players converge in an tensely drawn scene (reproduced by permission of the artist, Robert W. Jensen).

Some team sports, such as soccer and basketball, draw on a very different imagery, that of grace and strategy. It has been said of soccer that it is the elemental ball game. In its most basic form, it requires no goal, no demarcated playing field, no rules, no assigned positions. It requires only a kid, or two or more, kicking a ball around. Even the ball is not an essential component of the game. Where a ball is lacking, a bundle of rags or a tin can or a rock will do. It has even been observed that soccer appeals to a basic fact of human nature: Kids kick things.

When kicking things becomes formalized, as in the game of soccer, the game takes on new dimensions. At this point, it represents the expectations and aspirations of society as a whole.

The Cosmic Battle of Order and Chaos

As noted in Chapter One, ball games can represent the participation of human beings in the cosmic order. The Persian poet Nizami used polo as a metaphor for

John DeAndrea's 1971 image of *Boys Playing Soccer* captures the joyful exuberance of sports that often seems missing in international competitions (Everson Museum of Art, Syracuse, New York, Gift of Mrs. Robert C. Hosmer, 1972).

In a few sparse strokes, Robert W. Jensen's pen-and-ink drawing captures the intensity, grace and power of the soccer player (reproduced by permission of the artist, Robert W. Jensen).

human aspirations, but soccer and other ball games have also symbolized the playing field of life. A concept of this type is expressed in a poem about an early form of soccer or association football written by Li-Yu, a Chinese poet who lived from about 50 to 130 C.E.:

> A round ball and an oblong space
> With two teams standing opposed.

The ball flies across like the moon
At the full.
Captains are appointed and take their places
According to unchanging regulations.
In the game make no allowance for kith and kin
And do not let your mind be swayed by partialities.
Be cool and determined
And show no irritation when you fall.

This poem expresses several aspects of Chinese philosophy, as well as some characteristic of sports cross-culturally. The description of the ball and the playing field evokes geometric images of balance, with the opposing teams poised at opposite ends of the "oblong space." It echoes Taoist values relating to a balance of opposing forces. Also characteristic of Taoism, nature is invoked as the ball is compared to the moon. Confucian values emphasizing one's place in society are suggested by the captains taking their appointed places. Also Confucian-like, the players are governed by rules that were in place long before the game began and will continue long after it comes to a close. Finally, in the last four lines, the athlete is urged to transcend petty irritations and everyday loyalties, concentrating instead on the nobler demands of the game, a concept compatible both with Chinese values and with the stoicism universally demanded of athletes.

A game similar to soccer developed in China around 206 B.C.E., during the Han dynasty. The game was called *tsu chu* (*tsu* means roughly "to kick," while *chu* denotes a ball made of stuffed leather). Chinese emperors took part in the game, and one of them, Ch'eng Ti, was an accomplished player. However, both his empress and his ministers disapproved of such active participation.

Generally, monarchs are discouraged from participating in the give-and-take of ball games, activities seen as being more appropriate for combat soldiers. However, the pre–Columbian ball game of Central America was considered a noble activity suitable for gods, heroes and kings, though it could be brutal on several levels. The solid, heavy rubber ball, about eight inches in diameter, could be lethal when propelled at great speed. Teams of one to four players bounced the ball off their bodies, much like modern soccer players. They may have been aided (or hindered) in this by wearing heavy stone yokes, which could be used for controlling the ball. There are numerous depictions of ball players wearing yokes around their waist, as well as numerous stone yokes found in association with ball courts (See Wilkerson 1991). However, some scholars believe that the stone yokes were for ceremonial purposes only and that actual yokes worn by ball players during the game were made of some kind of padded material. Points were scored by directing the ball into a goal area of the court or by making contact with a stone ring at center court. Only rarely were players able to put the ball through the stone ring.

The game was associated with human sacrifice, and players were ritually killed to provide food for the gods. Ball courts, built in the shape of a capital "I", were often located at the heart of sacred centers. At several sites, including Tenochtitlan, located at the heart of what is now Mexico City, ball courts were close to skull racks used to display the skulls of sacrificial victims. According to Linda Schele and Mary Ellen Miller (1986), losers were sacrificed, their hearts were offered to the gods, and occasionally, their decapitated heads served as balls. There are numerous images of games with human heads as balls or with skulls inside balls.

There is evidence that ritual decapitations were carried out on the ball court, possibly at its center, the *itzompan*, or "place of the skull" (Gillespie 1991). Depictions of decapitation and disembodied heads or skulls are found in relief on walls of ball courts, on stelae (stone monuments), on jewelry, on vases, and in codices which describe life in Mexico and Central America at the time of the Spanish conquest. In addition, actual skulls have been found in association with ball courts at several Central American sites (Gillespie 1991).

The symbolic origin of the Central American ballgame is described in the Maya creation myth, the *Popul Vuh*, which centers on the exploits of the Hero Twins. According to the *Popul Vuh*, the twin brothers 1 Hunahpu and 7 Hunahpu were the best ball players on earth. They practiced endlessly, until the sound of the heavy bouncing rubber ball disturbed the lords who lived in Xibalba, the Maya Underworld. The angry Underworld gods of sickness and death sent messenger owls to the Hunahpu brothers summoning them to a ballgame. The boys stored their equipment in the loft of their house and followed the owls into Xibalba, where the gods deceived and killed them. The gods buried 7 Hunahpu's body in the ball court and hung 1 Hunahpu's head in a calabash tree to celebrate their victory.

One day the daughter of an Underworld lord walked past the calabash tree and spoke to the desiccated head hanging there. The head spat into her hand, impregnating her. When the girl's pregnancy became obvious, her outraged father ordered her sacrificed. To escape her father's wrath, the girl fled into the Middleworld and sought refuge with the mother of 1 Hunahpu and 7 Hunahpu. The mother of the dead brothers did not want to take the pregnant woman in, but grudgingly relented after the girl proved the twins in her womb were magicians by miraculously harvesting a large amount of corn from a single plant. The young women later delivered twins, whom she named Hunahpu (Hunter) and Xbalanque (Jaguar-Deer).

As the boys grew to maturity, they tried a number of occupations, but were unhappy with all of them. One day, guided by a rat, they discovered the ballgame equipment their father and uncle had left in the rafters of their house and learned that their true calling was to be ball players. They began playing the game, endlessly bouncing the rubber ball over the heads of the Underworld gods below. Once again angered by the racket, the lords of Xibalba invited the brothers to play on the ball court of the gods.

Unlike their father and uncle, the Hero Twins outwitted the Underworld gods as the games continued day after day, and the brothers were subjected to increasing danger. One night, the gods of sickness and death forced Hunahpu and Xbalanque to stay in the House of Bats, where there were many bloodthirsty vampire bats. The Twins slept inside their blowguns to avoid the bats, but Hunahpu, seeing a glimmer of light, stuck out his head to see if dawn had arrived. As he did so, a vampire bat decapitated him. Elated that they had at last succeeded in besting the twins, the lords of the Underworld hung Hunahpu's head over the ball court and announced that it would be used as the ball in the next match.

Xbalanque fashioned a temporary head for Hunahpu's body from a pumpkin and persuaded a rabbit to impersonate the real head. When the ballgame began, Xbalanque kicked the rabbit/ball over the walls of the court, and the animal in the guise of the ball bounced away, drawing the lords away from the game.

Xbalanque then restored his brother's head, and the two continued the ballgame, defeating the lords of Xibalba, thus symbolically conquering sickness and death. The Twins then allowed themselves to be sacrificed, asking that their bones be ground up and thrown into a river. They later returned as magicians to the court of the Underworld gods 1 Death and 7 Death, dazzling their audience by successfully dismembering themselves and a number of animals, then restoring them all to life. The gods 1 Death and 7 Death begged to be killed and restored to life so they could experience the miracle of rebirth. The Hero Twins obliged the two Underworld gods by killing and dismembering them, but did not restore them to life. Their labors complete, the brothers took their place in the sky as the sun and moon.

This mythical ballgame may have been acted out in real life among the Maya as part of the capture of a rival king. A series of images on stairs at a ball court at Yaxchilan may commemorate an event in the reign of Bird Jaguar, who became king in 752 C.E. In three scenes a Yaxchilan lord strikes a human whose neck is broken and snapped back. The body is bound and tied into the form of a ball, which is then rolled down a flight of stairs. Another scene shows Bird Jaguar preparing to strike his victim, who is identified in a caption within the ball as Jeweled Skull. Jeweled Skull was an important noble taken captive in the most important battle of Bird Jaguar's life. Linda Schele and Mary Ellen Miller (1986) suggest that the image represents a ritual sacrifice acted out in the form of a ball game over which Bird Jaguar presided, both as the predetermined winner of the game and as ritual executioner.

This custom gave the losing king an honorable way out. Rather than face an ignominious end on the battlefield, he would be offered a chance to acquit himself well on the ball court. At the same time, he would ensure that the order of the universe would be maintained by providing food for the gods. As a further enticement, one who ended his life as a human sacrifice could look forward to a glorious afterlife.

Sport is associated with divine warfare in Celtic mythology, in what may be a symbolic account of an early battle for control of the British Isles. The Fir Bolgs, or Men of Bolg, may have been early colonizers of Ireland, perhaps migrating from Iberia, now Spain and Portugal. The Tuatha De Danann were Gaelic gods said to have come from the sky. The battle between them began with a deadly hurling match, in which Tuatha De Danann participants were defeated and killed. The war then began in earnest, and all but 300 of the Fir Bolgs were slain. These courageous warriors demanded man-to-man combat until all were dead, but the Tuatha De Danann refused. Instead, the Gaelic gods offered the Fir Bolgs a fifth part of Ireland, and the Fir Bolgs chose to make their home in Connaught.

The American Indian sport that developed into lacrosse also had a more than passing association with warfare. The game, played from Canada to Florida, and west to the Great Plains, has been described as "halfway between sport and deadly combat" (Oxendine 1988:38). Each player was armed with a racquet, a stick with a curved end interlaced with netting. The racquet was used to catch the ball and throw it between the player's goal posts.

The games were apparently viewed as entertainment for both gods and humans. The Menomini of what is now the Great Lakes region of the United States tell a story of a great game of lacrosse in which all the animals representing the *above* beings (eagles, geese, pigeons, owls, and all other birds) played against all the animals representing the *below* beings (snakes, fish, otters, deer, and all beasts of the forest). One goal was established at what is now Chicago, the other at what is now Detroit. Forgetting himself in the excitement of the game and determined to get revenge because he was not invited, the hero Manabozho intervened on behalf of the *above* beings, firing arrows at the underground gods. As the gods dived into the water trying to escape his arrows, the water overflowed the field. All the animals followed the water to Manabozho, who climbed a tall pine tree in terror. As the waters rose, the tree grew taller until eventually the waters rose no more.

Ball games between rival human teams were preceded by elaborate ceremonies that began the day before, as the teams and their families arrived at the site of the match and set up camp on opposite sides of the playing field. American artist George Catlin (1841) described a scene among the Choctaw that reflects a balance of opposites similar to those expressed in the Chinese poem about soccer. Choctaw women arranged bets as four elders inspected and established the playing field. The elders then went to the center of the field, where they spent all night praying for wisdom and fairness. The ball-play dance began soon after dark when the players and their parties entered the playing field with lighted torches. Each group congregated around its own goal, while the officials remained in the center of the field. Players danced around their goals to drums and chants of the women. They vigorously rattled their lacrosse sticks and sang vociferously. Women also danced and sang, calling upon the Great Spirit to favor their team and urging the players to do their utmost to win.

Players also observed strict taboos. Among the Cherokee of North Carolina, participants refrained from eating rabbit for several weeks prior to major athletic contests to avoid becoming timid and witless like the animal. On the other hand, rabbit symbolism was used against the other team. Players would make a soup of the hamstrings of rabbits and pour it along the trails used by opponents before major games to make the players more vulnerable to defeat.

Cherokee players were not allowed to eat the young of any bird or animal and could not have contact with a human infant for seven days prior to the game. They avoided women during the seven days before and after the game. Any player whose wife was pregnant was not allowed to play because it was believed the man's strength was sapped by the developing child. If a woman touched one of the lacrosse sticks on the eve of the game, it was considered unfit to use.

According to anthropologist Kendall Blanchard (1981), the Choctaw version of the game, called *toli*, played an important part in rivalries, and major sporting encounters often substituted for warfare. When armed conflict threatened, community leaders named a date and location for a game, and selected players and ritual specialists to act as officials. From that day, as much as three to four months before the contest, elaborate preparations would distract the respective communities from their grievances and focus attention on the game itself.

Among the Ojibway, ball games were associated with tests of manliness, and participants were expected to prove their mettle in the game, suffering injury without complaint:

> No one is heard to complain, though he be bruised severely or his nose come in close communion with a club. If the last-mentioned catastrophe befall him, he is up in a trice, and sets his laugh forth as loud as the rest, though it be floated at first on a tide of blood [Copway 1972:570 (1851)].

Players decorated themselves with body paint as though they were going to war, and among some groups, there were other similarities to war. A U.S. military officer, Colonel Marinus Willett, describes a confrontation between two teams among the Muskogee in Georgia:

> The time of their arrival is so contrived, that the parties arrive near the field at the same time; and when they get within about half a mile, in a direction opposite to each other, you hear the sound of the war song and the yell; when presently, the parties appear in full trot, as if fiercely about to encounter in fight ... each player places himself opposite to his antagonist [quoted in Oxendine 1988:45].

The ritual meeting of opposing forces sometimes ended in an actual scuffle. Kendall Blanchard provides a description by the unofficial tribal historian of the Choctaw, Baxter York:

> In coming to the game, the teams would march down the trail, one-by-one, sometimes for as much as fifteen miles.... They would travel down the trail, the drum would beat, and the people would hear them coming. The leader of the group would lead a chant, and the rest of the group would answer with a "Yoo" [1981:30]!

As the two teams met, confrontation became more direct: "The other group that was their competition would meet them about half way, and there would be much shouting back and forth. Sometimes there would be wrestling.... Everyone was getting ready" (Blanchard 1981:30).

A game of lacrosse ended in warfare at Fort Michillimackinac on June 4, 1763. The fort, garrisoned by English troops, stood on what is now Mackinaw City, Michigan. A large number of Ojibway and Sac Indians went to the fort and invited the soldiers to come out to see a lacrosse game. The soldiers left the gates of the fort open while they went outside to watch the game. During the course of play, the ball landed near the open gate of the fort. The players pursued the ball, then dropped their lacrosse rackets and took hatchets from women who had concealed the weapons in their blankets. The athletes quickly became warriors as they killed the soldiers and burned the fort.

Modern soccer games have also been known to end in a form of warfare. British fans are notorious for unruly behavior and are sometimes banned from European competitions. However, they are not the only ones to expand the scope of the contest. The 1969 "Soccer War" between Honduras and El Salvador for the World Cup grew out of tensions that were already rising between the two countries before the matches when Honduras began expelling Salvadorean immigrants. The qualifying rounds of the World Cup are especially important because they are organized regionally. This means that a team from a region such as Central America, which has a number of excellent teams and enthusiastic fans, could be eliminated and never have a chance to play against less skilled teams from less hotly contested regions of the world.

When the Honduras soccer team was defeated in San Salvador, a number of Honduran spectators were set upon and mauled by the crowd. Honduras reacted by stepping up the number of Salvadorean expulsions. El Salvador closed its border to prevent the expulsions, but when this was unsuccessful, sent its troops into Honduras, the opening salvo of the Soccer War.

Sport often acts as a substitute for warfare, but when it fails, the heightened tensions of the game can exacerbate existing rivalries. Athletic contests reinforce group identity, which can either defuse hostilities or accelerate them. Even so, no matter how intensely they are fought, team sports never quite lose the exuberance of children's games, which is what lends them much of their emotional power. It is clear that on some basic level fans understand this, no matter how fervently they support the home team.

The Duel

When U.S. fans sing "Take me out to the ballgame," they are not referring to just any ballgame. The song refers specifically to baseball, which ranks with Mom and apple pie as a symbol of the American way of life. In 1909, President William Howard Taft initiated the custom of having the Chief Executive throw out the first ball of the season, underscoring the place of the game in American life. During the 1950s, the French-American historian and educator Jacques Barzun wrote: "Whoever wants to know the heart and mind of America had better learn baseball, the rules and realities of the game — and do it by watching first some high school or small-town teams."[65]

In one sense at least, the game may accord well with the American sense of fair play. J. A. Cuddon suggests that baseball is unique among major sports in that it is played without a clock, so that a loss cannot be blamed on time running out: "A baseball team that loses has beaten itself, in this sense, and certainly this is fairer than a sport in which the clock can be run out by the team ahead, with the team behind struggling vainly for a chance to score" (1979:90).

Baseball has produced some of the most illustrious of American sports heroes, including the paragon Joe DiMaggio and the champion of all rogues, Babe Ruth. Babe Ruth's career home run record of 714 stood until 1974 and his season total of 60 home runs stood until 1961, but his legend is bolstered almost as much by his personality and flair as by his batting ability. When, at the height of his career during the Great Depression of the 1930's, it was pointed out that he earned more money than U.S. President Herbert Hoover, Babe Ruth replied, "I had a better year than he did." His teammate Lefty Gomez described his style: "He was a circus, a play and a movie, all rolled into one. Kids adored him. Men idolized him. Women loved him. There was something about him that made him great."[66]

Artist Marjorie Phillips captures the essential drama of a baseball game in her paint-ing *Night Baseball.* She has caught the pitcher just before he throws, as all the other players and officials wait their turn for the action. At this moment, the drama is on the pitcher's mound, but the moment the ball is released, the drama shifts to the bat-ter (The Phillips Collection, Gift of the artist 1951 or 1952).

The Sultan of Swat could almost have served as a model for the fictional hero Casey. The real-life baseball player even went so far as to call his shot during the fifth inning of the third game of the 1932 World Series, in what has been called "the most magnificent gesture ever made on a baseball diamond" (Durant and Bettman 1979:239). The drama was heightened by the fact that it took place during a grudge match between the New York Yankees and the Chicago Cubs at their own Wrigley Field. The score was tied at four runs each when Babe Ruth came up to bat for the Yankees. He was greeted by a barrage of abuse from the Chicago bench. He took a strike and then defiantly pointed to the centerfield bleachers. He took another strike and again indicated his target as Cubs players jeered from the bench. On the next pitch, he hammered the ball to the deepest part of the centerfield bleachers, the exact spot he had indicated. Unlike Casey, the mighty Babe Ruth did not strike out.

Since the sport has long been a symbol of the American way of life, a baseball scandal hits particularly hard. A particularly traumatic event took place in 1919, when eight members of the Chicago White Sox conspired with gamblers to throw the World Series to the Cincinnati Reds. The scandal forced a reorganization of the governing body of baseball and produced what may be the most poignant phrase in the history of American sports when a little boy reportedly begged his hero "Shoeless Joe" Jackson, "Say it ain't so, Joe."

Sinclair Lewis cynically draws on the symbolic role of baseball to describe the pettiness of the title character in his novel *Babbitt*: "A sensational event was changing from the brown suit to the gray the contents of his pockets. He was earnest about these objects. They were of eternal importance, like baseball or the Republican Party."

Baseball may reflect national character in that it is one of the most individualistic of team sports. Though cooperation is essential in baseball, as in all team sports, the dynamic of baseball often pits an individual player against a shifting opponent. The batter goes out on the field alone. His most immediate opponent is the pitcher, and baseball is often portrayed as a duel between the batter and pitcher. If he hits the ball, the batter's fate is decided by the catcher, an infielder or an outfielder, depending on the course of the ball. Whether the athlete is at bat, on base, or on the pitcher's mound, he is essentially facing off against an individual player on the opposing team.

Modern baseball often takes the form of a war of nerves, but nineteenth-century games may have been more physically confrontational. One early ball player seems to imply that modern athletes lack the spirit of the old style of play:

> We used no mattress on our hands,
> No cage upon our face;
> We stood right up and caught the ball
> With courage and with grace [quoted in Durant and Bettmann 1979:45].

The origins of baseball are the subject of a debate that hinges on nationalistic fervor. Tradition would have it that baseball is a uniquely American sport, played according to rules drawn up by Abner Doubleday in 1839 in Cooperstown, New York. However, this creation myth probably owes more to national pride than to

Rhoda Sherbell has focused on the individuality of the athlete in her polychromed bronze *Charles Dillon (Casey) Stengel* (1981, from a 1965 plaster model). Stengel made his mark on baseball over a 54-year professional career, first as an athlete and later as a manager. He was elected to the National Baseball Hall of Fame in 1966 (National Portrait Gallery, Smithsonian Institution, Washington, D.C.).

Of all U.S. sports, baseball is considered the epitome of the American way of life, and baseball players are expected to set an example for youth. Robert W. Jensen's water-color *Young Boy and Coach* depicts a moment of instruction as a Little League player looks to his coach for guidance (reproduced by permission of the artist, Robert W. Jensen).

history. A children's reader published in England in 1744 called *A Pretty Little Pocket-Book* represents the letter "B" by the word "Baseball." The accompanying illustration suggests a game very similar to the American version. Since the book was reprinted twice in the United States, it would have been known to American sports aficionados long before baseball was "invented." It appears likely that the great American game is, like much of the country's population, an immigrant.

Baseball is similar to rounders, which may also have given rise to the British sport of cricket. There is no need for Americans to apologize for their chauvinism connected with baseball, however. The British tend to lose their reserve when it comes to cricket. In his monumental work *The International Dictionary of Sports and Games*, The British historian J. A. Cuddon puts aside his generally dispassionate appraisal of sports in this rhapsodic description of cricket:

> An 11-a-side bat-and-ball game the object of which is to score more runs than one's opponents. Less prosaically, it is the High Mass of sport, a sacramental devotion to the gods of skill and chance. It is probably the most complex and arcane recreation and game yet devised by man [1979:233].

Later, Cuddon wittily notes: "The major event towards the close of the 18th c. (apart, of course, from the French Revolution) was the creation of the MARYLE-BONE CRICKET CLUB in 1787-8" (1979:235). Cricket has inspired a number of poets to wax eloquent. R. W. Raper, a Fellow of Trinity College, Oxford, is noted for, among things, his parody of the American poet Walt Whitman. Raper links a number of heroic themes in "The Innings," dedicated to Whitman, from whom Raper draws his inspiration and his meter[67]:

1

To take your stand at the wicket in a posture of haughty
defiance;
To confront a superior bowler as he confronts you;
To feel the glow of ambition, your own and that of your side:
To be aware of shapes hovering, binding, watching around
— white flannelled shapes — all eager, unable to
catch you.

2

The unusually fine weather,
The splendid silent sun flooding all, bathing all in joyous
evaporation.
Far off a gray-brown thrush warbling in hedge or in marsh;
Down there in the blossoming bushes, my brother, what is it
that you are saying?

3

To play more steadily than a pendulum; neither hurrying nor
delaying, but marking the right moment to strike.

4

To slog:

5

The utter oblivion of all but the individual energy:
The rapid co-operation of hand and eye projected into the
ball;
The ball triumphantly flying through the air, you too flying.
The perfect feel of a fourer!
The hurrying to and fro between the wickets: the marvelous
quickness of all the fields:
The cut, leg hit, forward drive, all admirable in their way;
The pull transcending all pulls, over the boundary ropes,
sweeping, orotund, astral:
The superciliousness of standing still in your ground,
content, and masterful, conscious of an unquestioned six;
The continuous pavilion-thunder bellowing after each true
lightening stroke;
(And yet a mournful note, the low dental murmur of one who
blesses not, I fancied I heard through the roar
In a lull of the deafening plaudits;
Could it have been the bowler? Or one of the fields?)

6

Sing on, gray-brown bird, sing on! now I under-stand you!
Pour forth your rapturous chants from flowering hedge in the
marsh,
I follow, I keep time, though rather out of breath.

7

The high perpendicular puzzling hit: the consequent
collision and miss: the faint praise of "well tried."
The hidden delight of some and the loud disappointment of
others.

8

But, O bird of the bursting throat, my dusky demon and
brother,
Why have you paused in your carol so fierce from the
flowering thorn?
Has your music fulfilled the she-bird? (it cannot have lulled her
to sleep:)
Or see you a cloud on the face of the day unusually fine?

9

To have a secret misgiving:
To feel the sharp, sudden rattle of the stumps from behind,

electric, incredible:
To hear the short convulsive clap, announcing all is over.

10

The return to the pavilion, sad, and slow at first: gently
breaking into a run amid a tumult of applause;
The doffing of the cap (without servility) in becoming
acknowledgement;
The joy of what has been and the sorrow for what might
have been mingling madly for the moment in cider-cup.
The ultimate alteration of the telegraph.

11

The game is over; yet for me never over;
For me it remains a memory and meaning wondrous
mystical.
Bat-stroke and bird-voice (tally of my soul) "slog, slog, slog."
The jubilant cry from the flowering thorn to the flowering
willow, "smite, smite, smite."
(Flowerless willow no more — but every run a late-shed
perfect bloom.)
The fierce chant of my demon brother issuing forth against the
demon
bowler, "hit him, hit him, hit him."
The thousand melodious cracks, delicious cracks, the
responsive echoes of my comrades and the hundred
thence-resulting runs, passionately yearned for, never,
never again to be forgotten.
Overhead meanwhile the splendid silent sun, blending all,
fusing all, bathing all in floods of soft ecstatic perspiration.

This delicious poem unites a number of themes expressed in sports symbolism, placing it all in the context of a mystical union with nature, suggested by the "unusually fine" day and the song of the bird hidden in the bushes. It slyly hints at the competition between males and suggests that both the cricket players and the bird are putting on a fine display to win the admiration of onlookers.

When cricket leaves England, it sometimes takes on some interesting variations. The men of the Trobriand Islands in the western Pacific achieved a synthesis of war and sport in their adaptation of cricket. After colonial authorities outlawed warfare in the Trobriands, British missionaries introduced cricket as a substitute. The Islanders adapted the game to conform to their traditional form of warfare, while borrowing some artistic elements from American soldiers stationed in the Pacific during World War II.

Trobriander cricket is organized along lines of village rivalries. During the cultivating season, an entire village works hard planting extra taro and yams for the feasting and gift giving that will accompany the games, which are held during harvest time. The cricket matches are hosted by the village headman, who invites a team from a rival community. Teams are identified by names such as the "Tapiocas," or "Airplanes," which identify themes dramatically expressed in their body decorations, as well as in their dances and war chants. "Tapiocas" refers to a cash crop produced in the Islands. Since the Trobrianders associate the tapioca root with the male sex organ, chants and dances of the "Tapiocas" are enlivened by graphic sexual allusions and gestures. The name "Airplanes" hearkens back to occupation of the Islands by U.S. troops during World War II. When arriving on the playing field, members of the "Airplanes" team spread their arms wide in imitation of airplane wings and mimic the sounds of aircraft. Taking their cue from the marching rhythms of U.S. troops, Trobriander teams march in formation and chant the syllable "Hup" (as in "Hup, two, three) as they enter and leave the playing field.

The host team must always win, and there is no limit to the number of players on a team. British rules for the game specify eleven players to a side, but Trobriand teams may include as many as forty to sixty players, as many as would have traditionally taken part in warfare. Everyone connected with the game — from players to spectators to umpires — tries to influence the outcome with magic. Traditional magic used to guide war spears to their target is now applied to aiding the performance of the bat. There is no magic to help in catching the ball, since spears were not caught in warfare. However, Trobrianders used magic for their hands to help them guide the spear; they now use that magic to help them throw the ball.

Trobrianders feel their form of cricket is more interesting than the more conventional British form of the game. Innovations introduced by Trobrianders allow them to continue their traditional rivalries and social relationships unchecked and permit them to imprint their own distinctive stamp onto a sport that ordinarily reflects a British form of nationalism. However, it is unlikely that Trobriander cricket will ever be adopted by that bastion of sporting orthodoxy, the Marylebone Cricket Club.

Part 4. The Adversary Within

Six

Transcending Time and Space

> I can think of no better way to say it — those final holes played me.
> Michael Murphy, *Golf in the Kingdom*

In his book *Golf in the Kingdom*, Michael Murphy describes his encounter with a mystical golf instructor named Shivas Irons, whose approach to golf seems to transcend ordinary conceptions of space and time:

> 'Tis amazin' to me how these forms, these bodies, these ideas float in this emptiness … strange gravity," he said the words, then he cleared his throat. We looked at each other through the subtle presence that filled the room. "Just kites in that wind," he said with that bucktoothed grin and slowly stretched as he rose from his chair.[68]

Murphy gives the name Links of Burningbush to the legendary golf course that gave rise to the encounter, but afficionados of golf recognize it as St. Andrews, the spiritual home of golf in Scotland:

> In Scotland, between the Firth of Forth and the Firth of Tay, lies the Kingdom of Fife — known to certain lovers of that land simply as "The Kingdom." There, on the shore of the North Sea, lies a golfing links that shimmers in my memory — an innocent stretch of heather and grassy dunes that cradled the unlikely events which grew into this book.[69]

Though Murphy's ostensible opponent was the golf course, it becomes clear during his "course" of instruction that that Murphy's true opponent lies within, in his obsession with besting the legendary golf course by hitting par:

> Shivas came over to me then and put a big hand on my shoulder. "Dona' worry about the score so much," he said, "it's not the important thing." He squeezed my shoulder and turned back to MacIver with more instructions. Not the important thing, I thought as he walked away, not the important thing! I was touched by his reaching out — and dumfounded.[70]

Shivas' advice to Murphy would resonate with professional athletes, who avoid mentioning the score during a game or speculating on its outcome. They know that a seemingly certain victory can be snatched away by subsequent events in the game and that anticipating the outcome distracts them from playing the game (Womack 1982). As Murphy describes it, Shivas seems to be saying that obsessing over the score was preventing Murphy from playing his real game of golf, against the adversary within ourselves.

Though he cautioned Murphy about obsessing over the score, Shivas was exacting about the need to keep score carefully, to play by the rules of the game: "Ye must remember that ye're in the land where all these rools were invented. 'Tis the only way ue can play in the kingdom." Murphy adds, "I have thought of that line many times, "the only way you can play in the kingdom." I didn't fully appreciate it at first. Not until I realized that for him the Kingdom of Fife was very nearly the Kingdom of Heaven."[71]

Walking on Water

At another time and another place, Jesus Christ demonstrated his mastery over the physical world by walking upon the Sea of Galilee. He is one of the few who succeeded in transcending the limitations of time and space, though this is a pervasive theme in the heroic literature. Many have tried and failed. The most dramatic example is Icarus, son of the master craftsman of Greek mythology, Daedalus.

Daedalus constructed the wooden cow that allowed Pasiphaë, wife of King Minos of Crete, to have unlawful intercourse with a bull, and he built the labyrinth to house the monstrous offspring of that union, the Minotaur. Minos later refused the craftsman's request to leave Crete with his son Icarus and return to his home in Athens. Daedalus spelled out the dimensions of that contest of wills by saying:

> Though Minos owns this island, rules the waves,
> The skies are open: my direction's clear.
> Though he commands all else on earth below
> His tyranny does not control the air [Ovid, *Metamorphoses*, Book VIII].

Daedalus constructed wings of wax and feathers and instructed Icarus in the arts of flying, cautioning him to steer a middle course between the sea and the sun. Those who chanced to see Daedalus and Icarus soar above the island of Crete — a fisherman, a shepherd and a farmer — took them for gods, since they were challenging the heavens as only the gods can. But Icarus became intoxicated by the delights of flying and soared too close to the sun. His wax wings melted and he fell to his death.

There is an essential lesson in the stories of Jesus and of Icarus: Before challenging the limits of nature, one must first gain control over oneself. Jesus' mastery over nature is but the external manifestation of his mastery of himself. Icarus, on the other hand, raced greedily toward the sun because he lacked control over himself.

This lesson is expressed in stories about the life of the Bodhidharma, or Da Mo, who is credited with founding both the Zen and kung-fu traditions at the Shaolin monastery in China. According to legend, after Da Mo had meditated for nine years before the wall of a cave in the mountain where the Shaolin monastery is located, his shadow became engraved on the stone. Da Mo developed kung-fu movements to keep his body limber during his long hours of meditation. One day when Da Mo was meditating, he was visited by a poor and sickly young man named Ji Guang, who wanted to become his student. When Ji Guang arrived at the mouth of the cave, he watched the great monk meditate for several hours, afraid to enter and disturb him. At last the Bodhidharma emerged from the cave and began his physical training, several hours of rigorous thrusts and parries, punctuated by ear-splitting yells. Then, ignoring the young man, Da Mo re-entered the cave and sat down on a wooden bed. Ji Guang entered the cave and, bowing deeply before the great man, begged to be accepted as his student. The monk replied, "If you can pull me off this bed, only then will I teach you."

The young man pulled at Da Mo with all his might, but could not move him so much as a centimeter. When at last Ji Guang gave up, the Bodhidharma got off the bed saying, "I don't teach weaklings. Go back home. Do the exercises I did just now, and when you have perfected them you can come back. If you can pull me off this bed, then I'll pass my knowledge on to you."

Ji Guang went home and practiced for a year, learning and perfecting the techniques the Bodhidharma had shown him, and even inventing some of his own. He returned to the monk, who once again sat on the bed. Gathering his *qi*, or spiritual forces, Ji Guang grabbed Da Mo's collarbone with one hand and, with the other, banged on the head of the bed. At the same time, he yelled at the top of his voice and pulled the startled monk off the bed. Furious, Da Mo raised his massive fist to smash Ji Guang. At the same time, the young man reached over the side of the bed and pulled out its supports. The bed collapsed and Da Mo's fist passed harmlessly over Ji Guang's head. Without saying a word, Da Mo picked Ji Guang up from the floor and nodded once.

Just then, a flock of crows landed in the pear tree outside the cave and began to peck at the pears. "Go, get rid of them," Da Mo ordered Ji Guang. The young man walked over to the tree, flapping his hands and shouting. The birds flew away, but came back as soon as Ji Guang turned away from them. Without saying a word or leaving the cave, the Bodhidharma raised his arm and flicked his hand outward. This caused a cool wind to blow out from the cave toward the pear tree, frightening the birds so they did not return. Da Mo then said to Ji Guang, "Go home and train some more."

Ji Guang trained for more than a year, practicing the moves the monk showed him, as well as inventing new ones. When he returned, he found Da Mo in the hall of the monastery. As Ji Guang bowed in greeting, two sparrows flew into the room and landed on top of the shrine, where they sat twittering loudly. Da Mo was raising his hand to frighten the birds away when Ji Guang leaped into the air and grasped the swallows in his hands. The monk nodded twice and instructed the young man. "Wait over there for a while and I will teach you." Da Mo then took up his meditations and Ji Guang went outside to stand by a pine tree and wait.

As the young man waited, the snow began to fall, and he kept himself warm by practicing his exercises. For two days the snow grew deeper and deeper around Ji Guang, and ice accumulated in an enormous mass in the tree over his head. Only the area immediately around him remained free of snow and ice. On the third day, the ice in the tree broke and fell. Ji Guang neatly sidestepped it and caught it in his arms. With a powerful twist, he sent it flying into the rafters over Da Mo's head. The chunk of ice broke apart and fell in a shower around the monk, startling him out of his meditation. Da Mo went outside and discovered Ji Guang standing in his snow-free area, surrounded by banks of snow and ice. Nodding three times, the Bodhidharma said, "I bestow on you the religious name Hui Ke. From today you shall be my first disciple at the Shaolin monastery."[72]

After his initial confrontation with the Bodhidharma, all of Ji Guang's tests were against an opponent in nature. His preparation for these engagements involved a long process of learning self-control, even as he honed his physical skills. His teacher had already learned these lessons. The Bodhidharma could control nature because he had first mastered himself.

Humans have long aspired to conquer time, to soar through the air, to glide over the waves. They are seeking to transcend the limitations of their own bodies and minds. For those who actually make the effort, the greatest obstacles to overcome are the baser elements of one's own character. This is the essential dynamic of sports, as addressed in this chapter. In activities addressed in earlier chapters, humans have contended against the adversary in nature and the human antagonist. This chapter reintroduces the theme of contesting with nature, but in this case the object is not to kill her or even, in most cases, to defeat her. Rather, it is to challenge the prowess and courage of human beings. In these sports, there is a winner but no loser. In sports of transcendence, the outward challenge is but the external manifestation of that most formidable of all opponents — the enemy within.

Racing through Time

"Let us run with patience the race that is set before us" (Hebrews 12:1). The Apostle Paul was not alone in comparing the spiritual life to a race. Nor was he the first. The Nineteenth Psalm of the Bible celebrates the triumph of the word of the Lord: "Which *is* as a bridegroom coming out of his chamber, *and* rejoiceth as a strong man to run a race" (19:5). Writing in the sixth century B.C.E., the Greek writer of fables Aesop used the race as a metaphor to caution against overconfidence. His fable "The Tortoise and the Hare" contains the line, "Slow and steady wins the race."

The Upanishads, Hindu sacred scriptures dating from between 800 and 400

B.C.E. draw on the symbolism of the chariot race. The *Katha Upanishad*, which contains one of the first references to the doctrine of rebirth, compares spiritual striving with driving a chariot:

> Know that the Self (Atman) is the rider, and the body the chariot; that the intellect is the charioteer, and the mind the reins.
> The senses, say the wise, are the horses; the roads they travel are the mazes of desire. The wise call the Self the enjoyer when he is united with the body, the senses, and the mind.
> When a man lacks discrimination and his mind is uncontrolled, his senses are unmanageable, like the restive horses of a charioteer. But when a man has discrimination and his mind is controlled, his senses, like the well-broken horses of a charioteer, lightly obey the rein.
> He who lacks discrimination, whose mind is unsteady and whose heart is impure, never reaches the goal, but is born again and again. But he who has discrimination, whose mind is steady and whose heart is pure, reaches the goal, and having reached it is born no more.
> The man who has a sound understanding for a charioteer, a controlled mind for reins — he it is that reaches the end of the journey, the supreme abode of Vishnu, the all-pervading.[73]

The horse and chariot were of great symbolic importance to the authors of the *Upanishads*, who may have been descendents of Scythian (often called Aryan) invaders who swept down and overran the settled people of the Indus Valley. The invaders fought using horse and chariot, raiding settlements and capturing cattle for a prize. The horse was virtually revered by them and was at times sacrificed. Hymn 1.163 of the *Rg Veda*, dating from as early as 2000 B.C.E., sings the praises of the horse:

> The chariot follows you, Swift Runner; the young man follows, the cow follows, the love of young girls follows. The troops follow your friendship. The gods entrusted virile power to you. His mane is golden; his feet are bronze. He is swift as thought, faster than Indra [the most powerful of the gods].

Scholars once thought that the early Vedic scriptures were entirely products of the Scythian invasion. However, it is clear from their symbolism that both the settled agricultural traditions of Indus Valley dwellers and the nomadic horse tradition are represented in these texts. Cow sacrifice, discussed in Chapter Three, was probably already well-developed in the Indus Valley by the time the Scythians arrived.

The chariot race unites both traditions. In the race, which is reminiscent of raids and the seizing of cattle from settled people, cattle were often given as a prize. Uniting these two vigorous symbols — the horse and the cow — makes for rich metaphorical transformations. The contest repeatedly referred to in the Rg Veda can be a battle — metaphysical or mundane — or it can be a race. The race itself may take place in the cosmic realm or on earth.

It is evident that the obscuring of conceptual boundaries is deliberate, since it forms much of the basis for the imagery of the Rg Veda. The milk of the cow given as a prize is a metaphor for immortality. Hymn 3.31 of the Rg Veda beseeches the most powerful of the gods: "Soon, Indra, soon, make us winners of cows." This prayer can be interpreted, and was almost certainly intended, on several levels: Make us victors among men; make us more like you, O powerful one; and bring us immortality.

Milk is associated with seed, semen and rain, all life-giving forms. Hymn 10.102 of the Rg Veda describes a race in which a woman was the victorious charioteer: "The wind whipped up her robe when she mounted the chariot and won a thousand cows. For Mudgala's wife was the charioteer in the contest for cattle; becoming the very army of Indra, she gambled and won the spoils." Multiple imagery is engaged here. Scythian women were formidable warriors, and it seems likely they were also fierce competitors in horse races. The incident may also evoke fertility, or it may be a symbolic description of an erotic episode, since the woman's chariot is drawn by a bull with heavy testicles yoked to another bull by means of a wooden club.

Hymn 1.50 of the Rg Veda describes the Sun, Surya, as a charioteer: "You cross heaven and the vast realm of space, O sun, measuring days by nights, looking upon the generations. Seven bay mares carry you in the chariot, O sun god with hair of flame, gazing from afar."

Chariot races may have been held at religious festivals in Babylon and other parts of the Middle East. In Greek tradition the chariot race was the first event in the funeral games for Patroclus, slain in the battle at Troy. Patroclus' friend Achilles organized the race, and five warriors competed. The first prize was a woman and a cauldron, both captured at Troy. In this race, the best man did not win, due to the intervention of the gods. Eumelus, a skillful driver with fast horses, was in first place with Diomedes close behind when Apollo struck the second place driver's whip out of his hand. This infuriated Athene, who restored Diomedes' whip to him and inspired his horses to greater effort. She also avenged herself on Achilles by wrecking Eumelus' chariot. The hapless driver was thrown from his vehicle and suffered a number of minor injuries.

The race appears to have been a lesson in sportsmanship for Antilochus, son of Nestor, ruler of Pylos. Before the race Nestor advised his son that, if he wanted to win, he must rely on strategy since his horses were not the best. In a contest for second place with Menelaus, husband of Helen, Antilochus threatened his horses with death if they failed to overtake his opponent. Menelaus led as they entered a narrow gully, but slowed down to avoid a crash. Antilochus, seizing the moment and risking death or dismemberment, raced around Menelaus to capture second prize.

The last to arrive at the finish line was Eumelus, on foot, dragging his broken chariot behind him and driving his horses in front of him. Achilles pitied him and wanted to award him second prize, a mare in foal, but Antilochus vehemently protested:

"My lord Achilles," he cried, "I shall resent it keenly if you do as you suggest. You are proposing to rob me of my prize because Eumelus' chariot and horses came to grief—as did Eumelus, though he drives so well. The fact is that he ought to have prayed to the immortal gods; then he would never have come in last in the race."

Achilles laughed and awarded Eumelus a bronze breastplate which he had captured at Troy. Affronted by Antilochus' lack of sportsmanship, Menelaus remembered his own grievance. He accused Antilochus of winning by cunning and insisted that the second prize should be his. Antilochus apologized and offered Menelaus the prize. Touched, Menelaus cautioned Antilochus about using trickery in the future and refused his prize, taking instead the third prize of a cauldron.

The funeral games for Patroclus also included the footrace, with a first prize of a famous and magnificent silver bowl. Again, the outcome was decided by the gods. Ajax the Runner led most of the way, closely followed by Odysseus, who was older than most of the competitors. As they drew near the finish, Odysseus prayed to Athene, and the goddess came to his aid. She lightened all his limbs so he could run faster and caused Ajax to fall into a pile of cow dung. Spitting out dung as he claimed his second-place prize, Ajax exclaimed, "Damnation take it! I swear it was the goddess tripped me up — the one who always dances attendance, like a mother, on Odysseus."

The footrace is sometimes considered the most noble of modern Olympic events, and this may have been true of the ancient Games as well. The Olympic program included four races. The shortest at 200 yards, the *stade* was the most prestigious footrace, and Olympiads were referred to by the winner of the *stade*. Pindar's eleventh Pythian Ode, to Thrasydaios of Thebes, winner of the boys' footrace in 474 B.C.E., praises both the triumphs of the day and the exploits of the young man's forebears, winners of the chariot race:

> Now to the father Pythonikos
> and now to Thrasydaios, the son –
> > their liberality
> and reputation burn bright for all to see.
> In their victorious chariots, long ago they caught
> the glancing ray of fame from contests at Olympia.
>
> and at Pythos, stepping down
> > stripped for the races, they silenced
> > all Hellas by their speed.

The marathon was not a part of Greek athletics, but of warfare, and it has long been a symbol of total commitment to a cause. The origins of this event are shrouded in myth. According to Herodotus, when the Persians landed at Marathon in 490 B.C.E. on their way to attack Athens, the Athenians sent off the runner Pheidippides to summon help from the Spartans. The runner reportedly covered the 160 miles

Footracing was considered by the Greeks to be one of the more noble sports, as is still true for the modern Olympics. This Greek vase displays the strength and grace of foot racers (British Museum).

along a mountainous route in less than 48 hours. According to a much later story by Plutarch, an Athenian named Eucles returned to his home from abroad after the army had marched out to Marathon. Eucles ran out to fight in the battle, then ran back to Athens to announce the victory. After delivering his joyous news, Eucles died, not from injuries on the battlefield, but at the end of a triumphant race against time. That legend was commemorated in the first modern Olympics held at Athens in 1896. Those Games included a race from Marathon to Athens, a distance of 24 miles.

Women participated in foot races at Olympia, though not as a part of the men's events, nor were women allowed to observe the men's events. Instead, unmarried girls raced in the festival to Hera, the sister and wife of Zeus. Olive wreaths were awarded to the victors, who were allowed to erect statues of themselves, as were male athletes. Women also raced war chariots. Female victors won the respect of their male compatriots, as recorded in a number of inscriptions. One inscription dedicated to the Pythian Apollo reads, "Hermesianax son of Dionysius, citizen of Caesarea Tralles and also of Corinth, erected these statues of his daughters who themselves also hold the same citizenships" (Harris 1964:180). Another inscription

Alfred Boucher uses an image of three runners as a symbol of noble striving in his bronze *Au But! (To the Goal)*. This work may have contributed to the enthusiasm for establishing the modern Olympics when it was exhibited in France in the latter part of the nineteenth century. (Reprinted by permission of National Art Museum of Sport, Indianapolis, Indiana.)

from Delphi bears the legend, "I, Nicophilus, erected this statue of Parian marble to my beloved sister Nicegora, victor in the girls' race" (Harris 1964: 181). Perhaps because the runner competes against a field and no opponent is singled out as the "loser," racing represents an unselfish ethic of competition.

    Foot racing played a multi-faceted role among Native American groups. Prior to introduction of the horse by the Spanish in the sixteenth century, runners were required for war, trade, hunting and delivery of messages. Ancient Peruvians used a well-organized system of cross-country relay teams to deliver fresh seafood to the capital at Inca, located high in the Andes.

Delivery of messages by runners appears to have been quite efficient, and there are numerous reports of prodigious running feats by Native Americans. Within 24 hours of Hernan Cortes' landing on the east coast of what is now Mexico in May, 1519, local runners had described his ship, men, horses and guns to Moctezuma at Tenochtitlán, 260 miles away.

Secret running societies throughout the Americas promoted communication and trade. Ceremonial runners among the Mesquakie in Iowa took a vow of celibacy, adhered to strict dietary rules and dedicated their lives to running. The Senecas of New York had runners who represented the clans in races at religious festivals.

Native American groups in the Southwest and Tarahumara (or Raramuri) Indians from northern Mexico competed in a ball race, running at great speed while kicking a wooden ball along in front of them. These races appear to have had religious significance, and they certainly reflected clan affiliation. Both men and women participated. Zuni runners painted the symbol of their matrilineal clan on their chests and that of their father's clan on their back. The ball was believed to hold magical power that pulled the runner along with it.

The Tarahumara are still known as famous runners. In fact, the name Tarahumara may be translated as "foot runners." Their kick-ball race often lasted for two days and was lighted by torches. The event typically took place in the spring after planting. It was part of religious festivities and was preceded by a ritual that began the night before and lasted through most of the night and the following morning. The ceremonies were normally subdued and prayerful, and participants looked for omens to predict the outcome of the race. Seeing lightning bolts or shooting stars virtually guaranteed success, whereas hearing an owl was a bad omen and could cause the race to be postponed. The runners sought magical help before competing. The shaman, a ritual specialist, washed the feet of participants with warm water and herbs and helped to guard them against sorcery. A loss was always attributed to sorcery.

Footraces formed part of the mythology of the Blackfoot Indians. One such story pits the trickster hero Coyote against Old Man, who created the Blackfoot people and taught them to hunt. Old Man challenges Coyote to a footrace. On the day of the race, Coyote appears with one leg tied up and begs to be excused from competing because he is lame, but Old Man insists on going through with the race as planned. After much argument, Coyote says, "All right, but just for a short run." Old Man refuses, saying, "You agreed to a longer race, and it is just your bad luck that you are lame." After the race begins, Coyote continues to plead with Old Man to wait for him because of the great pain in his leg. As they arrive at the half-way point, Coyote suddenly takes off his bandages and runs the remaining distance, leaving Old Man far behind.

A legend among the Sioux attributes relations among the species to the outcome of a race. Many years ago, the "two-leggeds" of the earth, including humans and birds, competed against the "four-leggeds" in a great race that "circled the hoop of the earth." There was a great deal at stake in the event since, if the four-leggeds won, they would henceforth eat the two-leggeds. On the other hand, if the two-leggeds won, they could feed off the four-leggeds.

When the race began, the participants began running with all their might, but one wise bird, the magpie, hitched a ride by sitting on the ear of a bison bull. The race was hotly contested, and the lead changed many times between the two sides, as the magpie sat patiently on the ear of the bison and waited. Near the end of the race, a great rainstorm weighted down the wings of the birds so they could barely fly, so they fell far behind. The birds were the only real hope for the two-leggeds, since humans could not hope to compete against the mighty four-legged runners. As the four-leggeds drew near the finish line, they began celebrating a little prematurely. The magpie, who had been waiting for this moment, rose from the bison's ear and easily flew across the finish line ahead of all the four-leggeds. The Voice of Thunder proclaimed the magpie the winner, saying, "By thinking, you have won the race for all your relatives, the two-leggeds. Hereafter you shall wear the rainbow in your tail, and it shall be a sign of victory."

Wisdom assured a footracing victory for the elephant-headed Hindu god Ganesha, son of Śiva and Pārvatī. Ganesha and his brother Kārttikeya held a race to see who could most quickly circle the earth three times. Kārttikeya immediately began to run around the earth. When he returned, he found Ganesha still lounging where Kārttikeya had left him. Kārttikeya then ran quickly around the earth once again, only to find that Ganesha still had not moved from his place. Confident of victory, Kārttikeya began a third journey around the earth, but Ganesha rose and ran three times around his parents, explaining, "My parents are the world." As a reward for understanding the true nature of things, Śiva awarded Ganesha the honor of being worshipped before any other deity and before any important event. Thus, as the opener of significant events, Ganesha is known as the remover of obstacles.

Although the chariot race and the foot race have captured the romantic imagination, humans have employed many other vehicles to convey them at great speed over the earth's surface. Chariot racing may have given rise to horse racing, which may also have emerged out of the need for couriers in war. Perhaps because they could be bearers of death or messengers of death in warfare mysterious horsemen often seem to signify bad news. In the Book of Revelations (6:8), Death is seen as a horseman: "Behold a pale horse: and his name that sat on him was Death, and Hell followed with him." The Four Horsemen of the Apocalypse bear the names Famine, Pestilence, Destruction and Death. Biblical accounts may reflect the historical invasion of the Scythians from the Ukrainian plains, but the aura of death continues to surround the mysterious horseman. In the short story by Washington Irving, "The Legend of Sleepy Hollow," the schoolteacher Ichabod Crane meets a headless horseman on a lonely road at night.

According to Blackfoot legend, a dispute over a horse race led to resumption of hostilities between the Snake and Piegan tribes. After years of warfare, the two groups had made peace and the elders went back to their respective villages after a ritual observance of the peace, but some young men stayed behind to gamble. They decided to wrap up their games with a horse race. Each side was represented by a good swift horse, and they finished so close together it was impossible to determine who won:

The Snakes claimed that their horse won, and the Piegans would not allow it. So they got angry and began to quarrel, and pretty soon they began to fight and shoot at each other, and some were killed. Since that time the Snakes and Piegans have never been at peace [Grinnell 1917:12].

Horseracing has been an important sport in England for centuries and may date back to Celtic times. It is said that races were held at the festival of Lugh the sun-god on the first day of August. Manannan, the son of the sea-god Ler, owned a horse called "Splendid Mane," which raced at great speed over land and over the waves of the sea.

Modern horseracing has dual and somewhat contradictory associations. On the one hand, "playing the horses" has unsavory connotations, evoking images of working class men squandering their earnings. At the same time, horse racing is the "sport of kings," attracting the upper classes, both as bettors and as connoisseurs of magnificent animals.

Skating and Social Responsibility

Ice skating is the scene for acting out various forms of social responsibility in Mary Mapes Dodge's account of *Hans Brinker or the Silver Skates*. The story centers on a brother and sister in Holland who are economically impoverished, but rich in compassion and generosity. Hans and his sister Gretel are superb ice skaters, but are too poor to buy skates to compete for the prize in a race, silver skates. The story extols the nobility of sacrifice for others, suggesting that such generosity is ultimately rewarded.

Hans sells his skates to buy food for his father, who is semi-comatose after a work accident in which he fell from scaffolding during a storm, while he working to secure a segment of the elaborate system of dykes and sluices that prevented Holland from being engulfed by the sea. Significantly, the accident resulted from the father's dedication to meeting his social responsibilities, rather than from his own carelessness or lack of responsibility.

Hans' own dedication to social responsibilities, as well as his wood carving skill, earn the money to buy Gretel and himself skates to enter the race. But his "luck" results from the generosity of two members of the elite class, Hilda and her friend Peter, who deliberately buy Hans' hand-carved wooden necklaces to enable him to enter the race. After Hans sells his skates to benefit his father, they are returned to him through the kindness and generosity of a peasant girl named Annie, who later becomes his wife.

Because of Hans' virtuous ways, a dour old doctor is persuaded to treat the father for free, restoring him to health. When the father regains consciousness, he remembers a watch entrusted to him before his accident. Through the years, his faithful wife has respected his wishes to keep the watch, though she could have sold it to buy food for them all. Her loyalty — to her husband and to her word — is

Whereas the English artists such as George Stubbs painted portraits of horses, French artists such as Edouard Manet and Edgar Degas are less interested in rendering the horse with technical accuracy than in capturing the sensation of movement. Degas' bronze *Horse and Jockey, Horse Galloping, Turning the Head to the Right, the Feet Not Touching the Ground* focuses on the movement of body and leg. Degas finely models the horse's flank and forelegs, while permitting distortion of the animal's head and rendering the jockey into anonymity (The Metropolitan Museum of Art, Bequest of Mrs. H. O. Havemeyer, 1929. The H. O. Havemeyer Collection).

Robert W. Jensen's youthful skaters glide with ease around a carefully constructed composition. The relaxed confidence of these young skaters contrasts markedly with the same artist's intense representations of ice hockey players (reproduced by permission of the artist, Robert W. Jensen).

rewarded. Through an inscription on the watch, the doctor's long-lost son is restored to him. As a reward, the doctor provides Hans with the opportunity to become a doctor by paying his way through medical school and later hiring Hans as his own apprentice:

> Were you in Amsterdam to-day, you might see the famous Doctor Brinker riding in his grand coach to visit his patients; or, it might be, you would see him skating with his own boys and girls upon the frozen canal. For Annie Bouman, the beautiful, frank-hearted peasant girl, you would inquire in vain; but Annie Brinker, the vrouw [wife] of the great physician, is very like her — only, as Hans says, she is even lovelier, wiser, more like a fairy godmother than ever.[74]

In this story, virtue is rewarded through a network of social relationships. Because the doctor generously treats Hans' father, he regains his son; because Hans' mother resists the pragmatic impulse to sell the watch, she is able to repay the doctor's generosity.

Hans and his sister compete in the race for the silver skates, and Gretel wins the women's prize. However, Hans gives his skate strap to a faster skater, Peter, who has broken his own strap. Through Hans' generosity, Peter wins the race, and as a result of his own kind heart, he wins the beautiful Hilda as his bride. True to nineteenth-century American morality, virtue is rewarded by material gain, and lack of virtue results in material loss. The story has a happy ending for almost all those who displayed kindness and generosity, but fate was not so kind to an arrogant rich boy:

> Carl Schummel has had a hard life. His father met with reverses in business; and as Carl had not many warm friends, and above all, was not sustained by noble principles, he has been tossed about by Fortune's battledore until his gayest feathers are nearly all knocked off.

Even in describing Carl's misfortune, Mary Mapes Dodge cannot resist the sporting metaphor, in this case, the metaphor of badminton.

Scaling the Heights

> Kilimanjaro is a snow covered mountain 19,710 feet high, and is said to be the highest mountain in Africa. It western summit is called the Masai "Ngàje Ngài," the House of God. Close to the Western summit there is the dried and frozen carcass of a leopard. No one has explained what the leopard was seeking at that altitude.[76]

As Ernest Hemingway's preface to his short story "The Snows of Kilimanjaro" suggests, mountain-climbing is virtually synonymous with some type of quest. The activity is often considered the ultimate human challenge. The poet William Blake asserted:

> Great things are done when men and mountains meet;
> This is not done by jostling in the street.[77]

The acclaimed and controversial mountain climber Walter Bonatti was a boy in Italy as tensions mounted toward WWII. After the war, Bonatti notes, "There were hard times ... for a boy with no prospects facing life in a defeated country" (2001:3). He escaped from the tribulations of everyday life by trips to the mountains: "When I was a child I used to get away from home on one pretext or another during the school vacations and go where I could watch the eagles fly" (2001:3). For Bonatti, the flight of the eagles is a metaphor for transcendence. After his first climbs on the Grigna Peaks near his home, he became a devotee of mountain climbing:

> I was now devoted heart and soul to rock faces, to overhangs, to the intimate joy of trying to overcome my own weaknesses in a struggle that committed me to the very limits of the possible. More than that, I came to know the satisfaction of passing where others had not been able to go. In a sort of direct communion between thought and action I discovered more and more about my own powers, my own limits. Perhaps I was repaying myself for what life had denied me in other ways, but it became clearer to me how up there, in direct contact with unsullied nature in an uncomplicated environment, I felt alive, free, and fulfilled — more and more every day. In this way I was discovering adventure, rich in everything that uplifts and exalts humanity. Above all, I was discovering my way of life [2001:5].

In a song from the film *Sound of Music*, the Trapp family governess, played by Julie Andrews, advises her charges: "Climb every mountain; ford every stream." In other words, meet and conquer all of life's challenges. Mountain-climbing is important as a symbol not only because it is difficult, but because the rewards are intrinsic, rather than extrinsic. When George Mallory, a member of the first three expeditions attempting to scale Mount Everest, was asked why he climbed the mountain, he replied, "Because it's there." Mountain-climbing symbolizes the ultimate in disinterested achievement.

The dedicated naturalist John Muir worked hard to preserve the natural landscape. On a wilderness trek through the forests with Theodore Roosevelt in 1904, Muir persuaded the U.S. President to set aside much of the Sierras as a national park. Muir's notes written on a trek through the Sierras in 1869, when the naturalist was just 31 years old, describe his reverential awe at the splendor of Cathedral Rock:

> No feature, ... of all the noble landscape as seen from her seems more wonderful than the Cathedral itself, a temple displaying Nature's best masonry and sermons in stones. How often I have gazed at it from the tops of hills and ridges, and through openings in the forests on my many short excursions, devoutly wondering, admiring, longing! This I may say is the first time I have been at church in California, led here at last, every door graciously opened for the poor lonely worshiper. In our best times everything turns into religion, all the world seems a church and the

mountains altars. And lo, here at last in front of the Cathedral is blessed cassiope [a mountain plant], ringing her thousands of sweet-toned bells, the sweetest church music I ever enjoyed [1998:250].

As Muir's writing indicates, he did not set out to conquer nature, but to worship at her feet.

There is a widespread sense that the mountain is itself sacred. Greek gods were believed to live on Mt. Olympus, where they were presided over by Zeus. In Japan, Mt. Fuji is an important deity in the Shinto religion and is regarded as a guardian of the nation. Fujiyama[78] is devoted to the worship of Kono-hana-sakuyahime-no-mikoto, consort of the legendary great grandfather of the first emperor of Japan. Pilgrims may ascend the mountain only after purification of the body and mind. A classical eighth-century poem by Yamabe No Akahito, a deified poet in the court of Emperor Shomu, expresses the eternal mystery of the mountain:

> On Fujiyama
> Under the midsummer moon
> The snow melts, and falls
> Again the same night.[79]

In Judaic tradition, Yahweh chose Mt. Sinai to make his covenant with Israel and deliver his law in the form of tablets to Moses. A passage in the Book of Isaiah exhorts: "Get thee up into the high mountain ... say unto the cities of Judah, Behold your God!" (40:9) Both the Bodhidharma and Muhammad, the founder of Islam, meditated in caves on mountainsides. Muhammad received the call to be a prophet for Allah while meditating in a cave on Mt. Hira, now called *Jabal al-nur* (Mountain of Light).

Mountain-climbing has produced a number of flamboyant figures, not the least of which was George Mallory, who was known in England as the "golden boy" and as "Sir Galahad." Sir Edmund Hillary of New Zealand achieved a form of immortality when he reached the crest of Mt. Everest with his Sherpa guide Tenzing. Sir Edmund Hillary's feat has great symbolic significance because he scaled the highest mountain on earth, but height is not the only consideration in mountain-climbing. Enthusiasts also assess the degree of difficulty in making a particular assent, and much more subtly, style.

Modern climbers often use what are called "siege tactics" to scale mountains. This involves a series of climbs from a base camp, each pushing farther than the last. On each attempt, climbers leave fixed ropes from which they launch their next foray. The British sports historian J. A. Cuddon considers this strategy to be of dubious ethics: "Many think that pure rock climbs should not be sieged; others that there should be no sieging of any kind" (1979:554). Cuddon implies that sieging is an American corruption of the sport. Though he objects to the scaling of mountains by a series of controlled stages, Cuddon strongly supports innovations in technology and medicine:

The scientific and medical knowledge acquired over the years has been of enormous benefit in the development of more efficient and more sophisticated equipment. It has also enabled climbers to learn more and more about what the human body is capable of in extreme and hazardous conditions [1979:554–555].

Cuddon's negative view of sieging reflects some ironies in the symbolism and social context of sport. Attainment of some desired goal is not enough to be considered "sporting." The athlete must follow the rules, even when they are not explicitly stated. Sport by its very nature is defined by rules. It is not "sporting" to climb the mountain in the easiest possible way. Cuddon almost seems to suggest that this is cheating. According to this view, one must meet the mountain on its own terms, *mano a mano*, as it were. The very term "sieging" suggests a conquest, and Cuddon's disdain of this tactic is based on the idea that it is dishonorable to take unfair advantage of a worthy opponent.

Proponents of "sieging" could find equal justification for their cause. They could argue that strategy is an important part of sport, and that outflanking a formidable opponent is as honorable as overcoming him by brute strength. There is ample justification for both positions in the symbolism of sport. The athletic contest is multidimensional. It involves strategy, physical skill, and moral and intellectual commitment, as well as the sheer joy of meeting an opponent worthy of total engagement.

Skiing combines the exhilaration of altitude and confrontation with nature with the speed of the race. Unlike mountain-climbers, modern skiers rarely challenge nature in the raw. In fact, they typically confine themselves to well-charted trails. Yet skiers share with mountain-climbers the ineffable experience of standing alone on a mountain-top and looking down on an apparently somnambulant world. And this is part of the appeal for both sports. This is the mood captured in Andrew Wyeth's watercolor *From Mountain Kearsage*, which depicts three skiers at the pinnacle. From their elevated perspective they gaze out over a spectacular vista. This scene emphasizes the grandeur of the sport.

Although skiers seldom push beyond the known landscape, they do explore the limits of their own skills, striving for more speed, greater control or more challenging terrain. In skiing, danger is socialized and brought under control. The mountain is explored only tentatively and in company with others. Unbridled nature and untamed society meet on the ski slopes.

Braving the Depths

The quintessential conquest of nature is recounted in *Beowulf*, the oldest surviving Old English epic poem. Prior to engaging Grendel in battle on behalf of the Danish king Hrothgar, Beowulf and his men are drinking with the Danes in a beer hall when the hero is challenged by Unferth, Hrothgar's orator:

> Are you that Beowulf who contested against Breca swimming on the wide
> sea, where you two in your pride dared the deep waters and ventured
> your lives because of foolish boasting? No one, neither friend nor enemy,
> could dissuade you two from that sorry undertaking when you swam in
> the sea.... You both labored seven nights in the power of the water, but
> he had more might, and surpassed you in swimming. Then in the morn-
> ing the sea carried him up on Norwegian land....[80]

Swimming can be either a recreation or a sport. It generally becomes a sport when
it is a part of competition, and this represents a shift in the associated symbolism.
The recreational aspect of swimming, representing a relaxed appreciation of nature,
is exemplified by Paul Cézanne's image of languid sensuality *Bathers at Rest*. A similar mood prevails in a watercolor by Robert W. Jensen. In this case, the sea seems
to spurt forth youthful life.

The ultimate symbol of aspiration in swimming is the long-distance event, in
which the individual conquers a natural challenge. Attempts to cross the English
Channel or the Florida Straits continue to attract public attention. Like mountain-
climbing, braving the sea alone and unarmed metaphorically represents a courageous assault on a formidable obstacle, a contest that is meaningful only as a
conquest of self and a communion with nature. In a poem called "Swimming," the
conflicted British aristocrat, son of the Earl of Gainsborough and godchild of Queen
Victoria, Roden Noel describes a mystical journey:

> Reft him of his breath,
> To some far realms away
> He would float with Death;
> Wild wind would sing over him,
> And the free foam cover him,
> Waft him sleeping onward
> Floating seaward, sunward,
> All alone with Death;
> In a realm of wondrous dreams,
> And shadow-haunted ocean-gleams!

Of all those who would challenge the forces of nature, swimmers most closely
engage their opponent, and swimming metaphors often evoke death. From William Shakespeare to the American orator Daniel Webster, the ultimate effort is seen
as "Sink or swim." In an 1826 address at Boston's Faneuil Hall, Webster exhorts
his countrymen, "Sink or swim, live or die, survive or perish, I give my hand and
my heart to this vote." In his discourse in commemoration of John Adams and
Thomas Jefferson, Daniel Webster was committing himself to his fledgling nation,
the United States, whose Declaration of Independence had been signed just 50
years earlier, and had yet to prove itself. For this young nation, the adage "Sink or
swim," was particularly apt.

Robert W. Jensen's beach scene draws on another meaning of "sport," to play or cavort. Though there is a great deal of physical activity going on in this work, competition is entirely lacking. Overall, the image is one of youthful exuberance (reproduced by permission of the artist, Robert W. Jensen).

Riding the Waves

If there is a degree of melancholia associated with swimming, that mood is dispelled as soon as humans put wood between themselves and the sea. Yachting events combine speed, beauty and the excitement of contending with a worthy opponent. In his poem "The Yachts," William Carlos Williams depicts a yacht race as a mortal contest with a voracious ocean. He personifies both the vessels and the sea, describing the yachts as having glossy sides like horses and the sea as having a multitude of clutching hands:

> In a well guarded arena of open water surrounded by
> lesser and greater craft which, sycophant, lumbering
> and filtering follow them, they appear youthful, rare
> as the light of a happy eye, live with the grace
> of all that in the mind is feckless, free and
> naturally to be desired. Now the sea which holds them
>
> is moody, lapping their glossy sides, as if feeling
> for some slightest flaw but fails completely.
> Today no race. Then the wind comes again. The yachts

Vessels are the primary contestants in the sport of sailing, and human contenders are largely invisible, though their expertise in the contest is indispensable. In this computer-generated art by Julie Hill, entitled *2-2-TANGO*, sailboats are personified as dancers. The sailboat on the left appears to bow to the vessel on the right, thus establishing his role of the masculine partner. This role is emphasized by his display of a colorful banner, much like that of Central American male dancers (reproduced by permission of the artist).

move, jockeying for a start, the signal is set and they
are off. Now the waves strike at them but they are too
well made, they slip through, though they take in canvas.

Arms with hands grasping seek to clutch at the prows.
Bodies thrown recklessly in the way are cut aside.
It is a sea of faces about them in agony, in despair

until the horror of the race dawns staggering the mind,
the whole sea become an entanglement of watery bodies
lost to the world bearing what they cannot hold. Broken,

beaten, desolate, reaching from the dead to be taken up
they cry out, failing, failing! Their cries rising
in waves still as the skillful yachts pass over.

To William Carlos Williams, as to many others, gliding over the surface of the water represents freedom and triumph for the human spirit.

"Let's go surfing now; everybody's learning how. Come on a safari with me." That invitation in the 1960s by the rock group the Beach Boys was a call to drop arms and take up the surfboard. Though probably unintended by the Beach Boys, the song "Surfin' Safari" offered Americans a carefree alternative to the violent and bloody media images of an unpopular war in Vietnam. The song also evoked a California lifestyle for people who lived thousands of miles from the sea. The surf, surfers with sun-bleached hair and bikini-clad surfer bunnies came to represent California in a way that more momentous actions, like the Watts riots in Los Angeles of the same era, did not.

But it is to Polynesia, not California, that the origins of surfing must be traced, and the Beach Boy anthem would have stirred a chord in the breast of a legendary Hawaiian surfer, Kelea, a princess and sister to Kawao, King of Maui. According to legend, Kelea was so beautiful every man of rank wanted to make her his wife. Her brother urged her to marry one of her suitors, but she refused, preferring to spend her days surfing. "My surfboard is my husband," she said. "I will never embrace any other." In resisting her brother's entreaties to marry, she reminded him that the gods had predicted that she would find her husband in the surf. Her brother had to be content with these words, since even he could not challenge the gods.

On the island of Oahu, unknown to Kelea and her brother, a chief named Lo-Lale was looking for a wife. The chief hated and feared the sea because the woman he loved was drowned years before, so his cousin Kalamakua, a noble of high birth, set out on a quest to the neighboring islands, which required a long journey by outrigger canoe. Kalamakua promised to return with a wife for the chief. "If she does not suit you," he told the chief, "I will marry her myself."

Kalmakua's mission was unsuccessful at first, but as he traveled past Maui, he heard of Kelea's great beauty. As the decorated canoe neared her island, Kelea was swimming and, oblivious to everything but her own enjoyment, she almost ran into the canoe. Kalamakua invited her to come aboard to join them in the thrilling and

Yachting and sailing have entirely different connotations. James E. Buttersworth's painting *A Racing Yacht on the Great South Bay* expresses the elegance and privilege associated with yachting. However, yacht racing also requires great skill, which can only be cultivated through long hours of dedication (Virginia Museum of Fine Arts, Commonwealth of Virginia).

dangerous sport of surf riding. Again and again, he steered the canoe toward the beach until it appeared they were about to crash on the sand. At the last minute, he turned the craft around and headed back to sea, demonstrating his superb skills as a seaman. On each trip he journeyed farther out until they were caught in a storm. For some time they drifted on the ocean, and Kalamakua pretended to be lost. Finally he began guiding his canoe, not to her island, but to his own. Kelea was not fooled by his guise. She informed him that she had been following his progress by the stars and was fully aware that Maui was not his destination. As he took her to his island, Kalamakua told her of his cousin's search for a wife.

When they arrived on Oahu, the chief immediately fell in love with Kelea. They were married, and he indulged her in anything she wanted. Only one favor he begged of her, that she not risk her life in the sea. Kelea gave birth to three beautiful children, providing Lo-Lale with the heir he desired, but still she longed for the sea:

Though surfing is often associated with leisure, dedicated surfers see it as a quest. This is the mood of Robert W. Jensen's watercolor. This young surfer gazes toward a scene that is invisible to the viewer. The artist does not even provide us with a glimpse of the sea. We can only presume that is the object of his longing, as expressed in his intent gaze, the angle of his surfboard, and the orientation of his body (reproduced by permission of the artist, Robert W. Jensen).

> ...for the bounding surf which had been the sport of her girlhood; for the white-maned steeds of the ocean, which she had so often mounted and fearlessly ridden to the shore; for the thunder of the breakers against the cliffs; for the murmur of the reef-bound wavelets timidly crawling up the beach to kiss and cool her feet... [Kalakaua 1972:243 (1888)].

Eventually, Kelea told her husband that she wished to return to her island so she could realize her passion for surfing. Reluctantly, Lo-Lale agreed, so she left him, her children and her beautiful home and went down to the beach to find an outrigger canoe to take her back to her brother's island. At the beach she discovered that a surfing race was in progress and she could not resist joining in. She defeated all the chiefs and reached the shore amid the cheers of the onlookers. Kalamakua, who was resting nearby, asked a passerby the cause of the celebration. He was told that a beautiful woman had beaten all the chiefs at surfing.

Certain that the woman can be no other than Kelea, he met her just as she arrived on the beach after a second triumph. As he covered her with his mantle, she told him that she had separated from her husband and was about to embark for Maui. "In that case," he said, "you will go no farther. When I went in search of a wife for Lo-Lale, I promised that if he objected to the women I brought, or she to him, I would take her myself, if she so willed. Is Kalamakua better to your liking?" Kelea agreed to marry him, and for the rest of their lives they could be found surfing together off the beautiful island of Oahu.

For traditional Hawaiians, the sea is virtually sacred. Known as *kai*, the sea is described by a number of poetic metaphors. When she is calm, she is *kai malie*. When she is raging, she is *kai pupule*. Traditionally, if the waves were not suitable for surfing, the Hawaiians would call on a *kahuna*, a shaman, in the hope that he could "make waves." In *An Account of the Polynesian Race: Its Origins and Migrations*, a nineteenth-century Maui circuit court judge named Abraham Fornander described a surf-coaxing ritual involving a chant known as a *pohuehue*, named for the beach morning glory (*Ipomoea Pescaprae*). The kahuna would swing several strands of the vine around and lash them "unitedly upon the water until the desired undulating waves were obtained," while chanting in unison with the surfers:

> *Ku mai! Ku mai! Ka nalu nui mai Kahiki mai,*
> *Alo po 'i pu! Ku mai ka pohuehue,*
> *Hu! Kai ko'o loa.*

Or in English:

> Arise! Arise! You great surfs from Kahiki,
> The powerful curling waves. Arise with the *pohuehue*.
> Well up, long raging surf [quoted in Leuras 1984:33].

Hawaiians made offerings to the gods to pray for good surf at a seaside *heiau* or shrine at Kahaluu Bay on the Kona coast. A legendary woman named Laenihi was said to have great magical powers to wake the surf.

Although it has become associated with a carefree lifestyle, a certain poignancy is associated with surfing. Unlike other athletes who contend with nature as a form of transcendence, the surfer must wait until his opponent grants him the perfect wave. And the moment, when it comes, is fleeting. Thus, surfing often takes on the nature of a quest. The California surfer Greg Noll became a legend, known as "Da Bull" for his aggressive style. Noll reportedly spent twenty years looking for the ultimate wave. He found it one day in December of 1969, when a storm in the Aleutians drove massive swells onto the shore at Makaha Point in Oahu. His biographer notes that Noll's approach to surfing is experiential rather than discursive. According to Noll, "Talk is bullshit. You want to know the truth? Get a board and paddle out there, point your board down the face of a grinder and make a commitment. That's where you find the truth" (Noll and Gabbard 1989:v).

A poem composed in Hawaiian by a modern surfer, Larry Lindsey Kimura, demonstrates the lure of the wave and the sense of power and freedom that comes from mounting it. The poem also links the modern surfer to Hawaiian chiefs of old and describes an experience common to sports of transcendence:

> Here now a big wave rises
> An ʻonaulu loa, a wave of great length and endurance
> It swells, sweeping unbroken in the noon-day sun
> My board mounts the crest
> My loincloth flys in the spray of the sea
> I am like the ʻiwa bird crying wildly
> As it soars so high above
> But the finest delight
> Is there in the wave's cresting,
> Like a royal feathered helmet
> Upon my brow [Quoted in Leuras 1984: 168].

George Freeth was born on the island of Oahu in 1883 to an English sea captain and his half–Hawaiian, half–English wife. At that time, surfing had been banned in Hawaii by New England missionaries because of its "immodesty and idleness."[81] Freeth revived the sport, so impressing Jack London with his style that the novelist described him as "a Mercury — a brown Mercury. His heels are winged, and in them is the swiftness of the sea." In July 1907, when he was just 23, Freeth left Hawaii to promote Hawaiian tourism and introduce surfing to the mainland United States. Freeth arrived in California just as railroad baron Henry Huntington was developing Redondo Beach as a dream beach community and his friend Abbot Kinney had built a utopian residential community modeled after Venice, Italy, complete with canals. The popularity of the two beach communities was threatened when even experienced swimmers began drowning off the coast in alarming numbers.[82]

Rescue efforts of the day, using a life ring thrown from the pier or sending out a rescue team on a lifeboat, proved too cumbersome to be effective. Freeth's prowess at saving lives by swimming out to the rescue made him a legend. He earned the Congressional Gold Medal, the nation's highest civilian honor for bravery, by swimming out to save fishermen whose boat sank in a gale in the Santa Monica Bay. Freeth developed lifesaving techniques that are still in use today and organized water polo teams on the West Coast. He died at the early age of 35, not from his daring adventures on the water, but of the Spanish influenza epidemic of 1919, which killed 20 million people worldwide.

Perhaps the ultimate summation of the surfing art is contained in an inscription on a monument to George Freeth at Redondo Beach, California, where he introduced the sport of surfing to the mainland United States in 1907 and awed spectators with demonstrations of his surfing skills. Echoing early advertisements for his surfing events, the inscription describes Freeth as a man "who can walk on water."

Seven

Metaphors of Love, Death, and Rebirth

My heart is a lonely hunter that hunts on a lonely hill.
William Sharp (Fiona Macleod), whose poem
inspired the title for a novel by Carson McCullers,
The Heart Is a Lonely Hunter.

The two most elusive goals of human experience are romantic love and immortality. They are the source of the ache that cannot be eased, the question that cannot be answered, the prize that cannot be won. Not surprisingly, the most common sporting metaphor used to describe these universal quests is the hunt. However, other sporting contests — including races, wrestling and ball games — also figure prominently. There is a natural affinity between sport and the two most absorbing quests of human life, since the essence of sport is total commitment to an ineffable prize.

Even D. H. Lawrence, who expressed less interest in sport than in the game of love, drew on sporting metaphors to describe the sensual passions. In his poem "Women Want Fighters for Their Lovers," he advises males to emulate the cock, pun intended:

> Women don't want wistful
> mushy, pathetic young men
> struggling in doubtful embraces
> then trying again.
> ....
> Women want fighters, fighters
> and the fighting cock.
> Can't you give it them, blighters!
>
> The fighting cock, the fighting cock —
> have you got one, little blighters?
> Let it crow then, like one o'clock!

In a less aggressive mood, the poet compares the lighthearted mastery of a man poling a punt on the water with sexuality in "A Man at Play on the River":

184

His body pulsing with play

His full, fine body bending and urging like the stress of a
song.

Darting his light punt with the quick-shifting fancy of verse,

Among the shadows of blossoms and trees and rushes,

In-weaving the bright thread of his joy

Flashing his bright, brown arms as he leans on the pole.

His blue shirt glimmering in the water among the shadow of
trees,

Threading the round joy of his white-flannelled hips full of
play

Up the river, under the trees,

Down the river, in the gleam of the sun,

Across the river, bending low

In one swift bound to the house-boat.

There, among the flowers of the boat-roof

Passes the ever-changing joy of his active body;

His round, brown head bends like a bee above a blossom

Over a girl who has strewn herself in a hammock

As a white rose strews the ground,

His ruddy arms glow across her

His full round hips supporting himself above her

While the soft caress of her hidden laughter

Plays round him, as colour-ripples played

Round his bright joyful body

When he swung like the rhythm of a poem over the river,

And now hangs like the fragrant close of the measure

Over her strewn, white, laughing form.

Often, the quest for love involves the hero in a great adventure that forces him to overcome many perils to win his love. It is usually, though not always, the man who must endure many dangers. Often, the quest is assigned by the woman's father or male guardian as a condition for winning her. The outcome is uncertain and, until the end, it may not be clear whether the hero's prize will be the woman he loves or death.

Love may also be portrayed as a contest. In this case, the hero contends against the object of his love. He must "win her over." The contest can be lighthearted, so that the man and woman playfully contend against each other, and the outcome is just part of the "game." On the other hand, life itself may hang in the balance.

The hunt is prevalent in metaphors of love. Typically, the hunter is male, and the object of the hunt is female. As the poet Alfred, Lord Tennyson puts it: "Man is the hunter; woman the game" (*The Princess*, Vol 5). However, there are two stories in this chapter in which women pursue the husband they desire. In one case, the woman literally dons hunting gear; in the other case, the woman entices her future husband into the tender trap by using her cooking skills as bait.

The pursuit of love may result in transformation or transcendence. In this case, the stories do not end in consummation of physical love, but in transformation of the loved one or of the quest itself into a form of spiritual union. In other stories, the object of the adventure is not romantic love, but transcendence. The spiritual quest usually draws on the hunt as a metaphor. Finally, in the symbolism of the divine archer, the seeker merges with the object of his quest. He is no longer an actor in a great adventure; he is the arrow on its way to the target.

The Quest for Love

The story of Orion, one of the mightiest hunters of the Greek pantheon and reportedly the handsomest man alive, centers on a fatal quest for love. The object of Orion's passion is Merope, daughter of Oenopion, son of the god Dionysus. Oenopion promises Merope to Orion if the hunter will free the kingdom from the dangerous wild beasts that infest it. When the hunter accomplishes this task at last, he comes to claim Merope for his wife. However, Oenopion, who is himself in love with his daughter, refuses to give her up.

Enraged, Orion gets drunk and breaks into Merope's bedroom, where he rapes her. In retaliation, Oenopion blinds Orion and throws him onto the seashore. The hunter journeys over the sea and meets Eos the dawn, who falls in love with him. Her brother Helios, the sun-god who sees all, restores Orion's sight. Thus, Orion is both blinded by frustrated love for one woman and made to see through the generous love of another.

Orion returns to wreak vengeance upon Oenopion, who has fled. While searching for his enemy, Orion meets Artemis. The goddess of the hunt persuades Orion to abandon his quest for vengeance and join her in the chase for game. Orion's friendship with Artemis upsets Apollo, who fears his chaste sister will be seduced by the handsome hunter. Apollo sends a scorpion to pursue Orion, who discovers that his arrows and sword are no defense against the divine arachnid. The hunter dives into the sea to escape. Apollo then calls to Artemis, saying, "Do you see that black object bobbing around in the sea? It is the head of a villain who has just seduced one of your priestesses." Artemis shoots the object with her arrow. When she swims out to retrieve her quarry, she discovers that she has shot Orion through the head. In her grief, Artemis sets the hunter's image among the stars, where he is eternally pursued by the Scorpion.

There are a number of symbolic transformations in this story, all centering on sexuality and the hunt. The hunter's original prey is Merope. Through the intervention of her father, his quest is displaced upon the animals that are ravaging the

Opposite: **Auguste Renoir depicts *Diana* the goddess of the hunt (Artemis in Greek mythology) as a sensual and voluptuous beauty. The dead deer at her feet could almost be a metaphor for the men who died for gazing upon her beauty (National Gallery of Art, Chester Dale Collection).**

kingdom. He is successful in hunting them down and killing them, but is deprived of his rightful prize because of Oenopion's unnatural love for his daughter.

Orion seizes his prize illegally, thus transforming the story into a contest between the two men. He loses the first encounter, and this loss initiates his successful quest to regain his sight. This is clearly not a metaphor for spiritual enlightenment, since the hero returns to the hunt that darkened his vision in the first place. However, the prey is now transformed. Orion no longer pursues Merope, and his love for her is transformed into hatred for her father, the prey that again eludes him.

The hero sets out on a quest for Oenopion, but this is interrupted by Artemis, the divine huntress. Again, Orion's passion is diverted from the pursuit of human prey to the hunting of animals. The motif of sexuality re-enters the picture when Apollo fears his sister, the huntress, is about to become the prey. Apollo turns the tables on the hunter, transforming him into the prey of the Scorpion. Though it is hard to tell whether such imagery is deliberate, in astrology the Scorpion is ruler of the genitals or sex organs. Symbolically, then, the hunter is pursued by sexuality. He tries to escape his fate once again by swimming away from danger but this effort, which first saved him, now fails him. He becomes the prey of an even greater hunter, Artemis.

The handsome Celtic hero Culhwch, cousin of King Arthur, must undertake a great hunt, among other adventures, to win his beloved Olwen, daughter of the chief giant Ysbaddaden. According to the Welch epic *The Mabinogion*, the giant is reluctant to allow his daughter to get married because of a prediction that he can live only as long as she remains single.

Accompanied by a number of King Arthur's warriors, Culhwch journeys to Ysbaddaden's castle. After gaining entry by slaughtering the giant's guards, the hero approaches his prospective father-in-law and asks for Olwen's hand. The giant's response comes in the form of a poisoned spear. One of Culhwch's warriors catches it and throws it back, injuring Isbaddaden in the knee. The giant throws another spear, which is immediately thrown back at him, piercing his chest. The heroes try to be reasonable, saying, "Chief Giant Ysbaddaden, shoot at us no more, do not be the cause of your being injured and wounded and killed." But the giant is hard to persuade. He throws another poisoned spear. Culhwch catches it and throws it back at the giant, hitting him in the eye.

Ysbaddaden may already see the handwriting on the wall, because he screams at Culhwch, "You cursed barbarian son-in-law!" The heroes again propose a reasonable way out, saying, "Do not shoot at us any more; do not seek harm and injury and martyrdom for yourself, or even worse if you insist. Give us your daughter."

Ysbaddaden relents, but will surrender Olwen only if Culhwch performs a series of seemingly impossible chores. The ultimate task is to bring the giant a comb and scissors that lie between the ears of Twrch Trwyth, a ferocious and magical boar. To hunt the animal, Culhwch must first acquire wondrous hunting equipment — dogs, horse, and a hunter — each of which requires a major quest in itself.

The heroes accomplish all the endeavors in their turn, but before they even locate Twrch Trwyth, the boar has already destroyed a third of Ireland. King Arthur collects the warriors of Britain and the three offshore islands, as well as Brittany, France and Normandy, and leads them all to Ireland to hunt the animal. King Arthur's army locates Twrch Trwyth and his seven pigs, but after nine days and nights of fighting, as well as the destruction of much of Ireland, they succeed in killing only one pig. King Arthur tries to negotiate for the comb and scissors, but the great boar replies that he will not do anything for Arthur. In fact, he says, he next plans to destroy as much of Wales, Arthur's own country, as he can. The pigs then swim to Wales with all the armies of the world in pursuit.

The pigs slaughter many of Arthur's men. The army, along with a number of houndsmen and dogs, eventually manages to kill four piglets and drive Twrch Trwyth out of Wales. The ferocious boar heads for Cornwall, but after much more carnage, Arthur and his men succeed in capturing the comb and scissors. Twrch Trwyth escapes by swimming out to sea and is never seen again. Culhwch returns to Ysbaddaden to claim his bride. He kills the giant, cuts off his head and sets it on a stake on the wall. He then seizes his father-in-law's fortress and lands, and lives there with his bride Olwen.

Some scholars believe the story of Culhwch and Olwen is based on a historical invasion of Ireland by Wales. If so, the war may have been triggered by the quest for a bride. The story suggests that courtship by conquest may have been a custom in the British Isles. Culhwch's own father won his second wife by killing a neighboring king, seizing his land and marrying his widow.

A striking characteristic of stories of this type is that the object of love is typically only a spectator. Though it is her beauty or virtue or other fine qualities that trigger the quest, the story centers on the hero's efforts to prove himself worthy of possessing her. The contest is, in fact, about men. The woman is only the prize.

The Orion and Culhwch stories are similar in that the hero must wrest his bride away from a powerful father. Only one man can have her. The appropriate ending is that the hero should displace the father. Culhwch succeeds and brings about the old man's death. Orion fails, resulting in tragedy for all concerned. Not even the goddess Artemis escapes grief.

Women do not always wait passively for their lover to win the right to possess them. In the story of Hero and Leander, the lovers together face a different kind of opponent, an opponent in nature. However, it is the male, Leander, who must brave the depths to consummate his love. Hero stands as the beacon, the prize to be won. In an ironic twist, Leander must also defy the goddess and god of love.

Hero lives in a tower at a shrine dedicated to Aphrodite and Eros, whom she is committed to serve as priestess. The shrine, at Sestus, is on one side of the strait; Leander lives on the other side of the strait. They meet and fall in love at a festival of Adonis, but are forced to part and return to their respective homes. Each night, Leander swims the Hellespont, and Hero lights a lamp to guide his journey. They spend the night in each other's arms, and the next day, Leander swims back to his home.

The lovers continue in this idyllic way throughout the summer, but as winter comes, the waters of the Hellespont become more hazardous. One stormy night,

Hero knows she should not light her lamp and encourage her lover to brave the waves, but she cannot bear the thought of a night without him. She lights her lamp, and Leander plunges into the deadly waters. As he battles the raging waves, the wind blows out her lamp, and he loses his way in the darkness. Hero waits for her lover all night in vain. In the morning, she looks out her tower window and sees his battered body on the rocks below. Overcome with grief, she dives out of the window to join him in death:

> About her breast she tore the wondrous mantle,
> And from the sheer crag plunged in hurling headlong fall
> To find with her dead love a death among the waves,
> And the joy of love together in life's last separation
> [Musaeus, *Hero and Leander*].

Transformations: The Wild and the Tame

Hunting is equated with the quest for love in a number of European fairy tales recorded by the brothers Grimm. In the story of "The Skilful Huntsman" a man gains wealth and a beautiful bride through his prowess, cunning and sense of honor. The hero, a locksmith, leaves his father's house to learn to be a hunter. He encounters a huntsman who not only teaches him to hunt, but gives him an air-gun that always hits its mark. Already, there are three significant symbols in this story. The locksman can find his way through openings; the hunter tracks down his prey; and the air-gun is a potent symbol for male sexuality.

After completing his apprenticeship, the young man continues on his journey, which takes him through a large forest. One night he encounters three giants who are roasting an ox around a campfire. The hunter hides out of sight, and each time they start to take a bite, shoots the meat out of their hand. The giants are so impressed by his skill, they invite him to join them and enlist him in their efforts to steal a beautiful princess, who is hidden in a well-guarded palace.

The huntsman kills the king's guard dog with his magical air-gun and makes his way alone through the castle. In the first room he discovers a silver sword ornamented with a golden star and the name of the king. An envelope nearby contains a note saying that whoever has the sword can kill everything that opposes him. The young man takes the sword and finds his way through the castle to the bedroom of the princess, where she lies sleeping. Struck by her beauty, he resolves to save her from the giants, thinking, "How can I give an innocent maiden into the power of the wild giants, who have evil in their minds?"

He takes one of her slippers, which bears her father's insignia, as well as a similarly marked silk scarf and a piece of her sleeping gown, to prove his case to the giants. He leaves her sleeping and returns to the castle gates, where he calls to the giants, saying, "I have the princess, but you must climb through this hole in the gate to get her." As the first giant climbs through, the young hunter grabs him by the hair and cuts off his head. He does the same to the other two as they each climb through the hole. He cuts out their tongues and takes his booty to his father to show how well he has done in his career as a huntsman.

When the king awakens, he demands to know who has killed the giants, intending to give his daughter in marriage to the man who has so increased the security of his kingdom. A captain of the king's guards, a hideous and unworthy man, claims the feats as his own and insists that he has the right to marry the princess. She is not so willing a prize, however. She says she will give up her kingdom and live as a beggar rather than marry the captain. Her father, furious with his stubborn daughter, builds her a hut in the forest and sentences her to cook without pay for whoever passes by.

Drawn by the prospect of a free meal, the young huntsman goes to the hut in the forest wearing the sword he used to kill the giants. The woman recognizes her father's sword and demands to know how he came by it. "Are you the princess I saved from the three giants?" he asks. As proof of his deed, he shows her the slipper, the scarf and the piece of her nightgown, as well as the tongues of the giants, all of which he happens to be carrying in his knapsack. Overjoyed, the princess and hunter return to the castle and show the trophies to her father. The king gives his daughter in marriage to the heroic huntsman and gives orders to have the unscrupulous captain torn to pieces.

This story lends itself to several kinds of analysis, including Freudian, in which the various symbols could be interpreted as representing licit and illicit sexuality. It is also an ideal candidate for analysis according to the model proposed by the French anthropologist Claude Lévi-Strauss. He argued that humans think in binary oppositions, which are manipulated symbolically in myth. In the story of the skillful hunter, the oppositions focus on the dichotomy between the tame and the wild, good versus evil, the magical versus the grotesque, and honesty versus deception. These are acted out in a drama involving appropriate masculine and feminine behavior.

The young man leaves a domesticated (tame) occupation to become a hunter in the wild. This takes him from the town to the forest. It is there that he meets his mentor, a mysterious being who instructs him in manly skills and gives him the weapon of his calling. In Lévi-Straussian analysis, the guide represents an intermediate principle that mediates between the opposite poles.

Here, we digress from Lévi-Straussian analysis to consider another important model of the hero myth. The huntsman's meeting with the mysterious mentor marks it as representative of the third stage in the hero cycle model developed by Paul Radin, which he based on hero myths among the Winnebago Indians of the Great Lakes and Dakota regions of what is now the United States. In the third stage, the hero Red Horn is no longer represented as an animal, but as a human. In the Winnebago myth, the hero demonstrates his worth by, among other things, defeating giants by guile in a game of dice. He is accompanied and protected by a powerful companion in the form of a thunderbird called "Storms-as-he-walks." As in the story of the skillful hunter, Red Horn's mentor figure departs as the hero becomes powerful in his own right.

In "The Skilful Huntsman," the hero meets both his mentor in the forest and the personification of evil, the three giants, who are "wild" whereas the hunter is "tame." The giants are also grotesque, whereas the weapon of the hunter is magical. The hunter asserts dominion over the grotesque wild things of the forest by means of his magical weapon, the air-gun. The giants, who are of the forest, cannot pierce the fortifications of the castle, which represents the tame. The hunter, son of a locksmith, can move freely from the forest into the castle, killing the tame guard dog as he does so. At the moment of decision, the huntsman chooses the good/human princess over the evil/grotesque giants of the forest, at the same time rejecting the wild in favor of the tame. He then uses the tame/magical weapon, the sword that he finds in the castle of the princess, to kill the wild/grotesque giants, reversing the killing of the dog, in which he uses the "wild" weapon, acquired in the forest, to slay the "tame" animal. The guard dog died an honorable death in service to its master, whereas the giants died a dishonorable death in pursuit of prize that was beyond their station.

The deceitful captain is in opposition to the honest hunter. As a result of the captain's deception, the potential bride, the "tame" princess, is obliged to undertake her domestic duties in the "wild." Rather than assuming her rightful place as a bride in the castle, she must become a menial in the forest. The hunter once again releases her, this time from her servitude in the forest. When the rightful order is restored, the two are joined together in marriage, whereas the would-be bridegroom is torn apart. The hunter leaves the forest to take up his domestic role as a husband and later as a king.

The Persian epic *Shah-nama* describes the elusive romantic adventure of two warriors, Tus and Giv. The men go into the forest hunting one morning and turn up an unlikely quarry, a beautiful young woman. Thinking her a slave girl, they fight over who should have possession of her. Each claims to have seen her first, applying a rule of the hunt to an affair of the passions. Unable to settle their dispute, they bring the woman to their king, Kavus. Perceiving immediately that the woman must be of royal birth, Kavus tells his two warriors: "The hardships of your journey are now at an end. This is a mountain-doe, truly a heart-ravishing gazelle; but game appropriate only to the highest." Kavus makes the woman his queen, and she later gives birth to Siyavosh, who played the legendary game of polo before the Turkish king Afrasiyah described in Chapter Five of *Sport as Symbol*.

The symbolism of the hunt is pervasive in the story of how King Kavus found his bride. She is in the forest, where the two warriors are seeking game. According to the protocol of the hunt, the one who spots the game first gets the first shot, and the one who makes the kill claims the animal and has the right to decide how to distribute the meat. In the story of the Persian warriors, these basic rights of the hunt ultimately give way to superior social rank. Just as kings and queens may claim the right to administer the *coup de grace* during a hunt, King Kavus asserts his right to claim the game turned up by his two warriors.

Transformations: The Chased and the Chaste

In the Grimms brothers' story of "The Twelve Huntsmen," it is the woman who must become a hunter to win her lover. In this case, the heroine, a princess, is betrothed to a prince, and they are very much in love. As they are sitting happily together, the young man receives word that his father, the king, is dying. The prince leaves his beloved a ring and hastens to his father's bedside, where he learns that his father's dying wish is that he marry the daughter of a neighboring king. Sadly, the prince puts aside his first love and becomes engaged to the princess of his father's choice.

The prince's first love does not give up so easily. She bids her father to send messengers all over his kingdom and find eleven maidens like her in face, figure and size. She outfits them all in identical hunting clothes, and posing as men, they ride to her lover's castle, where he is now king. The new king does not recognize his former betrothed and accepts the maidens into his service as huntsmen.

Though they fool the king, the young women do not fool his lion, a magical animal who is able to learn people's secrets. The lion tells his master the twelve huntsmen are actually maidens in disguise. The king does not believe it, but the lion sets out to prove it. "Strew peas in the antechamber," the beast says. "A man has a firm step and will either crush the peas or pass over them without moving them, but maidens will come tripping or shuffling along and set the peas rolling." The king does as the lion suggests, but one of the king's servants warns the young women that the peas are strewn in the antechamber as a test. The princess instructs her handmaidens to step strongly upon the peas. The next morning, when the women meet the king in the antechamber, they tread so firmly upon the peas that not one rolls or even moves.

The king accuses the lion of lying to him, but the animal insists that the huntsmen/maidens were forewarned. "Now give them another trial," he says. "Have twelve spinning wheels placed in the antechamber, and when they see them they will look quite delighted, whereas no man would notice them." The twelve spinning wheels are placed in the antechamber, but again the women are warned, and they walk past them without so much as a glance. The king is then convinced that the lion is lying. From that day, the king takes his twelve huntsmen with him whenever he goes hunting.

One day while they are out hunting, they receive word that the king's new betrothed is coming to the castle. The chief huntsman — who is really the king's first love — falls from her horse in a swoon. Fearing that his favorite huntsman has been injured, the king dismounts from his horse and runs to help. As the king raises him/her up, the huntsman's glove falls off, and the monarch recognizes the ring he had given to his first love. He kisses her and claims her for his bride. He sends away the bride his father chose for him and restores the lion to a place of favor.

This story expresses some of the same themes as "The Skilful Hunter," but oppositions in "the Twelve Huntsmen" center axes. Oppositions between human-animal and mundane-magical are also expressed in the roles of the two kings, one a ruler of humans, the other the king of beasts. The human king has ordinary wisdom; the lion has magical powers of knowing.

The feminine is associated with the domestic realm, as represented by the spinning wheel, whereas the masculine is associated with the hunt. In this story, the power relationship is inverted, and it is the male who passively awaits the resolution of his fate, first from his father and later from his bride. The parent-child axis is represented in an opposition between the prince's father, who imposes his own desires upon his son, thus ignoring the son's desire to marry the princess of his choice. On the other hand, the father of the heroine heeds her desires and obeys her request to pursue her lover into the field dressed as a huntsman. In the end, the behavior of both the prince and his true bride are age and gender appropriate. He performs an act of filial piety by setting aside his own desires in obedience to his father. And though she was able to pass the tests of the peas and spinning wheel, she remains true to her lover and reveals herself to him in a classically feminine fashion, by falling into a swoon at his feet.

In the Grimm brothers' story, "The Princess in Disguise" the feminine hero transforms herself from hunted to hunter. The princess' problems begin when her mother the queen, the most beautiful woman on earth, becomes ill and is about to die. Before she dies, she makes her husband promise that he will not marry again unless he can find a woman who is as beautiful as she and has golden hair like her own. The king promises, and when he is ready to marry again, sends messengers throughout the world to find a wife who meets his requirements. Alas, there is none, and for many years, the king is without a wife and the kingdom is without a queen.

In the meantime, the king's daughter grows up. She is as beautiful as her mother and has her mother's golden hair. The king sends for his counselors and announces: "I will marry my daughter; she is the image of my dead wife, and no other bride can be found to enable me to keep my promise to her."

The counselors are greatly alarmed, fearing that so great a sin will bring ruin upon the kingdom, but the king will not be dissuaded. The princess tries to subvert his intentions by setting him to an impossible task. "Before I consent to your wish," she says. "I shall require three things — a dress as golden as the sun, another as silvery as the moon, and a third as glittering as the stars. Besides this, I shall require a mantle made of a thousand skins of rough fur sewn together and every animal in the kingdom must give a piece of his skin toward it."

Not to be diverted from his purpose, the king employees the most skillful women of the kingdom to weave the three dresses. He sends hunters into the forest to kill all the wild animals and bring their skins to make the mantle. When all is completed, he presents the three dresses and the fur mantle to his daughter, saying, "Tomorrow our marriage shall take place."

When the princess realizes there is no chance of avoiding her father's evil designs, she decides to run away. That night, she takes from her jewel-case three items of gold — a ring, a spinning-wheel and a hook — and packs them with the three dresses in a tiny parcel. She puts on the fur mantle and stains her face and hands with walnut juice. She then travels far away and enters a large forest to live as an animal. Like an animal, she crawls into a hollow tree and falls asleep.

The forest is owned by a neighboring king, unknown to the princess and her father. The next day, the king is out hunting. When his hounds come to the tree where the princess is sleeping, they sniff around and begin circling it, barking wildly. The king instructs his hunters to find out what the dogs are barking at. When the hunters return, they tell the king the most beautiful creature they have ever seen, covered with a thousand kinds of fur, is asleep in the hollow tree. The king says, "Go and see if you can capture it alive. Then bind it on the wagon and bring it home."

While the hunters are binding the maiden, she wakes up and cries out in terror, "I am only a poor child, forsaken by my father and mother. Take pity on me and take me with you." "Very well," they say, "you may be useful to the cook, little Roughskin. Come with us; you can at least sweep up the ashes." They take her to the king's castle, give her a place to sleep in the stable, and set her to work gathering wood, carrying water, stirring the fire, plucking the fowls and sweeping the ashes.

One day the king gives a festival. The cook allows Roughskin to go outside to watch the guests arrive, but warns her to return in time to sweep up the ashes and put the kitchen in order. The princess goes to the stable, throws off the fur mantle and adorns herself in the dress that is golden as the sun. She presents herself at the castle as a visitor. The king dances with her, thinking, "My eyes have never seen any maiden before so beautiful as this."

After the dance, the princess-in-disguise vanishes. The king sends his servants to search for her but no one knows where she is. The princess has gone back to the stable to exchange her dress for her fur mantle. As she is sweeping the floor, the cook orders her to make soup for the king. She makes the soup and puts her gold ring into it.

The king eats the soup, which is the best he has ever tasted, and discovers the gold ring lying at the bottom of the dish. He sends for the cook and demands to know who has cooked it. "I did," says the cook. "That is not true," says the king. "You have never made soup this good before." The cook then confesses that Roughskin made the soup. The king sends for the princess-in-disguise and questions her, but she denies knowledge of the ring.

Some time later, the king again gives a festival, and Roughskin is given permission to watch the visitors arrive. This time she puts on the dress that is silvery as the moon and appears at the castle. The king keeps her dancing all evening, but when the ball ends, she again disappears. She returns to the stable, takes off her silvery dress and dons her fur mantle. She goes to the kitchen to cook the king's favorite soup, dropping in the gold spinning wheel. Again she is summoned to the king, but she denies knowledge of the spinning wheel.

For the third time, the king gives a festival, and this time the princess attends in the dress that glitters like the stars. While they are dancing, the king slips a gold ring on her finger without her being aware of it. The ball lasts longer than before, and when it is over, the princess has no time to remove her beautiful dress before throwing on her fur mantle. She prepares soup for the king and drops in the golden hook.

The king summons Roughskin to explain the golden hook, and when she enters the room, he sees the ring that he has placed on her finger. He seizes her and holds her fast. As she struggles to get away, the fur mantle falls from her shoulders, and she is revealed in her full splendor, wearing the dress that glitters like the stars. The king recognizes her as the woman he has come to love. She tells her story, and he claims her for his bride.

There are several examples of symbolic inversion in this story. The princess is transformed into a social role that is more appropriate for her mother. As such, she is expected to become the bride of her father. To evade him, she instigates a hunt for all the animals of the forest. Her plan fails, and she symbolically takes the place of the animals that were hunted by her father in the forest. She escapes the dangers of inappropriate domesticity by hiding in the forest. However, the forest is not a safe refuge for a princess, and she is transformed from the object of a royal sexual pursuit to the object of a royal hunt.

She is again domesticated, though not to her rightful place as the bride of a king. Rather, she is relegated to the kitchen, where her great beauty and royal birth must be concealed. At this point, she transforms herself from prey into predator, and the king is her prey. Now, however, the metaphor shifts from hunting to fishing. She uses as bait her beauty and her domestic skill in cooking the king's soup. The symbols she drops into the soup are remarkably explicit. With the ring, she signals the object of the game, which is matrimony; the spinning wheel is a metaphor for domesticity; and with the hook, she manages to reel in her catch.

Woman as Prey

Ovid's *The Art of Love* abounds with sporting metaphors. In Book I, written "for the man who needs instruction in loving," the poet cautions his male reader to go where the game is:

> Hunters know where to spread their nets for the stag in his covert,
>   Hunters know where the boar gnashes his teeth in the glade.
> Fowlers know brier and bush, and fishermen study the waters
>   Baiting the hook for the cast just where the fish may be found.
> So you too, in your hunt for material worthy of loving,
>   First will have to find out where the game usually goes.[83]

Ovid provides some helpful suggestions as to where the game might be found. He describes the theater as "a place for the chase, not the chaste." He also advises young men to look for women at the racetrack, where people must sit close together and "contact is part of the game." Regardless of his imagery, Ovid is clear on the nature of the relationship: Man is the pursuer, woman the pursued. Or as he expresses it in yet another metaphor, "Women don't run after us; mousetraps don't run after mice."

The American poet Edna St. Vincent Millay describes a woman's attempt to transform the object of a hunt in her poem, "Hunter, What Quarry?" The woman encounters a fox hunter and asks the purpose of his quest:

> "To tame or to destroy?"
> "To destroy."

The woman then tries to divert the fox hunter from his course:

> "Huntsman, hard by
> In a wood of gray beeches
> Whose leaves are on the ground,
> Is a house with a fire;
> You can see the smoke from here.
> There's supper and a soft bed
> And not a soul around.

Noting that the sun was near setting, the hunter considers this unusual request:

> He thought, "Shall I take her
> For a one-night's bride?"
> He smelled the sweet smoke,
> He looked the lady over;
> Her hand was on his knee;
> But like a flame from cover
> The red fox broke —
> And "Hoick! Hoick!" cried he.[84]

The poet seems to suggest that, of the primordial drives, the urge to kill is greater than the urge to mate. A poem from the Confucian *Book of Songs* cautions women against becoming the hunter's quarry, comparing a woman who has been seduced to a dead doe:

> In the wilds there is a dead doe;
> With white rushes we cover her.
> There was a lady longing for the spring;
> A fair knight seduced her.[85]

Women are not always seen as victims of love in the Confucian epic. The *Book of Songs* includes many paeans of love written by women that draw on a hunting theme. In the following example, the singer lauds her lover's skill with the bow and arrow:

Hey-ho, he is splendid!
Magnificent in stature,
Noble his brow,
His lovely eyes so bright,
Nimble in running,
A bowman unsurpassed.

Hey-ho, he is glorious!
Lovely eyes so clear,
Perfect in courtesy,
Can shoot all day at a target
And never miss the mark.
Truly a man of my clan.

Hey-ho, he is lovely!
His clear brow Well-rounded,
When he dances, never losing his place,
When he shoots, always piercing.
Swift his arrows fly
To quell mischief on every side.[86]

The sensuality of this poem endures across the millennia. Since Chinese marriages of that era, probably around the seventh century B.C.E., were arranged, women did not typically meet their husbands until their wedding day. This is likely the tribute of a noble wife to the husband she has come to love. In this case, the imagery is subtle and sophisticated. The poem could be read as a tribute to the husband's noble qualities, as well as a metaphor for sexuality.

The Weapon That Never Misses

The image of a sexually appealing man with a weapon that never misses is a recurring theme in the mythology of love. In the story of Procris and Cephalus, the woman gives her husband a javelin that never misses its target. This legend links together the themes of love and death as expressed in the symbolism of hunting. The beautiful Procris marries Cephalus, and at first, they are rapturous in their love. Soon after their wedding night, Cephalus goes hunting. As he lays a trap for a deer, he is himself captured by Aurora (the Roman name for Eos, the dawn). The new husband stays with Aurora for some time, but continually proclaims his love for his wife. Finally, the infuriated goddess sends him home with a curse: "Someday you'll wish you never saw your wife."

As Cephalus leaves Aurora, he ponders the words of the goddess and, like many another lover, assumes that his wife has been unfaithful. Although he has spent many months with Aurora, he is maddened by the thought of his wife's faithlessness. He returns home in disguise and makes his way to Procris' bedroom. He finds her grieving for her lost husband. He tries to force himself on her, but she resists, saying, "I am given to one man — Wherever he may be, I'm his alone." Though he wants to put away his disguise and take her into his arms as her one true husband and lover, Cephalus' jealousy blinds him to her devotion and he persists in trying to seduce her:

> After wild promises I thought I saw
> A look of doubt tremble across her features,
> Then, conquered by my own deceit, I cried,
> "O you are cursed; I am your only husband,
> But now disguised as your adulterer.
> Look! You have stained your bed — I am your witness!"[87]

Ashamed and enraged, Procris leaves her "traitor-husband and his hateful bed," and goes to hunt with Artemis (Diana). Cephalus begs her forgiveness and she returns to him, bringing as gifts a hunting dog and a gold-tipped javelin of marvelous make:

> It never fails to strike the thing it aims at,
> And it returns with proof of blood upon it
> Back to the hand that threw it.[88]

Cephalus and Procris enjoy several years of happy married life. Then one day while hunting, Cephalus becomes overheated and tries to "court a gentle breeze" to cool his heated brow. "Come to me, Aura," he says, "and press your lips against my heated breast; look how I burn!"

Unfortunately, Cephalus' whimsical comment to the breeze is overheard by someone who repeats it to Procris, who assumes that her husband in the forest with a woman. The next day, when Cephalus leaves for the hunt, she follows him and hides in some bushes to watch him. After hunting for some time, he lies down to rest, and again, calls to Aura, the breeze, to cool him with her breath. He hears a stirring in the bushes nearby, and thinking it some kind of game, throws his always-fatal javelin at it. To his horror, he discovers that he has killed his own beloved wife:

> I saw her dying, and O what pathos there
> To see her hands still try to tear the gift —
> Once hers to me — out of her yielding breast.
> I raised her body in my arms and, folding
> Her torn dress where she bled, I held her fast,
> Nor could I stop the flow of Blood. I prayed
> She would not leave me tainted with her death.[89]

The dying Procris begs Cephalus not to share her marriage bed with Aura. The hunter then realizes that Procris has been lured to her death by jealousy. He tells her that Aura is not another woman, and reassured that Cephalus loves only her, Procris dies happy in her husband's arms.

Greek mythology is replete with stories that link hunting with erotic love. Eros, the god of love, is personified as a divine archer. Lovers are victims wounded by his arrows. Love and sexuality are also depicted as a trap. Eros' mother Aphrodite, the goddess of love, ensnares men with her magic girdle, which makes them fall hopelessly in love with her. However, she is herself ensnared by her passion for Ares, the god of war. Although her father Zeus gives her in marriage to Hephaestus, the lame god who crafts beautiful jewelry from silver and gold, the goddess' three children are actually fathered by Ares.

One night the lovers stay too long in bed at Ares' palace and are seen by the sun-god Helios as he begins his journey across the sky. Helios reports what he has witnessed to Aphrodite's husband, who sets a trap for his errant wife. Hephaestus hammers out an extremely fine but unbreakable bronze hunting net, which he secretly attaches to his marriage bed. He then tells Aphrodite he is going away on a holiday. As soon as he leaves, Aphrodite sends for Ares. At dawn, the two lovers try to get out of bed, but are unable to escape. As Ovid tells it, though Hephaestus (or Vulcan to the Romans) was successful at the hunt, he was less successful as a husband:

> Both were caught up and held within the net.
> Then Vulcan, fisherman, threw wide his doors,
> Which shone in burnished shafts of ivory,
> And called the other gods to see his catch,
> To see how lovers act within their chains.[90]

Hephaestus then demands that Zeus return his marriage-gifts, but the most powerful of all the gods refuses, saying that Hephaestus is a fool for making a public display of his wife's faithlessness.

Contesting for Love

Many mythological themes pit the hero against the object of his love. In the story of Atalanta, it is the woman who establishes the guidelines for winning her hand and metes out the punishment for failure. She is not dependent on her father or any other man, and in the dramatic context of the race, Atalanta is not only the prize, she is the opponent, and she sets the price of defeat as death. However, her harsh dominion over the game of love is provoked by a divine warning. Atalanta, who is as swift as she is beautiful, is told by an oracle:

> Run from the thought of sleeping with a man;
> You shall be caught with one, and yet alive,
> Lose all that's yours, nor ever get away.[91]

From that day, Atalanta refuses all suitors. If they persist, she challenges them to a race. If the suitor wins, she will marry him; if she wins, the suitor will die. Ovid says the young men still come in droves to seek her hand, "Brash lovers who saw danger as delight...." One, Hippomenes, comes only for sport, to see the foolish youths try their luck and die. As he watches Atalanta's fleet form in the race, Hippomenes falls in love:

> Her grace in flight had magic of its own.
> Ribbons at feet and knees whipped by swift motion,
> O glorious hair like wings across white shoulders;
> And as a purple curtain hung at doorways
> Flushes its light on stone, so her swift body
> Seemed to take colour as it glanced beyond him
> She'd won the race and wore the winner's garland,
> Indifferent to the boys who went to death.[92]

By falling in love with Atalanta, Hippomenes is transformed from spectator into contestant. He challenges Atalanta and she, looking upon his beauty, half wants to lose. Instead, she begs him to forget her and return to his home:

> "For he was made to live and love forever;
> If all were well and Fate had not said no
> To dreams of marriage, he alone could take me,
> To share my bed, to hold me in his arms."[93]

But Hipppomenes is not dissuaded and he is not above a little trickery. He enlists the aid of the love goddess Venus, who gives him three golden apples. During the race, Hippomenes throws the apples one at a time. Distracted by their beauty, Atalanta stops to pick them up, thus losing the race, her heart and her hand to Hippomenes. Unfortunately, Hippomenes fails to thank Venus for her aid, so the goddess uses their love to destroy their happiness. As they are walking in a wood near a shrine to Cybele, the goddess of fertility, Venus inflames them with an irresistible passion. They make love in the temple, thus enraging Cybele, who transforms them into lions for punishment. Venus assesses their fate in conversation with her own lover Adonis, himself soon to be transformed into an anemone flower through a reckless encounter with a wild boar. Forever after, the goddess of love says of Atalanta and Hippomenes, "When they made love they sought deep-wooded places."[94]

The story of Atalanta on one level represents a contest between women and men, with winning and losing as a metaphor for control. However, the contest takes place within the context of wilderness versus domestication, mediated by the intervention of the gods. The balance of power shifts from female to male in the course of the myth.

Because of the mandate of destiny, Atalanta takes control of her relations with men, and at first, she is always victorious. Even Hippomenes falls victim to the lure of her sexuality. Through divine assistance, he is able to defeat her in the race and win her as his wife, but Atalanta's defeat is not a loss. As husband and wife, they are equal in power and passion, and in their love for each other. Each has conquered the other, but both are powerless in the hands of the gods. Atalanta cannot resist her fate, nor can she prevail against Venus, the goddess of love.

Atalanta resists the domestication of romantic love, but is "tamed" by Hippomenes. Distracted by their joy in each other, the lovers neglect their responsibilities to the gods. Because of their heedless regard for the conventions, they are transformed into animals. Thus, they are no longer governed by the "tame," which is appropriate for humans, but are consigned to the "wild," which is appropriate for animals. They may no longer love openly as husband and wife, but must seek "deep-wooded places," the remote areas of the forest. They have been driven from the world of women and men.

Significantly, it is Cybele, the "Great Mother" and goddess of fertility, who exacts this terrible vengeance. She "Put bits between their mouth and drove them smartly." (Ovid, *Metamorphoses*, Book X) In the end, according to Ovid, the lovers who refused subjugation were domesticated and trained to the yoke. But is Ovid correct in defining the fate of Atalanta and Hippomenes as subjugation? Venus, the goddess of romantic love and passion, subjects them to the yoke of Cybele, the goddess of fertility, thus subjecting their passions to the demands of convention. But, for these two reckless lovers, convention is death, as ordained by the oracle.

Erotic Love Transcended

Atalanta is not the only woman who tries to escape the tender trap of love. The nymph Daphne, daughter of a river-god, flees in terror from the sun-god Apollo. But whereas Atalanta eventually succumbs willingly to her amorous opponent, Daphne's story has a different outcome. Her adventure results from Apollo's carelessness in incurring the wrath of Eros (Cupid). The sun-god first angers Eros by slaying the great serpent Python with his arrows. Not content with this affront, Apollo (Phoebus) then proceeds to insult the boy-archer:

> Still heated by his conquest of the snake,
> Phoebus saw Cupid wind a tight-strung bow,
> "Who is this lecherous child," said he, "who plays
> With weapons and is not a man? The bow
> Was made for me; I am the one who kills
> A worthy enemy, wild beasts — and look at
> Great Python wallowing in blood; his body
> Covers half the countryside. Your business
> Is not to play with arrows, but set afire
> Your little torch that guides unwary lovers."[95]

Undaunted, Cupid retorts that even great heroes cannot withstand the onslaught of love. He reminds Apollo that the power to kill is insignificant compared to the power to inspire love:

"Your arrows may be murder to us all,
But mine shall pierce your veins: as much
As mortals are less than the divine, so
Your poor glory is less than my poor skill."[96]

Then, just as Apollo killed Python with his arrows, Cupid uses his own arrows to inflame the sun-god with a passion for Daphne. At the same time, he inspires Daphne with a deep repugnance for the very thought of love. Even as her father urges her to marry and give him grandchildren, Daphne begs him to let her remain a virgin. Neither is a match for Apollo's passion. Daphne runs to escape the god, who follows swiftly after. In his pursuit of the nymph, Apollo makes explicit the metaphorical relationship between love and the hunt:

"O daughter of the deep green-shadowed River,
Who follows you is not your enemy;
The lamb runs from the wolf, the deer from lion,
The trembling-feathered dove flies from the eagle
Whose great wings cross the sky — such is your flight
While mine is love's pursuit....
....
My arrows never fail — and yet one arrow
More certain of its aim than mine wakes fire
Behind the chambers of an indifferent heart...."[97]

As she flees Apollo's amorous pursuit, Daphne is changed into a laurel tree. Deprived of the object of his desire, Apollo embraces the tree and declares the laurel to be the crowning ornament of emperors and victorious generals. Laurel wreaths were also used to crown victorious athletes. There is an additional link between the story of athletic contests and the story of Apollo and Daphne. As punishment for his slaughter of Python, Apollo was made to establish the Pythian Games, one of the four great Greek athletic festivals.

The motif of transcendence is also illustrated by the Buddhist legend of Suprabha. The daughter of a prominent citizen of Cravasti, Suprabha is so beautiful all the distinguished young men of the city want to marry her. However, she rejects her suitors to follow the Buddha as a nun. One day, as she is leaving the forested park where Buddha and his followers stay, she is recognized by one of her former suitors. He and his friends decide to carry her off to become his bride:

Before Suprabha is aware of it, she is surrounded, and they suddenly rush upon her. But as they are about to seize her, she directs her thoughts to the Buddha, and, immediately, she rises in the air. A crowd gathers; Suprabha soars above them for a while and then, flying with the grace and majesty of a swan, she returns to her sacred dwelling in the forest [Herold 1954:225].

On seeing the young woman take flight, the crowd calls after her: "O saintly one, you make manifest the power of the faithful; O saint, you render manifest the power of the Buddha. It would be unjust to condemn you to the earthly pleasures of love, O saintly one, O saint."

Symbolic transformation is evident throughout this story. As an object of desire, Suprabha is compared to the prey of a hunter. She dwells in the forest, a lair of game animals. She emerges from the forest, which is consecrated to the Buddha and therefore sacred. To avoid being trapped by humans, she is transformed into a bird-like creature and flies away, back to the forest. At the same time, she is transported from the mundane world of humans to the spiritual world of saints.

In the story of Suprabha, oppositions include male-female, hunter-prey, nurture-nature, clearing-forest, profane-sacred, human-swan, earthbound-aloft, desirous-transcendent and erotic love-spiritual power. Thus the forest is equated with nature and spirituality, whereas the cleared area represents the everyday earthbound world of humans. Just as Suprabha escapes the snare of her would-be lover, she transcends the social obligations incumbent upon ordinary mortals.

The Buddhist story of Suprabha has some commonalities with that of the sixteenth century Spanish mystic St. Teresa of Avila. Just as Suprabha rejected her suitors and left the world of men to follow the Buddha, St. Teresa left a life of worldly pleasures to become a "bride of Christ" as a Catholic nun in the strict Carmelite order. However, whereas the symbolism of Suprabha's story has clear associations with hunting, the pervasive metaphors of St. Teresa's writings are romantic love and war. She writes: "You, my true Lover, have begun this war of love...." Addressing God as her "Spouse" and as her "Conqueror," St. Teresa asserts that her only recourse is surrender. God both inflicts her wounds and is the source of their healing. As in the case of romantic and erotic symbolism mentioned earlier, St. Teresa ascribes her wounds to the "darts of love": "O true Lover, with how much compassion, with how much gentleness, with how much delight, with how much favor and with what extraordinary signs of love You cure these wounds, which with the darts of this same love You have caused!"[98]

There is a significant difference between the story of Suprabha and St. Teresa. At the time Suprabha leaves her father's house to follow the Buddha, he is in human form in his ultimate incarnation. She has followed an enlightened mortal man who has put aside sensual attachments as a discipline for spiritual transcendence. By following the Buddha, Suprabha will eventually be released from the cycle of birth and death.

St. Teresa, on the other hand, is barred from union with her divine Lover because she is trapped in her earthly body. Unlike Suprabha, she cannot fly away from the world of humans. She will see her Lover only after her own death. In describing her rapturous longing for God, St. Teresa is not seeking only a symbolic death to sensory attachments; she is speaking as well of her literal death:

> O my delight, Lord of all created things and my God! How long must I
> wait to see You? What remedy do You provide for one who finds so little

on earth that might give some rest apart from You? O long life! O painful life! O life that is not lived! Oh, what lonely solitude; how incurable! Well, when, Lord, when? How long? What shall I do, my God, what shall I do? Should I, perhaps, desire not to desire You? Oh, my God and my Creator, You wound and You do not supply the medicine; You wound and the sore is not seen; You kill, leaving one with more life![99]

In stories of feminine transcendence, erotic love is symbolically presented as a trap that binds the heroine to a world of domestic relationships, which prevent her from realizing other aspirations. In escaping or rejecting that snare, she achieves some form of transformation. Daphne becomes a triumphant crown; Suprabha transcends human limitations; St Terese achieves mystical union with her Lord. They represent the inverse of the story of Hero and Leander. Hero turns away from her duties as priestess to the God and Goddess of Love to embrace a real-life lover. She, too, is united with the object of her love — in death.

The idea that ordinary erotic love presents a barrier to, or is opposed to, spiritual aspiration underlies many religious beliefs and practices. It is the basis for sexual abstinence practiced by priests and nuns in both the Buddhist and Roman Catholic traditions. This view is related to the concept of an opposition between the sacred and the mundane. Those who seek union with the sacred must extricate themselves from the cares of the mundane world.

In Western tradition, this is often expressed theologically and in the scholarly literature as the barrier between the sacred and the profane. The idea that the ordinary world is profane dates back to the Romans, who philosophically framed the mind-body dichotomy. This found its way into Christianity through the writings of the apostle Paul, who announced that he beat his body in order to subdue it. As the Romans introduced Christianity throughout Europe, the idea of the body as traitor to the mind or soul prevailed in Western philosophy and theology.

In the European tradition, sexuality is especially stigmatized. In Roman Catholic theology, it is acceptable only for the purpose of procreation. A similar view is prevalent among the British nobility, among whom the production of sons is essential to continuance of hereditary titles and property rights. This view underlies the quotation attributed to the nineteenth-century monarch Queen Victoria. Though she was devoted to her husband, Prince Albert, she viewed sex as a duty rather than a pleasure. When she was asked by a friend how she was able to endure sex with such stoicism as to produce eleven children for the monarchy, she reportedly replied, "I close my eyes and think of England."

In many other traditions, sexuality is used metaphorically to produce fertility on many levels. In Japanese Shinto mythology, the sexual union of the god Izanagi and the goddess Izanami produced the sun, the moon, and the topography of Japan, as well as the present line of emperors. In Hindu belief, sexual union reflects the ultimate unity of the universe, Brahman, the creative force that is neither male nor female since it encompasses both. In Greek mythology, the offspring of primal parents govern both the forces of nature and cosmic events, as well as human affairs. In tantric Buddhism and Hinduism, sexuality is one path to enlightenment.

In general, however, humans must choose between sensual pleasures and the quest for immortality through transcendence. Both types of adventures are well represented in the symbolism of sport.

The Spiritual Quest

Even the medieval Christian mystic Meister (John) Eckhart, who lived in Germany from 1260 to 1328 C.E., used sporting terms to describe the individual's relationship to God. Like many other theologians in the Christian tradition, Meister Eckhart viewed the body as the enemy of the spirit or soul:

> The body is too strong for the spirit and so there is always a struggle between them — an eternal conflict. The body is bold and brave here, for it is at home and the world helps it. This earth is its fatherland and all its kindred are on its side: food, drink, and comforts are all against the spirit. Here the spirit is alien. Its race and kin are all in heaven.[100]

Meister Eckhart was not above mixing his sporting metaphors. He moves quickly from the wrestling mat to the stables. To keep the body from conquering the spirit, he recommended a number of penances — fasting, praying, kneeling, wearing hair shirts and lying on hard surfaces — as a way of weakening the flesh to give the spirit a chance to control it. The penances, he says, act like a bridle to curb the body. Not all of Meister Eckhart's disciplines are harsh, however. He adds that, "to make [the body] a thousand times more subject, put the bridle of love on it." In comparing the body to a horse, he did not have in mind anything so flighty as a racehorse. Rather, he wanted the body to be docile like a workhorse: "With love you may overcome it most quickly and load it most heavily." Meister Eckhart then moves from the stables to the stream by comparing God to a fisherman:

> That is why God lies in wait for us with nothing so much as love. Love is like a fisherman's hook. Without the hook he could never catch a fish, but once the hook is taken the fisherman is sure of the fish. Even though the fish twists hither and yon, still the fisherman is sure of him. And so, too, I speak of love: he who is caught by it is held by the strongest of bonds and yet the stress is pleasant.... To hang on this hook is to be so [completely] captured that feet and hands, and mouth and eyes, the heart, and all a man is and has, become God's own.

Meister Eckhart was concerned with the idea of mystical rebirth, what he calls the "eternal birth." The individual must die to the senses and surrender his will to experience the divine birth, which "Must come flooding up and out of man from God within him...":

> It is a fair trade and an equal exchange: to the extent that you depart from things, thus far, no more and no less, God enters into you with all that

is his, as far as you have stripped yourself of yourself in all things. It is here that you should begin, whatever the cost, for it is here that you will find true peace, and nowhere else.[101]

If one substituted the word "senses" for Meister Eckhart's word "body," the Roman Catholic mystic would be considered a good Buddhist. He is also Buddhist-like in his call for a surrender of the self to gain self-mastery:

> Holy Scripture cries aloud for freedom from self. Self-free is self-controlled, and self-controlled is self-possessed, and self-possession is God-possession and possession of everything that God ever made. I say to you, as true as God is God and I am a man, if you were quite free from self, free as the highest angel, then you would be as much like the highest angel as you would be yourself. This method gives self-mastery.[102]

The concept of mystical death and rebirth is pervasive among religions that emphasize direct experience of the divine. The thirteenth-century Sufi poet Jalalúddin Rumi writes similarly of the ecstasy of loving union with God. Whereas Meister Eckhart compares the mystical experience of God to a flood, Rumi follows Sufi convention in comparing religious ecstasy to being drunk from wine:

> Constantly serve the truth and you will become eternal.
> Lose yourself in the excitement and frenzy of true love.
> Boil like the wine in the barrel of your body
> Then see yourself becoming the divine companion and
>   the Saaqi.[103]

Saaqi, which means "cupbearer," is used by Rumi as a metaphor for a moment of divinely induced ecstasy. Like Meister Eckhart, Rumi also uses sporting metaphors to express surrender to God, but in his case, the sport is polo:

> Do you think I am in command here?
> Do you think that even a single breath belongs to me?
> I am like a pen in the hand of a writer, who is indeed
>   myself
> Like a polo stick, surrendered to the polo master,
>   who is me.[104]

However, Rumi also draws on the hunting metaphor to represent the spiritual quest:

> Little by little, wean yourself.
> ......
> From an embryo, whose nourishment comes in the blood,
> move to an infant drinking milk,
> to a child on solid food,
> to a searcher after wisdom,
> to a hunter of more invisible game.[105]

"Hunting" and Enlightenment

The symbolism of the hunt is widespread in Buddhist mythology. When Siddhartha Gautama (later Buddha Sakyamuni, the founder of Buddhism) leaves the palace of his father and sets out on his quest for enlightenment, his first garment, an emblem of his new life, is given to him by a hunter. Siddhartha is still wearing his princely robes and is looking around for plainer ones more appropriate for the life of an ascetic, when a hunter suddenly appears, wearing a coarse garment of reddish material. Siddhartha says to him: "Your peaceful robe is like those worn by hermits; it offers a strange contrast to your savage bow. Give me your clothes and take mine in exchange. They will suit you better" (Herold 1954:66).

The hunter replies: "Thanks to these clothes I can deceive the beasts in the forests. They do not fear me, and I can kill them at close range. But if you have need of them, my lord, I shall willingly give them to you and take yours in exchange." After the two exchange clothes, the hunter disappears into the sky and Siddhartha joyfully realizes the gods wished to present him with his hermit's robe, his new badge of office.

In Buddhist lore, the hunt is often used as a metaphor for transformation. The hunter becomes the prey; the selfish becomes selfless in an act of sacrifice. One such story involves the king of the city of Atavi, who is very fond of hunting. One day, he sees an enormous deer and starts to pursue it. The deer escapes and the king, now weary and discouraged, falls asleep under a tree in which dwells the man-eating demon Avalaka.

The king awakens just as the demon is about to make a meal of him. The distraught king pleads for his life, promising to give the demon precious gifts. Avalaka replies, "What care I for gifts? It is your flesh I want." In exchange for his own life, the king sends the demon the inmates of his kingdom's prisons. When all the prison populations are exhausted, he begins sending old people to Avalaka. At last, fearing that the population of his kingdom will be decimated, the king calls on the Buddha for help.

When the Buddha confronts Avalaka, the demon first tries to overpower the Holy One. When this fails, Avalaka poses four questions which the Buddha must answer or surrender his life: How can man avoid the river of passions? How can he cross the sea of existences and find safe harbor? How can he escape the tempests of evil? How can he be left untouched by the storm of desires? The Buddha responds:

> Man avoids the river of passions if he believes in the Buddha, in the law and in the community [the Buddha, the Dharma, and the Sangha]; he crosses the sea of existences and finds safe harbor if he understands works of holiness; he will escape the tempests of evil if he performs works of holiness; he will be left untouched by the storm of desires if he knows the sacred path that leads to deliverance [the Eight-Fold Path] [Herold 1954:251].

Hearing this, Avalaka falls down and worships the Buddha, promising to change his misanthropic ways. The two then go to the palace of the king, who also becomes a follower of the Buddha.

The Jatakas are stories describing episodes in the Buddha's previous lives, used to illustrate the Holy One's compassion and wisdom, as well as to provide instruction to devotees. The Banyan Deer Jataka uses the context of hunting to explain how the future Buddha, a Bodhisattva, wins amnesty for all creatures. In this Jataka, the Bodhisattva is reborn as a beautiful deer and is called the Banyan Deer King. He is one of two leaders of deer herds in a forest near Benares. The other is called Branch Deer.

The king of Benares is a passionate hunter, daily assembling the men of the kingdom as beaters to drive the game to him. The king's excessive love of hunting disrupts their work, so the men enclose the deer in a part to allow the king to shoot them at his pleasure. Because of their beauty — and no doubt their affinity with royalty — the man-king grants the two deer-kings immunity from being hunted and killed.

It soon becomes apparent that the plan contains a flaw. As soon as the deer see the bow, they become frightened and run away, injuring themselves, and eventually dying a horrible and painful death from their wounds. Seeing this, the Banyan Deer works out an agreement with the king and the Branch Deer. Each day a deer will offer itself for execution, sparing all the others agony and uncertainty of pursuit. The plan will also avoid waste, since it eliminates the possibility of a deer dying from its injuries in the forest, alone and unclaimed. The two deer-kings agree that the responsibility for offering a deer for execution will alternate between the herds of the Banyan Deer and the Branch deer.

One day the turn falls to a pregnant doe who is in the herd of the Branch Deer. She goes to her leader and begs to be excused, arguing that, in effect, two deer are being sent to the execution block. She says, "When I have brought forth my kid, we will go in our turn as two persons." The Branch King denies her plea, ordering her at once to the execution block.

The doe takes her case to the Banyan Deer, the future Buddha, who excuses her and offers himself for execution instead. When the king sees the deer-king on the chopping block, he exclaims: "Friend deer-king, did I not give you immunity? Why are you lying here?" The Banyan Deer tells the king of the pregnant doe, saying, "It was impossible for me to place the deadly trouble of one upon another. I, giving her my own life and taking the death that belongs to her, have lain down here."

The king replies, "Friend deer-king of golden hue, never have I seen even among men one who had such forbearance, goodwill and kindness. I am pleased with you. To both you and her I give immunity."

"Two have won immunity," the deer-king responds. "What will the rest do, ruler of men?"

"To the rest also I give immunity, master," the king answers.

"Your majesty, the deer in the park will have won immunity," the Banyan Deer king says. "What will the others do?"

"To these also I give immunity, master," the king of Benares replies. In this way, the Bodhisattva/deer-king wins immunity for all four-footed animals, the birds and the fishes.[106]

This story not only demonstrates the kindness, good sense and generosity of the Buddha in his previous lives, it also gives the symbolic origin of a number of cultural practices. Containment of the deer in the park parallels the domestication of animals for use by humans, though the relationship remains one of predator and prey. The institution of animal sacrifice, as expressed in the daily offering of a deer, emphasizes the role of animal as food, both for humans and gods, a pervasive theme in the history of sacrifice. The animal goes willingly to its death, the human refrains from wanton slaughter, and the gods are provided with sustenance appropriate to their nature. Ultimately, all animals are given immunity, which establishes equality between the lives of humans and animals. The story also gives the mythical origins of the prohibition against eating meat. It is virtually an account, in symbolic form, of the history of society and religion in India.

The story also expresses the relationship of the Buddha to Devadatta, a monk who sought to displace the Holy One as leader of the Buddhists. Devadatta, in a previous incarnation, was the Branch Deer. According to legend, Devadatta was a kinsman of Siddhartha Gautama, who on his enlightenment became the Buddha. Devadatta gave up his worldly wealth to follow the Buddha, but he did not give up his worldly ways.

Almost from the beginning, Devadatta's concern for rank becomes apparent, and eventually, he plots to depose the Buddha, enlisting the aid of a powerful king. However, the Buddha prevails because of his superior wisdom and virtue. The relationship between the Buddha and Devadatta is stated explicitly in stories about the life of the Buddha; it is expressed symbolically in the story of the Banyan Deer. The Branch Deer, like Devadatta, is bound to convention and unconcerned with the well-being of his herd. He lacks compassion for those in his care, whereas the Banyan Deer (Buddha) has compassion for all.

Rivalry is an important part of the hero myth, because the hero needs an enemy against whom to test his skills. The contest between the hero and his opponent also creates the dramatic interest that makes the story appealing to its audience. At the same time, those who hear about the trials of the hero experience them as metaphors for their own struggles. The eventual triumph of the hero contains the implicit message that the listener, too, can anticipate a positive outcome.

There is a key difference between the immortal deified hero, as opposed to the heroic human figure. The mortal hero wins every battle, except the one that eventually brings about his death. One message of these types of myths is that everyone must die. However, gods do not die. In fact, they must not die, since they control the fates of the mortals. Thus, the end of their story is not death but transcendence, and their character does not contain a fatal flaw.

Deities may be flawed, as in the case of Greek gods and goddesses, but their frailties do not bring about the end of the story or the death of the deity. The very human passions of the gods provide dramatic interest. The myth centers on working out conflicts engendered by the flaws. The story does not end with the death of the hero, but with his transcendence. The spiritual leader is transformed to another type of existence, from which exalted realm he assists his followers in their own struggles.

In stories of the Buddha or other religious leaders, flaws are typically externalized and personified in the form of a powerful enemy. The enemy is eventually defeated, but remains a potential threat to present-day followers of the religion. The implicit message is: "Be careful that you are not like Devadatta, or Judas, or Satan, because you will then become an enemy of the Holy One, Who will eventually triumph. Do not align yourself with Evil and defeat."

The Peyote "Deer" Hunt

The hunt as a metaphor for the spiritual quest is acted out in the ritual of Huichol Indians of Mexico. Huichol, who use the hallucinogenic peyote cactus in their rituals to achieve transcendence, describe their search for the cactus as a "hunt" and the cactus itself as a "deer." The "hunters" or *peyoteros* track down the peyote cactus in the sacred mountains where it grows. The first plant to be seen by the leader of the hunting party is believed to contain the essence of Elder Brother *Wawatsdri*, master of the deer. The peyote cactus is first "shot" with a bow and arrow before it is dug from the ground and ritually divided among the hunters.

The Deer-Peyote also embodies Maize, a sacred personification of corn, the plant that forms the subsistence base for the Huichol. Thus, the peyote hunt is directly linked to survival. When the Huichol go on the peyote hunt, they say, "We go to find our life."

The peyote ritual re-enacts a mythical first hunt led by *Tatewari*, "our grandfather," a deity who is the personification of fire. According to the myth, the ancient gods were summoned by Tatewari to a sacred assembly place he had constructed so that each might have his or her proper place. There they discovered that each suffered from some form of illness, and none was capable of fulfilling his or her function. Those responsible for rain were producing no rain, and the masters of animals were finding nothing to hunt.

Tatewari told the gods they were ill because they had not made a pilgrimage to the sacred mountains of *Wirikuta*, land of the peyote and the place to the east where the Sun was born. If they wished to regain their health, Tatewari said, they must prepare themselves ritually and follow him in their proper order on the long and difficult journey to the land of the peyote. They must fast and drink only small amounts of water. Only male gods would make the trek. Female gods would wait for them at the sacred lakes or water holes called *Tatei Matinieri* (Place of Our Mother), which are within sight of the sacred mountains.

Not all the divine peyote seekers completed the journey. Some, like Rabbit Person and Hummingbird Person, dropped out along the way and remained in animal form. However, the principal male and female gods — the Rain Mothers and those of the Earth-Ready-for-Planting and of fertility and children — followed Tatewari to the sacred mountains at the end of the world to the fifth level, where the Deer-Peyote revealed itself to them in the ceremonial hunt. This is how the gods "found their life" in the primordial hunt and taught the Huichol to do the same.

The quest takes place following the "ceremony of the drum and the squash," after fall harvests. The drum ceremony probably has sexual connotations. The drum or *tepu* has a hole or "mouth" in front. Sacred smoke emerges from the hole when burning pitch pine brands are placed beneath the drum to tighten and tune the deerskin drumhead. The drum is believed to be female; the fire and pitch pine brands are male.

The anthropologist Peter Furst suggests that the peyote hunt symbolizes ritual rebirth. It begins with ceremonial confession and purification. Everyone who plans to participate in the hunt must confess his or her sexual adventures, identifying each sex partner by name. A shaman (ritual specialist) — the modern representative of Tatewari — ties a knot in a cord for each escapade. After each confession, he brushes his ceremonial arrow with pendant hawk plumes over the peyotero's face, shoulder, arms and chest, down the thighs and knees to the feet. The shaman then directs the seeker to face *Tatewari*, the purifying fire, and ask that he "burn away everything, everything, burn away all your transgressions, burn it all away, so that nothing will remain, so that you will be new" (Furst 1972:156). The peyotero holds first one hand and then the other to the fire, then does the same with his feet. Some leap over the flames. After everyone has been purified, including the shaman, he places the cord, now covered with knots, into the fire, thus ritually burning away their transgressions.

The shaman then takes a longer cord and holds one end to the back of his hunting bow, beats the bowstring several times with an arrow and then chants quietly. Then he touches each peyotero with the cord and ties a knot in it for each. He passes the cord around all those assembled, linking them to the back of the bow and to each other. This cord is taken along on the peyote hunt.

On the way to the sacred mountains, novice peyoteros, who are "new and delicate," are blindfolded before passing through the Gateway of Clashing Clouds, considered to be a dangerous place. They walk blindfolded until they get to the "Place of Our Mothers." The novices are told to squat near the water holes, make themselves small and keep their heads down, thus assuming a fetal position. The shaman dips his ceremonial arrow into one of the water holes — viewed as a rain or fertility Mother — and ritually purifies a gourd bowl. He then removes the blindfold of each novice, allowing him to see the sacred mountains for the first time. The shaman then pours a gourdful of water over the novice's head and gives him another gourdful to drink. The novice is then given his "first food," consisting of bits of tortilla softened by being soaked in sacred water, much as a child's first food is softened. Everyone one on the quest, including the shaman, is ritually bathed.

The anthropologist Peter Furst (1972) suggests the entire first part of the ceremony represents a ritual of rebirth. Confession reduces the peyoteros to the innocence of the newborn. The cord represents the umbilical cord, and the knots represent those tied by the midwife at birth. The ritual bath at the "Place of Our Mothers' evokes the first washing by the midwife. The novice then "emerges into the light" at the feet of the sacred mountains.

When they arrive at the sacred land of the peyote, the male adepts and initiates stalk the "deer" with bow and arrow, look for "tracks," and when the peyote is located, shoot it with arrows to "kill" it. They sob and pray as Elder Brother-Deer-Peyote lies dying. When the peyote dies, experienced peyoteros can see its rainbow-colored spirit rise from its body. The shaman implores:

> Do not be angry, Elder Brother, do not punish us for killing you, for you have not really died. You will rise again. We will feed you well, for we have brought you many offerings, we have brought you tobacco, we have brought you water from Our Mothers, we have brought you arrows, we have brought you votive gourds, we have brought you maize and your favorite grasses, we have brought you tamales, we have brought you our prayers. We honor you and we give you our devotion. Take them, Elder Brother, take them and give us our life. We offer our devotion to the *kakauyarixi* who live here in *Wirikuta*; we have come to be received by them, for we know they await us. We have come from afar to greet you [Furst 1972:175].

The shaman then uses his ceremonial bow to push the life essence back into the Peyote-Deer, chanting as he does so. All around the dead deer, he says, peyotes are springing up, growing from his horns, his back, his tail, his shins, his hooves.[107] The shaman then cuts away the peyote, leaving a piece of root so that more peyote can "grow from his bones." The shaman cuts the peyote into five pieces and gives them to the peyoteros, who chew them for their hallucinogenic effect.

The peyote hunt is viewed as a process of "completing oneself," and peyoteros are believed to be transformed into spirit beings for the duration of the hunt. An experienced leader is said to have what the Huichol call "balance": "that special, ineffable capacity to venture without fear onto the 'narrow bridge' across the great chasm separating the ordinary world from the world beyond" (Furst 1972:152). Though "balance" is believed to be a quality of spirit, it can be manifest through physical control. Peter Furst describes a demonstration by Ramon, a Huichol shaman, who was able to leap great distances over a great chasm. Ramon later explained, "Those who do not have balance are afraid. They fall and are killed." The concept of spiritual "balance" expressed through physical power is one the Bodhidharma, legendary founder of Zen and kung fu, would understand very well.

The Divine Archery Contest: Transcending Love and Death

The bow and arrow point the way to transcendence in the Japanese archery tradition. The term *kyudo*, "the way of the archer," involves much more than the ability to hit a target. Kyudo is in the Zen tradition of Japanese Buddhism. The object is to achieve balance among mind, body and bow, which gives rise to a unity that links the spirit to the target. Hitting the target is less important than attaining perfect technique and self-discipline. The archer practices correct breathing to control the mental and physical force — or *ki*— that is believed to be centered below the navel. Proper technique ultimately leads to perfect serenity. According to an ancient Zen saying, "You can find your own character in the moment of shooting."

Kyudo begins with a series of formal bows. The bow is drawn and released in eight stages which, when skillfully executed, appear to be one continuous movement. At the sixth stage, the body of the archer is on a line with the target, which is also the focus of his attention. As the archer holds the pose, *ki* is believed to be concentrated and flows downward the feet. The name for this stage is *kai* or "meeting."

At the seventh stage, when the archer feels he is in a state of oneness with the target, the arrow is released. This is seen, not as an act of volition by the archer, but as a result of the unity the archer has achieved with the target:

> Like a heavy drop of water…
> that decides to be free,
> the arrow liberates itself.

The term for this stage is *hanare* or "release." At this point, it is believed that there is an explosion of energy flowing through the body of the archer, who then completes the stage in a cruciform position. His arms are at a ninety-degree angle to his body, level with his shoulders, his feet are apart, his gaze is on the target, and his entire body is in line with the flight of the arrow.

Archery is a metaphor for spiritual striving in the *Upanishads*. In Hindu belief, Brahman is the creative energy that underlies all the phenomenal world. The *Mundaka Upanashad* urges readers to aim for unity with Brahman: "He is immortal. He is real. Attain him, O my friend, the one goal to be attained." The poet-priest who authored this Upanishad then gives a graphic illustration of how unity with Brahman is to be achieved:

> Affix to the Upanishad, the bow, incomparable, the sharp arrow of devotional worship; then, with mind absorbed and heart melted in love, draw the arrow and hit the mark — the imperishable Brahman.
>
> OM is the bow, the arrow is the individual being, and Brahman is the target. With a tranquil heart, take aim. Lose thyself in him, even as the arrow is lost in the target.[108]

The OM is the sacred syllable that evokes Brahman in Vedic and Hindu tradition. It is used both as a mantra, or chant, and an object of meditation.

Although there are parallels between the imagery of archery in the Hindu and Japanese Zen tradition, there are significant differences in the use of symbolism. For both, the ultimate goal is transcendence. For Hindus, this means union with

Brahman, the creative spirit that underlies all being. Archery is used as a metaphorical image to help the believer visualize his relationship to Brahman so that he can transcend ordinary reality.

Zen Buddhists, on the other hand, strive to transcend symbols for a direct experience of *satori* or *nirvana*. In the Hindu example presented in the Upanishads, the target represents Brahman; in Japanese archery, the target represents merely itself. Kyudo is a ritual that transforms the archer. It does not "stand for" anything else. Performing the act *is* the transcendent experience.

PART 5. SYMBOLIC ACTORS AND SOCIAL DRAMAS

Eight

High Priests and Super Stars

All his friends rejoice in the friend who emerges with fame and victory in the contest. He saves them from error and gives them food. He is worthy to be pushed forward to win the prize.

The Rg Veda

"You know me," he said, trembling from Parkinson's disease. "I'm a boxer." It may have been Muhammad Ali's most eloquent moment in a long career marked by *bon mots*. He often described his boxing style as "Float like a butterfly; sting like a bee." Coming ten days after the destruction of the Twin Towers of the World Trade Center in New York in 2001, an event that transformed the New York skyline, Ali was appearing on an international multimedia program featuring top entertainers to raise money for victims. Eighteen hijackers, believed to be Islamic fundamentalists, had diverted four U.S. commercial airliners to use as guided missiles against the country's cultural icons.

Ali, a living cultural icon, then delivered his own message: Don't add to the list of horrors by directing hate crimes against Muslims. "I wouldn't be here representing Islam if it were terrorist," he said. "I think all people should know the truth, come to recognize the truth. Islam is peace."

Though directed to non–Muslims in the United States, the message went out to Muslims and others around the world, reminding them of what he believed was the true contribution of one of the world's great religions. It was a powerful example of symbolic inversion. The hijackers, in attacking cultural icons of the United States, had also hijacked Islam and subjected other Muslims to reprisals in the form of hate crimes directed against them and in U.S. military sorties against Muslim countries. Muhammad Ali attacked the hijackers, not with his fists, but with words.

Ali's appeal was a rare event in the history of sports symbolism. In most cases, the eloquence of sports symbolism takes place on the field, not the stage, in actions, not words.

A less scripted moment of sports symbolism took place on the same day, when New York Mayor Rudolph Giuliani "sought to serve as chief grief counselor to a suffering city."[109] "You can mourn and you can be very sorrowful," he said. "But at the same time, you can go on with your life. It's OK, I mean, that's part of grieving. When people feel comfortable with it, they really should go out and do things they normally do." Giuliani then described his plan for taking his own advice: "I'm gonna go to a Mets game."

Baseball games in the United States had been cancelled in the wake of the tragedy, and the New York Mets were scheduled to play their first game, at home in Shea Stadium, since the fall of the Twin Towers. Also in the audience for that first game was 7-year-old Jack Hord, whose father died in the north tower of the World Trade Center. Draped in the American flag and with the Stars and Stripes painted on their faces, the boy and his friend — along with the mayor — watched the Mets pull off a 3-2 win over the Atlanta Braves. Mike Piazza, who hit the winning home run for the Mets, said after the game, "We just wanted to give the people something to cheer about."

"We Have Met the Enemy, and He Is Us"

One of the greatest of Persian kings described in the *Shah-nama*, Key Khosrow, personally led his armies against Afrasiyah, the Turkish king who represented the forces of evil for the Persians. Key Khosrow, commander of the forces of good, prevails after a hard-fought battle. Despite Afrasiyah's please for mercy, Key Khosrow cuts off his head, and for 60 years reigns in peace. At the end of that time, Key Krosrow meditates upon his accomplishments as king:

> I have now exacted vengeance for my father and adorned the world with prosperity. I have killed all who deserved death, all whose way was crooked and who behaved in barbarous fashion towards the pure gods. There remains no land, whether cultivated or waste, in which the proclamation of my sword is not recited. The great ones of the world are my vassals, thought they be possessed of throne and diadem. Praise be to God, who granted me this *Farr* [kingly radiance], this phase of the stars, my foothold and my power to give protection.... No man will achieve greater fame and success, power and fortune, peace and satisfaction, than I have done. We have heard and seen the secret of the world, its evil and its good, whether revealed or hidden [Ferdowsi 1985:175].

But Key Khosrow recites his achievements in a voice of despair, not of triumph. Now that all his earthly enemies have been vanquished, the king fears that he will at last give way to that most treacherous of opponents, the enemy within:

> Many a long day has passed over my head and from the gods I have received all my desires. Yet I have turned my mind to war, my spirit finds no defense against lust, against the contemplation of evil or the belief in Ahriman [the Prince of Darkness]. I shall become a malefactor [like some of my forebears].... I shall without warning turn ungratefully away from

> God and bring terror into the serene souls of men. The divine *Farr* will break away from me and I shall turn to crookedness and unwisdom, after which I shall pass away into darkness and my head and diadem will enter into the dust. In the world, all that will remain of me will be ill repute; an evil end will await me in the presence of God [Ferdowsi 1985:175].

For five weeks the great king remains awake, praying for guidance on how to avoid falling prey to the demons who threaten him from within. When at last he sleeps, he is visited by an angel, who advises him:

> King of felicitous star, monarch of happy fate, you have been accustomed for long to the collar of kingship, the crown and the throne, and now you have achieved all you have sought. If you depart immediately from this world, you will find an bode in the shade of the pure Lawgiver. Linger no further in this darkness [Ferdowsi 1985:178].

Heading the words of his heavenly visitor, Key Khosrow yields his throne to his son. He bids goodbye to his family and subjects, and journeys to the mountainous frontiers of his kingdom, where he disappears in a snowstorm. Like all great heroes, Key Khosrow has learned that he can never completely subjugate the enemy within — he can only fight the monster to a draw.

It is the ultimate lesson of all great legends and of all great sporting contests. Whether it involves a ritual battle against the forces of evil, a ball game against a feared rival, or the conquest of Mount Everest, the enemy will return again and again. In fact, the enemy is never vanquished; it is merely transformed. As one avid surfer succinctly put it, every wave is different.

From Angel to Athlete

The same existential conflict that lies at the heart of religion also gave rise to the sporting contest. Originally, the parallel symbolic systems of religion and sport operated in tandem. However, they diverged through time. Religion has adhered to the realm of the sacred, whereas sport has undergone a process of secularization. As a result, athletic contests have had to leave the protection of the gods and enter the forum of public debate.

Scholars and sportswriters alike scan the athletic form for divine stigmata and are disappointed to find them absent. Critics rail against the commercialism of professional sports with the fervor of a Christ casting moneylenders out of a temple. Johan Huizinga, who exalted play as the creative wellspring of all human endeavors, took a dimmer view of sports: "sport has become profane, 'unholy' in every way, and has no organic connection whatsoever with the structure of society" (1950:197–198).

In fact, sport may reflect the values and structure of the society in which it occurs with an accuracy we would prefer to ignore. If professional athletes in the

United States appear to emphasize monetary rewards over the sheer joy of playing, this may well be because the society as a whole values material achievement over less tangible rewards. In their cross-cultural study of games and sport, B. Sutton-Smith and J. M. Roberts (1970) conclude that the organization and style of play of a particular sport is directly correlated with the social organization of the society in which it occurs. According to Sutton-Smith (1973), games are scaled down versions of real life relationships. In his essay on The American Boy, published in 1900, Theodore Roosevelt, the leader of the Rough Riders, emphasized the importance of sports for moral education:

> There are always in life countless tendencies for good and for evil, and each succeeding generation sees some of these tendencies strengthened and some weakened; nor is it by any means always, alas! That the tendencies for evil are weakened and those for good strengthened. But during

The French artist Jean-Pol D. Franqueuil depicts these two football players as part of the fabric of American life. This work was inspired by a Super Bowl party, in which the artist observed that the televised football game provided a backdrop for the social interactions of guests (reproduced by permission of the artist).

the last few decades there certainly have been some notable changes for good in boy life. The great growth in the love of athletic sports, for instance which fraught with danger if it becomes one-sided and unhealthy, has beyond all question had an excellent effect in increased manliness.

The American President believed that rigorous sports were especially important for developing character in the sons of the elite. Sons of the poor were more likely to develop character naturally, by doing hard physical labor. In the absence of the need for physical labor, Roosevelt asserted, sons of the rich were likely to become effeminate:

> Forty or fifty years ago the writer on American morals was sure to deplore the effeminacy and luxury of young Americans who were born of rich parents. The boy who was well off then, especially in the big Eastern cities, lived too luxuriously, took to billiards as his chief innocent recreation, and felt small shame in his inability to take part in rough pastimes and field-sports. Nowadays, whatever other fault the son of rich parents may tend to develop, he is at least forced by the opinion of all his associates of his own age to bear himself well in manly exercises and to develop his body — and therefore, to a certain extent, his character — in the rough sports which call for pluck, endurance, and physical address.

Roosevelt's distinction between sports for the elite and work for the masses is still reflected in the rules and organization of the International Olympic Committee. When the modern Olympics were organized in the 1890s under the guidance of Baron Pierre de Coubretin, they were aimed at combating a growing trend toward professionalism in sport and reviving the spirit of the Greek Olympics. On a subtler note, they were intended to showcase the physical skills of the European aristocracy, who had the time and economic resources to train for nonessential activities. The events at the first Olympics, held in Athens in 1896, reflect this emphasis on competition for the love of sport. They included cycling, fencing, gymnastics, lawn tennis, shooting, swimming, track and field, weightlifting and wrestling.

When Americans began to compete in the Olympics, early in the twentieth century, they were criticized for their mechanistic mode of training, which allowed them to dominate many track and field events. Eventually, in the late twentieth century, professionalism crept into the Olympic Games, primarily from two sources: (1) nationalistic competition and (2) the dominance of the marketplace in professional tennis, soccer, basketball and hockey.

Because they overtly recognized the importance of Olympic competition, Eastern European nations early identified Olympic potential in young athletes and supported them through training, housing and other benefits. Therefore, they came to dominate such sports as gymnastics and figure skating. U.S. Olympic officials protested these interventions, saying that Eastern European athletes were de facto professionals, thus forcing American amateur athletes to compete against athletes who could devote full time to training. The U.S. Olympic Committee was forced to support its athletes covertly and was, therefore, always subject to disciplinary action.

The issue was essentially cultural and economic. Americans have an ethic of selfless competition and consider the applause they give an athlete sufficient compensation. They do not acknowledge the tremendous expense of training for a world-class sporting competition. The American view is derivative of the Western European aristocratic model but reflects the uniquely American ideal of equal opportunity for all. The American view is expressed in quintessential form in the Horatio Alger novels of the nineteenth century, in which a poor boy rose to great economic heights through his own efforts. As expressed in sports, this ideal is expressed in the view that athletes should support their own training and excel through their own efforts. Whereas the Horatio Alger heroes were rewarded by financial success, the prevailing American view suggests that athletes are rewarded by public acclaim.

On the other hand, Eastern European nations hold the view that athletes, like soldiers, compete on behalf of the state. Therefore, just as a nation trains and outfits its soldiers for war, the nation also trains and outfits its athletes for competition.

As noted so far, the modern Olympics expresses three models for athletic competition: (1) the Western European aristocratic model, in which an athlete of high birth competes for the love of excellence and is supported by his lineage; (2) the American democratic model, in which an athlete demonstrates his or her worth by overcoming great obstacles; and (3) the Eastern European model, in which the athlete competes on behalf of the state.

There is yet a fourth model represented in the modern Olympics. Countries that do not have the resources, either private or public, to train and support athletes are still eligible to compete in the Olympics, even if they have no hope of winning. In some cases, where athletes show promise, they may be fostered by countries such as the United States, which trains athletes from several African nations. In other cases, such as Trinidad, athletes compete with little training or resources, but are adopted by audiences as representative of the Olympic spirit of competition for its own sake. Thus the Olympic model comes full circle, from the disinterested aristocrat to the disinterested proletarian.

Historically, sports have undergone a more profound transition from the sacred to the secular. Whereas they were once part of religious festivals, sporting events have become associated with the idea of escapist entertainment. In his book *From Ritual to Record*, Allen Guttman takes the devolution[111] of sports a step further. He argues that the secularization of sport has reduced athletic achievement to an accounting procedure. Modern sports, he suggests, are no longer aimed at appeasing the gods, but at making a mark in the record books:

> When we can no longer distinguish the sacred from the profane or even the good from the bad, we content ourselves with minute discriminations between the batting average of the .308 hitter and the .307 hitter. Once the gods have vanished from Mount Olympus or from Dante's paradise,

we can no longer run to appease them or to save our souls, but we can set a new record. It is a uniquely modern form of immortality [1978:55].

Secularization is not unique to sports. Since the Enlightenment of eighteenth-century Europe, the arts, literature, theater, science and government have all been weaned away from the church and left to proliferate on their own. It is significant that the same scholars who bemoan the secularization of sport are not equally distressed by the same trend in science and government. Are these institutions "profane" because they have become separated from religious insitutions? Have art, music, literature and drama become "unholy" because they are no longer sponsored by the church and dedicated to praising God? It is unlikely that contemporary scholars would willingly surrender their secular universities to ecclesiastical authority.

A novel by murder mystery writer P. D. James is set in an about-to-close theological college on the East Anglican coast of Britain. During the investigation of a series of murders, Emma, a visiting college professor, visits George Gregory. Gregory inhabits St. Luke's Cottage, where he listens to Handel and considers the human condition:

> She watched him as he poured the coffee. The goatee beard gave a slightly sinister Mephistophelean look to a face which she had always thought more handsome than attractive. He had a high sloping forehead from which the graying hair sprang back in waves so regular that they looked as if they had been produced by heated rollers. Under thin lids his eyes regarded the world with an amused or ironic contempt.[112]

Emma observes: "You're not in sympathy with St. Anselm's, are you? Is that because you're not a believer yourself, or because you don't think they are either?" Gregory replies:

> Oh, they believe all right. It's just that what they believe has become irrelevant. I don't mean the moral teaching: the Judaeo-Christian heritage has created Western civilization and we should be grateful to it. But the Church they serve is dying. When I look at [the painting] the *Doom* I try to have some understanding of what it meant to fifteenth-century men and women. If life is hard and short and full of pain, you need the hope of heaven; if there is no effective law, you need the deterrent of hell. The Church gave them comfort and light and pictures and stories and the hope of everlasting life. The twenty-first century has other compensations. Football for one. There you have ritual, colour, drama, the sense of belonging; football has its high priests, even its martyrs. And then there's shopping, art and music, travel, alcohol, drugs. We all have our own resources for staving off those two horrors of human life, boredom and the knowledge that we die.[113]

The importance of drama, emotion and conflict resolution in sports was recognized by FIFA[114] President Joseph "Sepp" Blatter when he refused to allow the use of video replays and other technical devices to help referees resolve disputes over calls at the 2002 World Cup: "If our game [soccer] is becoming scientific then we will take away its emotion and nobody would have any discussion any longer if it was offside, not offside; if it was inside, not inside the penalty box."[115]

Blatters' decision, and U.S. reporters' interpretation of it, reflected cultural differences intrinsic to international competition. As noted earlier, when U.S. athletes began to compete in the modern Olympics, the Games were organized around Western European models of aesthetics and sportsmanship. Western Europeans scorned the American emphasis on scientific precision in athletic training as being antithetical to the essential nature of the sporting contest, which Europeans viewed as extolling the virtue of noblesse oblige. Since then, American scientific precision and commerce have permeated the Olympics.

International football (soccer) is not based on an elitist model. Instead, it draws on the passionate commitment of a mass audience. Blatters' decision came during a World Cup competition in which the United States made its first respectable showing, displaying superb form in defeating Mexico to advance to the quarterfinals, thus drawing the attention of U.S. sportswriters and audiences. Having been socialized into the American sporting tradition, U.S. sportswriters were assuming that scientific precision is more important than symbolic expression. In affirming the importance of emotion and discussion, Blatter chose symbols over science.

The fact that sport has followed the same process of secularization as other social institutions confirms its "organic connection with the structure of authority," rather than disputes it, as Guttman suggests. However, the disquiet expressed by scholars regarding sport is significant, because it suggests that sport remains intimately linked with the social forces and psychological motivations that underlie religion.

Myth and Ritual of Sport

The process of evolution from ritual to record described by Guttman is more complex than he suggests and is probably related more to mass communication than to secularization alone. The symbolic value of sport is ideally expressed through participation, just as religious engagement is enhanced through participation in ritual. It is the athlete, intently engaged in performance, who experiences the process of transformation directly. He enacts the ritual of conflict, and he experiences the catharsis of conflict resolution. Those who watch from the sidelines are privy to the mythology, the symbolic story of conflict resolution. Myth provides a coherent story that explains the moral and social order; ritual allows one to act out the symbols and is therefore a more powerful transformative experience.

The symbolic experience of spectators comes from watching the enactment of heroic themes of transformation. Being present at a sporting event increases the sense of participation. In company with others, the sports fan shares the thrill of victory or the agony of defeat. Watching a sporting event "live" on television or other media is a step removed from being in the arena of conflict. However, the context is still more immediate and conveys a greater sense of urgency than reading a summary in the newspaper. Reducing an athletic contest to scores or statistics is the ultimate impoverishment of the sporting myth. It shifts the focus from the process to the product, whereas in a symbolic contest, the *dynamic* of conflict resolution is far more intrinsically rewarding than the *result*.

Secularization has deprived athletes of symbols for explaining and codifying transformative aspects of athletic achievement. Competing in sports needs no explanation, however, since it is pure experience, and impassioned acting out of conflict. Participation in sports in sports retains the force of ritual to dedicated athletes. The sense of achievement resulting from physical excellence is not simply mastery over an external opponent, but mastery over oneself.

It is not at all clear that the gods have vanished from Olympus. Modern representations of athletes express the same mood of exuberant achievement or intense commitment to a goal as earlier works. To a scholar protected from the heat of the chase, or to a sportswriter viewing the athletic contest from a safe distance, the gods may appear remote. But to an athlete sprinting to a glorious finish, or to a mountain climber seeing the world for the first time from the pinnacle of the highest mountain on earth, the gods seem very close indeed.

The Secularization of a Symbol

Although sports have become secularized, they remain intricately linked to their social context — and this accounts for their seemingly inexplicable appeal. People remain concerned about issues of survival, of life and death, even though they may no longer take to the forests and veldts in pursuit of game. Conflict remains a fact of social life, and people must still deal with flaws in their own characters that prevent them from realizing their aspirations. Humans must still deal with the "dark night of the soul."

All these issues are acted out in the drama of sports. The symbolic content of athletic competition has remained the same, even though it has been severed from its twin — religion. Religion and sport are related symbolic systems, though religion operates in the spiritual realm and sport in the secular arena. Both provide a context for transcending everyday reality. They are mutually enhancing.

Sport was included in religious festivals because it was thought to please the gods, who were interested in the outcome of sporting events. The action in the sports arena was, and still is, an enactment of the conflict and crisis described in religious myth: good versus evil, moral courage versus cowardice, and competing for the good of the group rather than for one's own glory. The stakes in religious belief are high, nothing less than life and salvation. Sport encapsulates the tension and drama of religion in an all-out contest that is often as unpredictable as life itself. And it is sometimes comforting to remind ourselves that life is, after all, "just a game."

In small-scale or traditional societies, there is typically one religion that all people share. If they agree on nothing else, they agree that the gods must be placated,

This bronze of a pole vaulter by R. Tait McKenzie focuses on the agility and beauty of the athlete. Just as the athlete vaults over the barrier, it would seem, it is possible to transcend earthbound distractions. It is an image of athletics as an idealized metaphor for striving (from *The Sport Sculpture* of R. Tait McKenzie, 2nd Ed. p. 97 by R. Tait McKenzie, 1992, Champaign, IL: Human Kinetics. Copyright 1992 by Andrew J. Kozar. Reprinted by permission).

In virtually all societies, sport is part of the socialization of boys. This boy seems to be gazing into the future as he balances on his soccer ball (reproduced by permission of the artist, Robert W. Jensen).

the rules must be obeyed. One of the most dramatic shocks resulting from colonial conquest is the overthrowing of native gods. Those spirit beings who have the power to control human affairs are revealed to be powerless in the face of threat from humans who come from outside the society.

In a pluralistic society, sport makes mythological themes accessible to people from many different backgrounds. It is a fact of modern life that no one religion has a secure hold on the imagination of its adherents. No matter how strongly we believe, we know that others do not believe. This challenges the absoluteness of our faith. Challenge from outside can promote solidarity within a religious group, but it accelerates the fragmentation of a pluralistic society. The various competing religions do not provide an overarching symbolic system that explains ultimate reality, including right and wrong, for all members of the group. Though the subgroup may be solid, the society as a whole is fragmented. Precisely because it is secularized, sport provides a symbolic system that unifies rather than divides. It addresses overarching symbolic themes, not specific theological issues. It deals not with the nature of God, but with the nature of human beings.

> If I could paint you, friend, as you stand there,
> Guard of the goal, defensive, open-eyed,
> Watching the tortured bladder slide and glide
> ………
> My sketch would have what Art can never give,
> Sinew and breath and body; it would live [E. C. Lefroy, A Football Player].

Notes

1. Los Angeles *Herald Examiner*, February 23, 1980. The U.S. team went on to defeat Finland for the gold medal.

2. Siddhartha was not conceived in the usual way. His mother Maya was impregnated when she dreamed of a snow-white elephant that descended from the sky and entered her womb.

3. Homer, *The Odyssey*, W. H. D. Rouse, trans. New York: Mentor, 1937.

4. I owe this insight to Annmarie Virzi, a student in my psychological anthropology class at California State University, Northridge.

5. Yanomami is spelled differently depending upon which author writes about them. The spelling is dependent upon the transcription of Yanomami pronounciation, which is not the same as English.

6. The Book of Songs. Arthur Waley, trans. New York: Grove Weidenfeld, 1960.

7. Ibid.

8. Ibid.

9. The dates of Ferdowsi's birth and death are based on conjecture. According to some scholars, Ferdowsi probably died between 1020 and 1025 C.E.

10. Charles University, Praha, Czech Republic.

11. Drawn from the website http://www.ibiblio.org/gaelic/celts.html.

12. Ibid.

13. Ibid.

14. Ibid.

15. Rowan Fairgrove, "What We Don't Know About the Ancient Celts." Internet site http://www.conjure.com/whocelts.html. Among Tibetan Buddhists to this day, human skulls have ritual significance. For the Buddhists, use of the skull in rituals symbolizes liberation from attachment to the body. We have no way of knowing what significance Celts ascribed to the use of human skulls in their rituals.

16. Fairgrove, ibid.

17. Ibid.

18. See http://www.harappa.com/indus2/91.html.

19. *Bhagavad-Gita*, Swami Prabhavananda and Christopher Isherwood, trans. New York: Mentor, 1972.

20. David Fingrut, SEED Alternative School, Toronto, *Mithraism: The Legacy of the Roman Empire's Final Pagan State Religion.* rome/E/Gazetteer/Periods/Roman/Topics/Religion/Mithraism/David_Fingrut**.html.

21. *The Bundahishn ("Creation"), or Knowledge from the Zand*, E. W. West trans. From *Sacred Books of the West*, Vol 5. Oxford: Oxford University Press, 1897.

22. Christopher B. Siren, "Cannanite/Ugaritic Mythology FAQ, ver. 1.2," http://pub pages.unh.edu/~cbsiren/canaanite-faq.html.

23. See http://has.brown.edu/~maicar/Theseus.html, for a summary of the adventures of Greek gods and heroes, by Carlos Parada, author of *Genealogical Guide to Greek Mythology*.

24. Http://www.xmission.com:8000/~dderhak/index/moors.htm.

25. Ibid.

26. I am indebted to Johnathan Game, my research assistant, for this analogy.

27. *Reflections on the Revolution in France* (1790).

28. Http://www.shaolinwinchun.com/en/origins/origins_kungfu.html.

29. Ibid.

30. Ibid.

31. Http://members.tripod.co.uk/wingchun/wingchun.htm.

32. Http://www.leejkd.com/about_jeet_kune_do.htm.

33. Ibid.

34. Http://home.clara.net/buddhistwingchun/descr.htm.

35. Ibid.

36. Ibid.

37. Http://www.agmen.com/etruscans/pag_engl/museum/giochi.htm.

38. Ibid.

39. Http://www.dalmacija.net/sinj/sinj_1.htm.

40. Ibid.

41. I owe this characterization to my son, Greg Womack.

42. http://www.magma.ca/~sumo/s101miri.htm.

43. Stephan A. Hoeller, "On the Trail of the Winged God,"http://www.webcom.com/~gnosis/hermes.htm.

44. Http://keith.martialartsman.com/pug/pugOrigins.html.

45. Http://www.ibhof.com/molineau.htm.

46. During the 1991 Persian Gulf War, President George Bush, Sr. repeatedly underscored the idea that the U.S. Army was all-volunteer.

47. Fred Ayer, *Before the Colors Fade: Portrait of a Soldier, George S. Patton, Jr.* Boston: Houghton Mifflin, 1964.

48. "The Battle of Brunanburh" in *Beowulf and Other Old English Poems*. Constance B. Hieatt, trans. Second edition. Toronto: Bantam Books, 1982.

49. Grahame L. Jones, "Cup Conductors: Brazil's Scolari, Germany's Voeller master art of coaching, *Los Angeles Times*, Friday, June 28, 2002, D8.

50. Http://www.coachgumby.com/sport_soc2.htm.

51. Ibid.

52. Guttman builds on the analogy noted by Mike Holovak and Bill McSweeney in *Violence Every Sunday*. New York: Doubleday, 1965, p. 17.

53. http://www.personal.psu.edu/users/w/x/wxk116/romeball.html.

54. Ibid.

55. This is the standard paraphrase of Hitler's assertion. The Fuehrer's own prose was much more verbose.

56. Trans. By J. B. Bury. Provided by Paul Halsall, http://www.fordham.edu/halsall/source/priscus1.html.

57. Http://www.imh.org/imh/kyhpllb.html.

58. Http://www.hempbc.com/magazine/jul95/scythians.html.

59. "Only Rule of the Game: Don't Drop the Headless Calf," *Los Angeles Times*, January 27, 2002, p. A6.

60. Ibid.

61. Ibid.

62. Grahame L. Jones, "Cup Conductors: Brazil's Scolari, Germany's Voeller master art of coaching." *Los Angeles Times*, Friday, June 28, 2002, D8.

63. Http://www.bartleby.com/58/10.html.

64. The Rose Bowl game, formerly held on New Year's Day following the Rose Parade, in Pasadena, California, reflects similar pageantry. In this case, the rivalry is more democratic, pitting West Coast champions against rivals in other parts of the country.

65. *God's Country and Mine*, 1954.

66. Http://www.thebaseballpage.com/past/pp/ruthbabe/default.htm.

67. See Walt Whitman, *Leaves of Grass*, 1855.

68. Michael Murphy, *Golf in the Kingdom*. New York: Penguin Compass, 1997, p. 102.

69. Ibid., p. 3.

70. Ibid., p. 27.

71. Ibid., p. 22.

72. From *Tales of teh Shaolin Monastery*, collected and edited by Wang Hongjun, translated by C. J. Lonsdale. Hong Kong: Joint Publ., 1988.

73. *The Upanishades: Breath of the Eternal*. Swami Prabhavananda and Frederick Manchester, trans. New York: Mentor, 1948, 1957, p. 19.

74. Mary Mapes Dodge, *Hans Brinker or The Silver Skates*. New York: dilthium Press, Childrens Classics Division, p. 342.

75. Ibid., p. 344.

76. Ernest Hemingway, "The Snows of Kilimanjaro." In *The Snows of Kilimanjaro and Other Stories*. New York: Collier Books, 1961, p. 3.

77. From Blake's notebook, *Great Things Are Done*, 1807–1809.

78. Fujiyama is the Japanese term for Mt. Fuji.

79. *One Hundred Poems from the Japanese*, Kenneth Rexroth, ed. New York: New Directions, 1964.

80. *Beowulf and Other Old English Poems* Constance B. Hieatt, trans. Toronto: Bantam Books, 1983, pp. 15–16.

81. Cecilia Rasmussen, "Surfer King, Swimmer Extraordinaire, Lifesaving Hero," Los Angeles Times, Sunday, February 10, 2002, p. B4.

82. See Lt. Karl Bohn and Arthur C. Verge, http://www.cmp.ucr.edu/exhibitions/oceanview/essays/verge/default.html.

83. Ovid, *The Art of Love*. Rolfe Humphries, trans. Bloomington: Indiana University Press, 1957. Book I, p. 106.

84. Edna St. Vincent Millay, *Collected Lyrics* (New York: Harper and Row, 1917).

85. *The Book of Songs: The Ancient Chinese Classic of Poetry*. Alex Waley, trans. (New York: Grove Wiedenfeld, 1960. p. 60.)

86. Ibid., p. 22.

87. Ovid, *The Metamorphoses*, p. 209.

88. Ibid., p. 207.

89. Ibid., p. 212.

90. Ibid., p. 116.

91. Ibid., p. 290.

92. Ibid., p. 291.

93. Ibid., p. 291.

94. Ibid., p. 294.

95. Ibid., pp. 43–44.

96. Ibid., p. 44.

97. Ibid., p. 45.

98. *The Collected Works of St. Teresa of Avila*, Vol. I, Kieran Kavanaugh and Otilio Rodriguez, trans. (Washington, D.C.: Institute of Carmelite Studies, 1976, pp. 388–389).

99. Ibid., p. 379.

100. From "Another Sermon on the Eternal Birth."

101. "Talks of Instruction." Additional sayings of Meister Eckhart are available on the websites http://www.op.org/eckhart/meister.htm and http://members.wwisp.com/~srshanks/Meister_Eckhart/Sayings.html.

102. Http://members.wwisp.com/~srshanks/Meister_Eckhart/Sayings/html.

103. Rumi, "Thief of Sleep." Shahram Shiva, trans. Prescott, AZ: Hohm Press, 2000, p. 56.

104. Ibid., p. 63.

105. *Rumi: We Are Three*, Coleman Barks, trans., 1987, p. 10.

106. *Stories of the Buddha: Being Selections from the Jātaka*. Caroline A. F. Rhys Davids, trans. and ed. (New York: Dover, pp. 14–22)

107. The resemblance to the symbolism of the Mithraic sacrifice described in Chapter Three is striking.

108. *The Upanishads: Breath of the Eternal*, Swami Prabhavananda and Frederick Manchester, trans. New York: Mentor, p. 46.

109. David Zucchino and John J. Goldman, "Foreign Victims List Complicates Count," *Los Angeles Times*, September 22, 2001, A6.

110. From *Pogo* Earth Day cartoon 1971, Walt Kelly.

111. I adopt this term from H. P. Lovecraft, the great writer of bizarre fiction, who suggests that humans not only evolve, they can devolve into a more brutish state.

112. P. D. James, *Death in Holy Orders*. New York: Ballantyne Books, p. 279.

113. Ibid., p. 281.

114. Fédération Internationale de Football Association.

115. *Los Angeles Times*, Friday, June 28, 2002, D8.

Bibliography

Armitage, John. *Man at Play: Nine Centuries of Pleasure Making.* London: Frederick Warne, 1977.

Barthes, Roland. *Mythologies.* Annette Lavers, trans. New York: Noonday Press, 1972.

Bhattacharyya, N. N. *History of the Tantric Religion.* New Delhi: Manohar, 1992.

Blanchard, Kendall. *The Mississippi Choctaws at Play: The Serious Side of Leisure.* Urbana: University of Illinois Press, 1981.

Bonatti, Walter. *The Mountains of My Life.* Robert Marshall, trans. and ed. New York: Modern Library, 2001.

Boutros, Labib. *Phoenician Sport: Its Influence on the Origin of the Olympic Games.* Amsterdam: Gieben, 1981.

Catlin, G. *North American Indians.* Volume 1. Minneapolis: Ross and Haines. (Originally published 1841.)

Chagnon, Napoleon A. *Yanomamö,* 4th ed. Fort Worth: Harcourt Brace, 1992.

Copway, G. *The Traditional History and Characteristic Sketching of the Ojibway Nation.* Toronto: Coles, 1972. (Originally published 1851.)

Courtney, Nicholas. *Sporting Royals Past and Present.* London: Hutchinson/Stanley Paul, 1983.

Cuddon, J.A. *The International Dictionary of Sports and Games.* New York: Schocken Books, 1979.

Cumont, Franz. *The Mysteries of Mithra.* Thomas J. McCormack, trans. New York: Dover, 1956. (Originally published by the Open Court Publishing Co. 1903.)

Dowson, John. *A Classical Dictionary of Hindu Mythology and Religion: Geography, History and Literature.* New Delhi: Heritage, 1992.

Duffié, Mary Kay. *Through the Eye of the Needle: a Māori Elder Remembers.* Fort Worth: Harcourt Brace, 2001.

Durant, John, and Otto Bettman. *Pictorial History of American Sports.* Cranbury, NJ: A.S. Barnes, 1952.

Durham, William H. *Scarcity and Survival in Central America: Ecological Origins of the Soccer War.* Stanford: Stanford University Press, 1979.

Elliot, Sir Charles. *Hinduism and Buddhism,* Vol II. London, 1921. (Reprint 1957.)

Estioko-Griffin, Agnes. "Daughters of the Forest." In Mari Womack and Judith Marti, eds., *The Other Fifty Percent.* Prospect Heights, IL: Waveland, 1993. (Originally published in *Natural History,* May 1986.)

Faulkner, William. *Uncollected Stories.* Joseph Blotner, ed. New York: Vintage Books, 1979.

Ferdowsi. *The Epic of Kings.* Reuben Levy, trans. London: Routledge and Kegan Paul, 1967.

Furst, Peter T. *Flesh of the Gods: The Ritual Use of Hallucinogens.* New York: Frederick A. Praeger, 1972.

Gillespie, Susan D. "Ballgames and Boundaries." In Vernon L. Scarborough and David R. Wilcox, eds., *The Mesoaamerican Ballgame.* Tucson: University of Arizona Press, 1991.

Gluckman, Max. *Rituals of Rebellion* (Frazer Lecture). Manchester: Manchester University Press, 1952.

Goodhart, Phillip, and Christopher Chataway. *War Without Weapons.* London: W.H. Allen, 1968.

Grinnell, George Bird. *Blackfoot Lodge Tales.* New York: Charles Scribner's Sons, 1916.

Guttman, Allen. *From Ritual to Record: The Nature of Modern Sports.* New York: Columbia University Press, 1978.

Harris, H. A. *Greek Athletes and Athletics.* Bloomington: Indiana University Press, 1964.

Herold, A. Ferdinand. *The Life of Buddha.* Paul C. Blum, trans. Tokyo: Charles A. Tuttle, 1954.

Hikoyama, Kozo. *Sumo: Japanese Wrestling.* Tokyo: Board of Tourist Industry, Japanese Government Railways, 1940.

Huizinga, Johan. *Homo Ludens: A Study of the Play-Element in Culture.* Boston: Beacon Press, 1950.

Ixtlilxochitl, Fernando de Alva. *Obras Historicas.* México, D.F.: Editora Nacional, 1952.

Jung, Carl. *Symbols of Transformation.* R. F. C. Hull, trans. Bollingen Series XX. Princeton, NJ: Princeton University Press, 1956.

Kalakaua, His Hawaiian Majesty King David. *The Legends and Myths of Hawaii: The Fables and Folk-Lore of a Strange People.* R. M. Daggett, ed. Boston: Charles E. Tuttle, 1972. (Originally published 1888.)

Leuras, Leonard. *Surfing: The Ultimate Pleasure.* New York: Workman, 1984.

Lizot, Jacques. *Tales of the Yanomami: Daily Life in the Venezuelan Forest.* Ernest Simon, trans. Cambridge: Cambridge University Press, 1984.

Mackay-Smith, Alexander, Jean R. Druesedow, and Thomas Ryder. *Man and the Horse.* New York: Simon and Schuster (Metropolitan Museum of Art), 1984.

McCormick, John, and Mario Sevilla Mascareñas. *The Complete Aficionado.* Cleveland: World Publishing, 1967.

Merrill, William L. "Religion and Culture: God's Saviors in the Sierra Madre." In James P. Spradley and David W. McCurdy, eds., *Conformity and Conflict: Readings in Cultural Anthropology,* 6th ed. Boston: Little, Brown, 1987. (Originally published as "God's Saviors in the Sierra Madre," *Natural History* 93[3], 1983.)

Muir, John. *My First Summer in the Sierra.* Boston: Houghton Mifflin, 1998. (Originally published 1911.)

Nadel, Siegfried Frederick. *The Nuba: An Anthropological Study of the Hill Tribes in Kordofan.* 1947.

Noll, Greg, and Andrea Gabbard. *Da Bull: Life Over the Edge.* North Atlantic Books, 1992.

Ohnuki-Tierney, Emiko. *The Ainu of the Northwest Coast of Southern Sakhalin.* New York: Holt, Rinehart and Winston, 1974.

Oxendine, Joseph B. *American Indian Sports Heritage.* Champaign, Il: Human Kinetics Books, 1988.

Poliakoff, Michael B. *Combat Sports in the Ancient World.* New Haven: Yale University Press, 1987.

Radin, Paul. *Winnebago Hero Cycles: A Study in Aboriginal Literature.* Baltimore: Waverly, 1948.

Sandars, N. K. *The Epic of Gilgamesh.* London: Penguin, 1972.

Santley, Robert S., Michael J. Berman, and Rani T. Alexander. "The Politicization of the Mesoamerican Ballgame and Its Implications for the Interpretation of the Distribution of Ballcourts in Central Mexico." In Vernon L. Scarborough and David R. Wilcox, eds., *The Mesoamerican Ballgame*. Tucson: University of Arizona Press, 1991.

Saso, Michael. "Chinese Religions." In John R. Hinnells, ed., *A Handbook of Living Religions*. New York: Penguin Books, 1991.

Satguru Sivaya Subramuniyaswami. *Dancing with Śiva: Hinduism's Contemporary Catechism*. Concord, CA: Himalayan Academy, 1993.

Schele, Linda, and Mary Ellen Miller. *The Blood of Kings: Dynasty and Ritual in Maya Art*. Fort Worth: Kimbell Art Museum; and New York: Braziller, 1986.

Squire, Charles. *Celtic Myth and Legend*. Hollywood, CA: Newcastle, 1975.

Sutton, Donald S. "Ritual Drama and Moral Order: Interpreting the God's Festival Troupes of Taiwan." *Journal of Asian Studies* 49:535–554, 1990.

Sutton-Smith, B. "Games, the Socialization of conflict." In *Sport in the Modern World—Chances and Problems*. Heidelberg: Springer-Verlag Berlin, 1973.

_____, and J. M. Roberts. "The Cross-Cultural and Psychological Study of Games." In G. Luschen, ed., *The Cross-Cultural Analysis of Games*. Champaign, IL: Stipes, 1970.

Takuan Sōhō. *The Unfettered Mind: Writings of the Zen Master to the Sword Master*. William Scott Wilson, trans. Tokyo: Kodansha Intl., 1986.

Turnbull, Stephen. *The Lone Samurai and the Martial Arts*. London: Arms and Armour Press, 1990.

Wang, Hongjun. *Tales of the Shaolin Monastery*. C. J. Lonsdale, trans. Hong Kong: JPC, 1988.

Wayman, Alex. *The Buddhist Tantras: Light on Indo-Tibetan Esotericism*. Delhi: Motilal Banarsidass, 1973.

Weber, Max. *The Protestant Ethic and the Spirit of Capitalism*. Talcott Parsons, trans. New York: Scribner's, 1958. (Original work published 1904–1905.)

Whitley, David S. "By the Hunter, for the Gatherer: Art, Social Relations and Subsistence Change in the Prehistoric Great Basin." *World Archaeology* 25(3):356–373, 1994.

Wilkerson, S. Jeffrey K. "And Then They Were Sacrificed: The Ritual Ballgame of Northeastern Mesoamerica Through Time and Space." In Vernon L. Scarborough and David R. Wilcox, eds., *The Mesoamerican Ballgame*. Tucson: University of Arizona Press, 1991.

Willetts, R. F. "Hermes." In Richard Cavendish, ed., *Man, Myth and Magic: An Illustrated Encyclopedia of the Supernatural*. New York: Marshall Cavendish, 1970.

Wilson, H. H. *Essays and Lectures on the Religion of the Hindus*. Vol I. London, 1875.

Womack, Mari. "Anthropology and the Sport Hero." Paper presented at the conference of the Association for the Anthropological Study of Play, Fort Worth, TX, 1981.

_____. "Sports Magic: Symbolic Manipulation Among Professional Athletes." Ph.D. dissertation, University of California–Los Angeles, 1982.

_____. "Professional Athletes: Heroes for Hire." Paper presented at the Conference on Sport, Clemson, South Carolina, 1983.

_____. Introduction to "On the Nature of Things." In Mari Womack and Judith Marti, *The Other Fifty Percent: Multicultural Perspectives on Gender Relations*. Prospect Heights, IL: Waveland, 1993.

Index

DATE DUE

GAYLORD

PRINTED IN U.S.A.